BACK

CAMOUFLAGE +

Vulnerability = foil predator =
(BIRDS + 1Bpres Druj Nesting)

Boldly

Mucly less Moving = a) Autonomously = Attention-
Sexual
Competency { b) Homoserally = Rivalry + Followships
{ c) Heteroserally = Hukems
{ d) Socially = frog STATUS
Amicially = "Males Which The
Aggressive" —

Woundedness Moving
a) Bodily = Onplasan Sexual
Competence
b) Homo } rodents
c) Hetero
d) Grou

SCIENCE AND PSYCHOANALYSIS

Preceding volumes of *Science and Psychoanalysis*

Volume I: *Integrative Studies* (1958)
Volume II: *Individual Familial Dynamics* (1959)
Volume III: *Psychoanalysis and Human Values* (1960)
Volume IV: *Psychoanalysis and Social Process* (1961)
Volume V: *Psychoanalytic Education* (1962)

Science and Psychoanalysis. Volume VI.

VIOLENCE AND WAR

with Clinical Studies

Edited by

JULES H. MASSERMAN, M.D.

Professor of Neurology and Psychiatry,
Northwestern University
Chicago

President, Academy of
Psychoanalysis
1958-59

GRUNE & STRATTON

New York · London · 1963

Library of Congress Catalog Card Number 58-8009

Printed and bound in the United States of America (B)

CONTENTS

CONTRIBUTORS

ABELL, RICHARD G.: Lecturer in Mental Hygiene and Psychiatrist, Barnard College, Columbia University, New York, New York.

BERKOWITZ, LEONARD: Professor of Psychology, University of Wisconsin, Madison, Wisconsin.

BONIME, WALTER: Associate Clinical Professor, New York Medical College, New York, New York.

COSER, LEWIS A.: Professor of Sociology, Brandeis University, Waltham, Massachusetts.

DAHLBERG, CHARLES CLAY: William A. White Psychoanalytic Institute, New York, New York.

ECKHARDT, MARIANNE HORNEY: Washington Psychoanalytic Institute, Washington, D. C.

EIBL-EIBESFELDT, IRENAUS: Max Planck Institute für Verhaltensphysiologie, Seewiesen bei Starnberg, West Germany.

FINK, MAX: Director, Missouri Psychiatric Institute, St. Louis, Missouri.

GRINKER, ROY R.: Director, Institute for Psychosomatic and Psychiatric Research and Training of Michael Reese Hospital and Medical Center, Chicago, Illinois. President, Academy of Psychoanalysis, 1961-62.

HOCH, PAUL H.: Commissioner of Mental Hygiene of the State of New York, Albany, New York.

JACKSON, DON D.: Palo Alto Medical Clinic and Mental Research Institute, Palo Alto, California.

JAFFE, JOSEPH: Director of Research, William Alanson White Institute, New York, New York. Assistant Clinical Professor of Psychiatry, Columbia University, New York, New York.

LEEDS, ANTHONY: Chief, Program of Urban Development, Pan American Union, Washington, D. C.

LIEF, HAROLD I.: Professor of Psychiatry, Tulane University School of Medicine, New Orleans, Louisiana.

MARK, JOSEPH C.: Psychologist, Child Guidance Clinic, East Orange, New Jersey.

MARKOWITZ, IRVING: Director, Child Guidance Clinic, East Orange, New Jersey.

MARLOWE, DAVID H.: Division of Neuropsychiatry, Walter Reed Army Institute of Research, Washington, D. C.

MARMOR, JUDD: Clinical Professor of Psychiatry, School of Medicine, University of California, Los Angeles, California.

MEAD, MARGARET: Associate Curator of Ethnology, American Museum of Natural History, New York, New York.

MILLET, JOHN A. P.: Associate Professor of Psychiatry, New York School of Psychiatry, New York, New York. President, Academy of Psychoanalysis 1959-60.

NAGLER, SIMON H.: New York Medical College, New York, New York.

vi

RIOCH, DAVID McK.: Director of Research, Walter Reed Army Institute, Washington, D. C.

ROMM, MAY E.: Training Psychoanalyst, Los Angeles, California.

RUBINS, JACK L.: Psychoanalyst, New York, New York.

SALZMAN, LEON: Associate Professor of Clinical Psychiatry, Georgetown University School of Medicine, Washington, D. C.

SEIDERMAN, STANLEY: Child Guidance Clinic, East Orange, New Jersey.

SPIEGEL, HERBERT: Associate Attending, Department of Psychiatry, St. Luke's Hospital, New York, New York.

TOOLAN, JAMES: Assistant Clinical Professor of Psychiatry, New York University, New York, New York.

WASKOW, ARTHUR I.: Peace Research Institute, Washington, D. C.

WEIGERT, EDITH: Washington Psychoanalytic Institute, Washington, D. C.

WEISS, FREDERICK A.: Training and Supervising Analyst, American Institute for Psychoanalysis; Attending Psychoanalyst, Karen Horney Clinic, New York, New York.

PREFACE

"Neo-Analysis" *vs* Neo-Atavasim: Another Dialogue

AMONG the most significant measures of progress in any field are the evidences of consternation and active hostility evoked in the self-styled guardians of threatened dogmas. Socrates, Buddha, Jesus, Galileo, Spinoza, Darwin, Freud, et. al., aroused such responses in their time, and suffered the calumny accorded to all innovators. Unfortunately, their followers—being far less great than their preceptors, else they would not constitute themselves merely disciples—soon tend to erect yet another arrogant orthodoxy of their own, and thus repeat the cycle.

These reflections are relevant to a Jeremiad entitled "Communication about the Neoanalytic Movement" published by Maxwell Gitelson, immediate past president of the International Psychoanalytic Association, in the final pages of the 1962 journal of that organization. In brief, Dr. Gitelson asserted the following:

1. That all deviations from Freudian doctrine are "diluted and distorted."

2. That the "American Academy of Psychoanalysis" and the "International Forum for Psychoanalysis [which is] strongly supported by the American Academy," engage in perversions of psychoanalytic theory and practice: e.g., as in the "neo-analytic schools of Horney, Sullivan, Fromm-Reichmann and others."

3. That the Academy and Forum are also "politically active" in these pursuits.

4. That some of the members of the Academy are not "qualified analysts," presumably because they were trained in Institutes sponsored by universities rather than by the American Psychoanalytic Association; that others have remained members of the American Psychoanalytic and International, despite an implicit apostasy; that still others have never desired membership in the American, or are merely "former analysts . . . disappointed in their experience"; and worst of all, that the Scientific Associates of the Academy have only a "remote . . . or non-existent" relationship to the field.

5. That the Academy is "not sympathetic" with the American Psychoanalytic Association.

6. That the wisest course for loyal bearers of the "torch of self-knowledge which we received from Freud" is to avoid all contact with "so-called liberalism" and "attend to our own knitting."

7. That the latter pursuit should include a more rigid selection of psychoanalytic trainees to exclude those whose intractable "narcissism" or "persistent transference neuroses" may lead them to free or progressive thought, and the

recognition of a past "failure to be uncompromising in the application of our psychoanalytic insight into our *authoritarian* [italics mine] roles as teachers and educators [to prevent] . . . some of our colleagues and students [from finding] . . . solace for narcissistic injury in alliance as dissident coteries." It might well be argued that this harangue, written in the pose of Moses bearing the Decologue to those tempted to worship Baal, did not merit a reply; nevertheless, the fact remains that Dr. Gitelson's tract was published in the official Journal of the International Psychoanalytic Association, where it would be read by many who, being unacquainted with the field, might be misled to condemn all of psychoanalysis as a cult still pre-empted by dour mystics, pseudoscientific practitioners, or coercive trade-unionists. But as a 22 year member of both the American and International Psychoanalytic Associations, as one of the founders and Past Presidents of the Academy of Psychoanalysis, and as Editor of this series of volumes on Science and Psychoanalysis, I had no wish to have any of these organizations and endeavors identified with Dr. Gitelson's statements. I therefore addressed the following letter to Dr. John Sutherland, Editor of the International Journal, London, England:

Dear Sir:

Dr. M. Gitelson's recent "Communication From the President About the Neoanalytic Movement" (Int. J. Psychoanal. XLIII:3, 1962) seems to require some correction in order to restore the balance of probity and professional dignity of your respected Journal. This reply is therefore addressed to your readers rather than to Dr. Gitelson, who in past correspondence* has proved to be a nebulous and eventually uninteresting protagonist inclined to evade issues by orotund sentences like this one, except that his nouns generally have no consistent meanings, and are followed six lines later by predicates that connote no consistent processes. However, in the particular "Communication" referred to, Dr. Gitelson made his allegations slightly more explicit than usual and it is with reference to these that your readers may appreciate the following facts:

First, there is no "American Academy of Psychoanalysis." The Academy of Psychoanalysis, founded in 1956 by some of the leading psychoanalysts in the United States—nearly all of them members of the International Psychoanalytic Association—has in six years grown so greatly in scientific prestige and influence that:

(a) Its Fellowship now includes some of the world's most renowned senior

---

*Cf. my previous exchange of letters with Dr. Gitelson in "Transference: Counter and Countered—a Dialogue," p. 160-172 of Salzman, L. and Masserman, J. (Eds.): Modern Concepts of Psychoanalysis, New York, Philosophical Library, 1962.

Since the Editorial Board of the International Journal of Psychoanalysis declined to publish the response to Dr. Gitelson's harangue, it is reproduced here.

psychoanalysts: e.g., Franz Alexander, Carl Binger, Dexter Bullard, Roy Grinker, Martin Grotjahn, Abraham Kardiner, Judd Marmor, John Millet, George Mohr, Sandor Rado, Janet Rioch, May Romm, William Silverberg, Edith Weigert, et. al. Five of these have been Presidents of the Academy, which now numbers over 350 prominent analysts on both American continents.

(b) Dr. Gitelson correctly notes that many of these Fellows of the Academy are also dues-paying members of the American Psychoanalytic Association and thereby the International; indeed, the number is increasing monthly. However, it is not true, as Dr. Gitelson avers, that they "have no sympathy for the American Psychoanalytic Association"; on the contrary, they are deeply sympathetic with the current travails of the American Psychoanalytic, and therefore retain their membership and influence in that Association in the hope that, to use Freud's phrase, "the soft voice of the intellect" would eventually prevail in its doctrinal, administrative and pedagogic councils.

(c) Dr. Gitelson also inveighs against the Academy's designation of non-voting Scientific Associates—a widely sought elective honor which has been reserved for about fourscore of America's leading anthropologists, sociologists, psychiatrists and other behavioral scientists, including many of the Chairmen of the Department of Psychiatry in United States universities, each of whom had rendered outstanding contributions to psychiatry and psychoanalysis. In this connection, it appears incredible that Dr. Gitelson is serious in his implied strictures that analysts should be unique among scientists in not being interested in, and avidly receptive of, developments in other fields that could advance understanding and skill in their own science. Let us trust that our potential friends in these related fields will not take his attitude as representative.

Second, Dr. Gitelson's allegation that the Academy is "politically active" is, to use two of his favorite panchestons,* more "tendentious" than "diatrophic"—unless Dr. Gitelson reads the latter term as *di-atrophic*. The Constitution of the Academy specifically confines its purposes to research and communication, and to the promotion of psychoanalysis as a scientific discipline; indeed, it expressly forbids not only the establishment, but the "approval" or "disapproval" of Institutes, Societies, Standards of Training or other pre-emptive or quasi-official regulative activities. The only approach to "political" action in which the Academy was ever even distantly involved occurred in 1959 when the American Board of Psychiatry and Neurology, considering the Academy an authoritative and impartial body, sought its advice as to whether or not to establish a subspecialty Board of Examiners in Psychoanalysis and invited the Academy to nominate such examiners if the Board were established. The Academy, after serious deliberation, counselled against the establishment of such a Board, and the wisdom of this advice was later confirmed when the American Psychoanalytic Association reversed its previous stand and echoed the Academy's recommendation.

Third, Dr. Gitelson's somewhat free-wheeling accusation that the activities of the Academy constitute "active opposition to psychoanalysis which leaves no doubt about the wish to negate its discoveries" must have led to many a doubt

---

*Garrett Hardin's term for words so protean in their connotations that they are essentially meaningless.

as to Dr. Gitelson's accuracy of reporting and impartiality of judgment on the part of readers acquainted with the following facts:

1. The semiannual scientific meetings of the Academy are invariably attended not only by its Fellows and Scientific Associates but my many other members of the American Psychoanalytic and guests from various scientific societies who desire to learn of fundamental progress in this field.

2. The Academy has been designated as a constituent body of the American Association for the Advancement of Science, and the two associations, under the Chairmanship of Dr. Sandor Rado, held an historic Joint Meeting in Philadelphia on December 26-28, 1962.

3. The Scientific Proceedings of the Academy, published by Grune and Stratton under the title *Science and Psychoanalysis*, has attained world-wide circulation and acclaim.

Fourth—and this time a minor but perennially necessary correction of Dr. Gitelson's writings: the Academy had and has no official connection whatever with the International Psychoanalytic Forum. Finally, Dr. Gitelson's dictum that we must "be uncompromising in the application of our psychoanalytic insight into our authoritarian roles (sic!) as teachers and educators" is so scholastically anachronistic—and so contrary to the asymptotic but free and productive seeking for truth upon which both science and ethics are based—that it would be charitable to regard it is a *lapsus* rather than a credo. However, this leads me to a more general comment about the necessity of recognizing reactionary movements in all branches of human endeavor. Perhaps a trenchant analogy in current history would here be apropos:

The Catholic Church, too, has its Alfredo Cardinal Ottaviani, Secretary of the Supreme Sacred Congregation of the Holy Office, whose Coat-of-Arms proudly bears the motto *Semper Idem* and whose creed is "Scripture must be read under ecclesiastical guidance." At the recent Ecumenical Council, progressive elements of the Church, led by Augustine Cardinal Bea, Head of the Secretariat for Promoting Christian Unity, deplored Ottaviani's doctrinal intransigence because it "would close the door to intellectual Europe and the outstretched hands of friendship in the old and new world." The Council, cognizant of broader vistas of scholarship and new obligations to humanity, rejected Ottaviani's rigid concepts of "orthodoxy" and followed a greater destiny.

Shall scientific societies seeking knowledge of, and service to mankind in other fields, do less?

Since the dispatch of this letter many other members not only of the Academy, but of the American and the International Psychoanalytic Associations have expressed their concern and regrets over Dr. Gitelson's "Communication," and are awaiting an official disavowal of his sentiments from responsible officials of the latter two organizations. However, much more important than such rear-guard realignments are the continuous advances that are the major concerns of every science. Many of those achieved in psychoanalysis and its interrelated fields during 1962 are presented herewith. The volume is arranged in three parts as follows:

Part I, which records the Symposium on Human Violence held jointly by the Academy and the American Association for the Advancement of Science.

Parts II and III, comprising the outstanding multidisciplinary contributions to psychoanalytic theory, research and practice during the preceding Scientific Meeting of the Academy.

Thus constituted, Volume VI of this series is, respectfully, submitted to the scientific world in the hope that it will merit the kind reception accorded to its predecessors.

—Jules H. Masserman, M.D.

January 2, 1963

Part I. Violence and Warfare

VIOLENCE: AN INTRODUCTION

By DAVID McK. RIOCH, M.D.

THE ROLE of violence in behavior is a broad topic. The exertion of physical force, possibly with destructive effects, may characterize the course of any one of a number of patterns of overt behavior. The language referring to or associated with violence may be used in an even greater variety of conventional forms of symbolic behavior.

In this Symposium attention is being paid chiefly, therefore, to aggressive behavior and to its socially organized expression in warfare, although other aspects are also considered. The problem of formulating the relevant aspects of behavior has not yet been solved and, hence, the difficulties encountered in developing a comprehensive statement of a pattern of behavior, which includes data from several different sources, are considerable. In abstract terms we need to know the general setting in which the behavior is probable; the signals which are likely to evoke (or release) the behavior; the consummatory act or state, attainment of which terminates the behavior; and the complexity of the course from release to termination. By "complexity of the course" I refer to problems such as whether the behavior—in this case, violence—is a part of a thought-out plan; a considered strategy; a ritualized reaction to an appropriate signal; a stage in the breakdown of the organism's capacity to think; or some other type of performance. In addition to these formal aspects we need, further, to consider the objective of the formulation itself—that is, whose behavior it is proposed to influence by the formulation, under what circumstances and to what end. The objectives of the critical biologist, of the psychiatric therapist, of the military tactician and so forth often lead to very different formulations

1

which can only be compared through our knowledge of the cultural pattern of which the respective formulations are a part. It is, clearly, the purpose of this Symposium to provide an opportunity for clarifying a number of aspects of these problems.

The plan of the Symposium extends from studies of animal behavior and controlled experiments on human subjects to psychiatric approaches to the problems of disturbed behavior and to consideration of social anthropological data. The chief interest in surveying this field is the problem our civilization now faces with respect to modern technological developments in warfare. I should like to take this opportunity to note briefly two other views of the role of violence in behavior, namely, those of professional studies of warfare and of experimental investigation of the central nervous mechanisms mediating "violent" behavior.

Although his work is widely and well known I will start by recalling to our attention a few of the remarkable observations described by Karl von Clausewitz in his treatise, "On War." Just as in modern biology we describe the general setting in which a behavioral event occurs, the cues which evoke it, the character of its course, and the consummatory states to which it leads, so von Clausewitz points out that war is never an isolated event, without antecedent and succedent states. He regards war as a form of communication between nations, stemming from preceding political communication and leading to different, but continuing, communication. The conduct of the war itself is planned whether, for example, it is to be mainly offensive or defensive, whether the end-state is to be a limited acquisition of territory or a total occupation, and so on. Despite policies, plans and preparations, however, he finds that war is a matter of chance to a large extent. The unexpected happens. Here he finds, further, that human subjects tend to distrust their logic and their intellects. They prefer the already accepted, much simpler images of themselves and the world and, relying on "courage," they throw themselves into danger and physical effort in order to get an immediate answer to some immediate question. Finally, von Clausewitz was under no illusions as to the fundamental difference between theory and practice, between analyzing a situation and living it. He is emphatic on the superiority of empirical data over theoretical explanations and on the even greater value of experience. Written between 1818 and 1830, von Clausewitz's "On War" still stands as an historical landmark of simple, pithy discussion of the relevant aspects of one of the most complicated, organized patterns of human behavior. As such, if for no other reason, it is worthy of attention by behavioral scientists.

At a quite different level, namely, that of the man engaged in combat, probably the best source of data on the characteristics of violence in human behavior is a series of books by Marshall.[8, 9] Marshall's information was obtained through interviews with all the men available from a unit as soon after they had come out of an action as feasible. I was fortunate in being able to accompany General Marshall on several occasions in Korea. He asked only the simplest questions about actions, weapons, terrain, and so forth, and maintained the continuity of the narrative, as different members of the group contributed to it, by adhering rigidly to the temporal sequence of events. By cross-checking differing reports as they were given he was able to piece together a coherent account. In the course of the group interview one or another man would add observations on behavior, always stated in terms of action or desire for particular action. Subjective terms were scarcely ever used. In these interviews, Marshall[10] seldom found a man with reasonable comprehension of the action as a whole and most men remembered only parts of a few, scattered episodes, sometimes in the wrong order. This chaos, as far as retrievable memories were concerned, had not prevented superior performance from moment to moment during the action. Reports obtained a few days after an action, Marshall found, did not show the startlingly clear memory of isolated events, objects, etc., presented in the immediate interviews, and the amnestic periods were forgotten or evaded. The later accounts also were colored by factors or considerations extrinsic to the action itself and the use of subjective terminology increased.

It is of particular interest that a man can "steel himself" to face death or wounding, or he can throw himself with his fellows into an attack. Marshall found, however, that the greatest threat of the battlefield was its "lonesomeness." A man can rarely stand the *sense*, the *conviction*, of being left, deserted and alone—a sense which may develop quickly when, under stress, he fails to see or hear the other members of his outfit or his leaders. This is the point at which he almost always turns back toward his own lines or seeks shelter in which to hide. These observations are well supported by a great deal of other evidence. The "loneliness" reaction, of course, does not occur merely from the fact of being alone, as the work of trained agents behind the lines and of trained commandos, etc., shows. It is rather, a function of training and anticipation in the particular setting. The data thus would support the proposition that violence in human behavior is part of social communication, even when it is associated with considerable reduction in the capacity to think. Under secure conditions our symbolic behavior may be quite different and we may use the conventional cliché of the universal "fear" of death to assert our normality and explain the awesome experiences of the threat of lonesomeness.

It is of interest that von Clausewitz and Marshall, dealing with different data, came to comparable conclusions. Both were excellent observers and both wanted reliable information on the behavior of armies and men for their professional use. They had a "need to know" how men behave, how violence is used in human behavior and how it is lost. They were also concerned with the problem of the degree to which violence is exerted to accomplish a given end, as well as with the problem of the transition to another pattern or objective.

To consider, now, a few of the many experimental studies on aggressive behavior, I should like first to mention a careful investigation of such behavior in the Northern Grasshopper Mouse, *Onychomys leucogaster*, recently published by Clark.[4] Clark studied the environmental contingencies which evoked or which inhibited this behavior and also the previous experiences of individual mice which resulted in a modification of the standard responses to the environmental contingencies. He concluded that aggressive behavior is a pattern that is, in part, genetically determined but that is only elicited by particular circumstances. He further found that the aggressive pattern of behavior could be modified by experience and that an animal could learn to find other solutions to situations than that of attacking. He further found that the tendency in a group of mice was to organize in such a way that aggressive behavior tended to diminish. The incidence of overt aggressive behavior increased when the group became disorganized through changes in either social or territorial factors. One may say that there is no such occult force as a "need for aggression" but that aggressive behavior may be used, as it were, "reasonably" in answer to certain situations or it may be "resorted to" in situations of uncertainty and social disorganization.

The literature of experimental studies on the brain and aggressive behavior is too extensive to review here in detail. I will, therefore, limit my comments to a few observations which illustrate certain general principles. In the historical development of the problem of "localization of function" in the brain, there has been an unfortunate tendency to take concepts from one discipline and to correlate them with concepts from another discipline without paying sufficient attention to the data underlying the respective concepts. Thus, for example, the concept of "emotions" became important on the basis of considerable clinical psychiatric work and on the basis of various psychological tests and studies early this century. During the 1920's and 1930's Walter B. Cannon studied the functions of the sympathetic system and the relationships of the hypothalamus to this system. During the same time Bard[3] described in meticulous detail the behavior he observed in cats which had survived ablation of the cortex. He was most careful to avoid any statement as to localization of function. Nevertheless, by the latter part of the 1930's there was a widely accepted, absolute statement that the hypothalamus was the "center of the emotions." Later work failed to support this concept. Macht and Bard (Bard[1]) showed that the sham-rage reaction could be evoked in experimental preparations with complete transection of the brainstem just caudal to the hypothalamus. These experiments demonstrated that the necessary neural mechanisms for mediating the limited pattern of sham-rage were located caudal to the hypothalamus and probably in the midbrain. Confirming certain incidental observations of Kelly et al.[7] in their studies on the "facio-vocal center," I have found in more recent, unpublished studies that the "rage" reaction is abolished following a lesion which destroys the dorso-lateral part of the reticular formation and the central gray at the level of the superior colliculi. Bard and Mountcastle[2] have also demonstrated that if the ablation of the cortex is carried out in such a way as to preserve the ventral lateral parts of the limbic lobe the sham-rage reaction fails to appear. Secondary ablation of the amygdaloid nuclei on both sides allows one, however, to evoke the sham-rage in the classical manner.

Additional observations on decorticate cats and a review of earlier data strongly suggest the so-called sham-rage reaction is not to be considered a unique pattern of behavior. Rather, it represents aspects of behavior which occur in three distinct, stereotyped patterns seen in decorticate preparations. One finds spitting, growling, biting and clawing in what may be called a pattern of attack behavior, in a pattern of struggle-escape behavior and in a pattern of threat-escape behavior. In each case one finds dilatation of pupils and increase of heart rate but it is only in the threat-escape pattern that one gets maximal erection of the hair as in the typical "Hallowe'en cat." The attack pattern is evoked by a nociceptive stimulus; the struggle-escape is evoked by partial restraint but is increased by adding a nociceptive component, and the threat-escape is evoked by a loud, high-pitched noise. Not only are these patterns in the decorticate preparations so stereotyped as to be virtually caricatures of the related patterns in intact cats but also the decorticate patterns lack some of the most effective maneuvers of which the intact animal is capable. Thus, the decorticate struggle-escape response is a straight pulling away from the restraint, clawing and biting anything in the neighborhood of the head and front paws. In the correlated normal pattern the cat uses twisting, rolling and turning. Also, it alternatively attacks the source of the stimulus and tries to pull away. In addition, the intact animal's behavior is very much under the control of a variety of environmental contingencies rather than under the control of a limited stimulus, as is the decorticate.

A number of small bilateral but limited lesions of different parts of the brain have been described as reducing the threshold for the expression of aggressive behavior. The studies by Wheatley,[12] Bard and Mountcastle,[2] Shreiner[11] and others have provided a wide variety of data. It is of interest that not only do these lesions change the threshold of aggressive behavior but in addition they change the character of the situation which releases the behavior and they also change certain aspects of the character of the behavior itself. It would appear, however, that it is only extensive, bilateral destruction of the dorso-medial thalamic nuclei which produces the phenomenon of "attack on sight." Other lesions result in aggressive behavior which appears defensive in cats. Similarly, experiments on electrical stimulation of particular areas will evoke different patterns depending on the area and also depending on the situation in which the experiment is conducted.[6]

When we take the results of stimulation and ablation studies, such as those which have been described and consider these in the light of current anatomical and physiological information on the structure and the nature of information flow in the brain, we come to the conclusion that we do not deal with *centers* which *produce* certain patterns of behavior. Rather, we are dealing with mechanisms which direct the interaction of the organism with the environment in patterns of behavior which, to a large extent, are related to the anatomically determined capabilities of the organism. The adequacy and complexity of these patterns appear to be related to the capacity of the brain to perceive and to process the environmental data and to use the results of previous experience for building more complex patterns of behavior. With brain damage or with functional disturbance the patterns become simpler and more stereotyped and also more under the control of certain limited stimuli from the immediate environment. The data are not yet sufficient to permit us to say which parts of the central neuronal networks are necessary for mediating patterns of aggressive behavior; nor can we say that any part of the brain is completely uninvolved in the repertoire of aggressive behaviors of intact animals.

In conclusion I should like to repeat that in the study of the role of violence in behavior one cannot take concepts from one discipline or from a study conducted for a particular purpose and apply these concepts to another area. It is necessary to "translate" the concept, taking the data and the point of view of the original author into account. It is the purpose of this Symposium to provide the opportunity for the participants to learn more of each other's methods, objectives and findings in order to clarify our thinking on the role of violence in behavior.

REFERENCES

1. BARD, P.: The Central Nervous System. *In:* Medical Physiology, edited by Bard, P. 10th Ed. St. Louis, C. V. Mosby, 1956, pp. 1055-1056.
2. — AND MOUNTCASTLE, V. B.: Some forebrain mechanisms involved in expression of rage with special reference to suppression of angry behavior. Res. Publ. A. Nerv. Ment. Dis. 27: 362-404, 1948.
3. — AND RIOCH, D. M.: A study of four cats deprived of neocortex and additional portions of the forebrain. Bull. Johns Hopkins Hosp. 60:73-174, 1937.
4. CLARK, L. D.: A comparative view of aggressive behavior. Amer. J. Psychiat. 119:336-341, .
5. CLAUSEWITZ, VON K.: On War. Washington Infantry Journal Press, 1950.
6. EGGER, M. D., AND FLYNN, J. P.: Amygdaloid suppression of hypothalamically elicited attack behavior. Science 136:43-44, 1962.
7. KELLY, A. H., BEATON, L, E., AND MAGOUN, H. W.: Midbrain mechanism for facio-vocal activity. J. Neurophysiol. 9:181-189, 1946.
8. MARSHALL, S. L. A.: Men Against Fire. New York, William Morrow, 1953.
9. —: The Soldier's Load and the Mobility of a Nation. Washington, D. C., The Combat Forces Press, 1950.
10. —: Island victory. Infantry Journal. New York, Penguin Books, 213 pp., 1944.
11. SCHREINER, L., RIOCH, D. M., PECHTEL, C., AND MASSERMAN, J. H.: Behavioral changes following thalamic injury in cat. J. Neurophysiol. 16:234-246, 1953.
12. WHEATLEY, M. D.: The hypothalamus and affective behavior in cats. A study of the effects of experimental lesions with anatomic correlations. Arch. Neurol. Psychiat. 52: 298-316, 1944.

AGGRESSIVE BEHAVIOR AND RITUALIZED FIGHTING IN ANIMALS

By IRENÄUS EIBL-EIBESFELDT, Ph.D.

FIGHTING is a term that is often functionally defined as any sort of behavior which leads to flight, surrender or destruction of a member of the same or another species. Scott[24] defines "agonistic" behavior more widely as "any sort of adaptation which is connected with a contest or conflict between two animals, whether fighting, escaping, or freezing" (p. 16). Aggression can be generally conceived as any attack, which if allowed to continue will result in physical damage of the opponent. However, most animals show clear and discrete responses to varying situations leading to such an attack, and the behavior patterns involved in intraspecies and interspecies fighting are often different.

As one example the Oryx-Antelope never uses its rapier-shaped horns to gore another Oryx, but fights its rival in a tournament-like way. They "fence" with the upper portion of their horns and, finally, push against one another, forehead against forehead. This is never done to predators, who are attacked with lowered head and impaled.[32] Male giraffes, in rival combat, use their short horns, whereas against predators, they use their hooves.[2] Animals also distinguish between aggression carried out against a predator and that against prey. A polecat, when hunting, is silent and does not fluff its fur or empty its olfactory gland when attacking a prey, but does so and emits sharp cries when attacking a predator.

On the basis of the different behavior patterns involved, there seems no reason to attribute intraspecies aggression, aggression against a predator, and aggression against prey to a single motivational system. Only occasionally does one find indications that prey-catching behavior gradually shifts into predator defense, e.g., as the size of the prey gets larger.[5] Ardrey,[1] e.g., tried to trace the aggressivity of modern man to the fact that *Australopithecus* was a "ferocious carnivore," but this is hardly convincing. Herbivores, too, are not at all peaceful, as two fighting bulls demonstrate.

Our special concern in this report is with *intraspecies fighting behavior*. Every animal keeper knows that animals of the same species tend to fight each other, while often they ignore members of other species, as long as they are not predators. One can easily demonstrate this by placing a tree shrew, some guinea pigs, or an Aguti into a cage with a resident male European squirrel; the latter will not fight until another male squirrel is introduced. The tree shrew, in turn, will ignore the squirrel, but ferociously attack another tree shrew put in the cage. This principle is applicable for many fishes, birds, and reptiles.

In intraspecies fighting behavior we can distinguish aggressive attack and defensive fighting. We find attack usually being elicited by the perception of a conspecific prior to bodily contact; in contrast, defense is brought about by painful stimulation after bodily contact. Aggressive attack is often released by simple sign stimuli of the rival; e.g., Tinbergen's[30] sticklebacks fought a crude dummy as long as it had a red belly, but ignored a detailed copy of another stickleback, which lacked the red characteristic of the breeding male. Lack[15] demonstrated that the male robin (Erithacus rubecula) blindly attacks a brush of red feathers mounted on a branch in his territory, but ignores a stuffed male without red breast feathers. Peiponen[21] confirmed this observation and showed that a male blue throat (Luscinia svecica) reacts in a similar way to another male's blue breast feathers. Noble and Bradley[18] found that male iguanas (Sceloporus undulatus) fought with a female whose belly had been painted blue to resemble a male, but court males with bellies painted female grey.

Many vertebrates show solitary habits, attacking other conspecifics that enter their territories; yet they allow, for short periods, a sexual partner to enter for purposes of propagation. Our European hamster (*Cricetus cricetus*) is an example of an animal of this sort. Other animals (e.g., the Norway rat) live together in groups composed of several males, females, and young, showing a common territory but defending this against any intruding conspecific not belonging to the group. There are, furthermore, species that live in families constituted of a pair and their young or just the mother and her babies, while others live in herds dominated by one male, as, e.g., the sea lions. All these groups have one thing in common: they do not allow the approach of a conspecific of another group. Their behavior is usually associated with the possession of a certain area, which they defend. In migrating birds, one often observes that individuals maintain a rather constant distance from each other, called the individual distance; they carry, so to speak, their territory with them.

Fighting with the *sexual rival*, especially in males is also often observed. A number of studies have revealed that the fluctuations in male aggressivity coincide with fluctuations in the levels of male sexual hormones; castrates tend to show peaceful habits, but become aggressive when injected with testosterone.[3] During the breeding season, tame male European squirrels (*Sciurus vulgaris*) chase other males with which they previously had peacefully shared their cage, or attack the caretaker if prevented from fighting a rival conspecific. When the rutting season is over, they behave peacefully again.

Increased general activity also seems to be controlled by an inner urge, similar to that found by v. Holst and v. Saint Paul.[12] By electrical brain stimulation they not only released aggressive behavior patterns but also the typical appetitive behavior preceding it. The brain stimulated cock or hen does not blindly start a fight, but first becomes aroused, then searches for specific releasing stimuli, which allows the discharge of aggressive behavior. Stimulated in other areas, a cock might similarly search for other stimuli, e.g., those releasing courtship, while at the same time ignoring stimuli that elicit fighting. This demonstrates that one has activated the physiological system of a drive.

At the moment we keep a number of male lava lizards (*Tropidurus albemarlensis*), in cages separated by a piece of cardboard. If we remove this, then neighboring lizards persistently try to get at each other through the glass and fight, ignoring food, hurting themselves, and biting and beating at the glass. The same phenomena can be observed in land iguanas (*Conolophus subcristatus*) and some fishes.

In man intraspecies aggression is considered as a destructive, unwanted force. Lorenz[16] emphasized the drive nature of human aggression, pointing to its inherited background. Kuo[14] and Scott[24, 25] differed with this opinion. Scott found that he could condition a mouse to be either peaceful or aggressive; however, after repeated defeats, an aggressive mouse became nonaggressive and of lower rank order. Conversely, a nonaggressive mouse could be conditioned to become aggressive; ergo, aggression was a result of individual experience. Scott therefore concluded that "there is no such thing as a simple instinct for fighting, in the sense of an internal driving force, which has to be satisfied" (p. 62), and "From a more general viewpoint, the experiments with mice show us that aggression has to be learned. Defensive fighting can be stimulated by pain of an attack, but aggression in the strict sense of an unprovoked attack can be produced only by training" (p. 20). Scott hoped that peaceful children could be raised in an environment that lacked stimulation to fight. McNeil[17] in his excellent review, remarks in this context. "Whether such passivity would be at the cost of initiative is an unanswered question" (p. 197). So also, Kuo caged cats, rats, and dogs together from infancy and found that they remained peaceful. This and similar experiments brought him to the conclusion: "Our hope for a peaceful and tranquil society without fighting and social domination lies in the prevention of the development of such behavior patterns. The developmental approach seems to have encouraged us to hope that the day may not be so far off, when it will be just as feasible to immunize against social domination and fighting as immunization against smallpox or poliomyelitis" (p. 225).

But do their experiments really support this conclusion? They certainly prove that aggressive behavior can be enhanced or inhibited by experience, but that it has to be learned in order to occur was not shown. When we protected grey Norway rats from a conspecific conflict by raising them in isolation, they, nevertheless, attacked conspecifics that were put in their cage, prior to any painful stimulation, with the patterns of threat and fighting used by experienced animals.[9, 10] On the other hand, rats that were raised in groups and had competed over food, remained peaceful toward their cage mates and attacked only foreign members of their species.

But if aggressive behavior is a product of evolution it must have some survival value. Comparative studies reveal the two main functions of aggression. First, the conspecific competes for the same food, nesting material, nesting sites, etc., so that aggression serves the function of spacing out. The mechanism of aggression in such cases prevents overcrowding and is, furthermore, a most effective mechanism for the distribution of species acting as "population pressure." Second, fighting serves to select the fittest male for propagation even though fights between individuals of the same species normally do not result in death and rarely even in serious injury to either combatant. On the contrary special mechanisms have often independently evolved to spare the loser. In animals that are in a position to hurt each other, e.g., by the possession of strong or poisonous teeth, the mode of fighting has become ritualized to a tournament, in the course of which the animals measure their strength without biting each other. The animal that loses the fight is often a healthy but immature male that cannot withstand the attack of a mature individual. If the conspecific were killed, the species would be endangered by exterminating the necessary reserve of young males. One might expect, in view of the disadvantage of serious injury to a member of the same species, that this acted in some instances as a strong selection pressure against aggressivity. But spacing out, through combat, was apparently too important to permit a weakening of aggressive tendencies. In order to allow this mechanism to work, the most complicated ways of fighting have developed in the course of evolution, as a direct result of these two counter-directed selective pressures.

This does not mean that all species show tournamental fighting. Species which cannot hurt each other seriously do not engage in tournaments whereas other species, outfitted with strong weapons, sometimes engage in damaging fight, as in hamsters or rats. But these species are capable of quick flight and after the exchange of a few bites, the loser makes a fast getaway. If one keeps such animals in close captivity, then they often kill each other; however, in some species this is prevented by the loser assuming a special submissive posture, which the winner respects.

Lorenz[16] has described such fights in dogs and wolves. In both species fighting starts with the exchange of bites. But as soon as one contestant begins to lose, it exposes its vulnerable throat to its opponent by turning its head away and this immediately stops the attack. A young dog will throw itself on its back when attacked by an older dog or when its master raises his voice. Similar submissive postures are known in many birds. Young rails turn the back of their head toward the aggressor and so do the young of the great crested grebes (*Podiceps*). The latter, as they turn, display a type of signal light: a featherless spot flushes red. A turkey that has lost a fight assumes a submissive posture by lying flat on its belly in front of the victor. Similar behavior is shown by the lizard (*Lacerta agilis*) who in submission lies flat on the belly at the same time making intention movements to run away.[13] In most of the submissive postures the loser places himself at the mercy of the winner by exposing vulnerable parts to attack. At the same time, it often makes itself smaller by folding its fins as do the cichlid fishes. Darwin called this the "principle of antithesis: i.e., the animal hides stimuli that normally release aggression. This concealment can take many forms. In the blackheaded gull (*Larus ridibundus*) the black face mask releases aggression and looking at the partner is a gesture of threat. During pair formation the animals turn the back of their heads toward each other, looking at the partner only out of the corner of the eye. This facing away or "headflagging" has been proved to have an appeasing effect.[30] The coot (*Fulica atra*) in a similar way hides its aggression—releasing white lobe by dipping its head in the water. Some species turn their weapon away, as in the case with the albatross, who appeases his sexual partner by pointing its beak toward the sky.[7] A similar gesture is shown by submissive boobies.[30] In some species infantile behavior is used for appeasing. Male hamsters, e.g., use infantile call notes during courtship.

Interesting ceremonial fights can be studied in many species. In the cichlid fishes, (*Aequidens portalegrensis*), an initial display with erected fins is followed by a phase during which the animals beat at the opponent with their tails, sending a strong current of water against the opponent's body. If this does not bring about the decision, the animals grasp each other's mouths and begin pulling each other forward and back, in a sort of wrestling; when one finally gives up, it folds its fins and disappears. A damaging fight might follow if the loser cannot escape, as the victor often bites and rams it, tearing its fins and breaking off scales, but this never happens except in captivity.

In different species of cichlid fishes, different stages of this fight are emphasized. Some hardly fight at all, but have elaborate displays (*Cichlasoma meeki*). Others emphasize tailbeating while rarely mouth pulling (*Apistogramma wickleri*), while the latter pattern is prominent in other species (*Cichlasoma biocellatum*).[19]

Another way of ritualized fighting has been described in the anemone fish (*Amphiprion percula*). The rivals stand opposite each other, each trying to bite the opponent's side, which the other shields with the spread-out pectoral fin. This special parrying movement prevents ram thrusts and thus the contest appears rather as a tournament.[8] Recently Schapitz[22] described rival fights in the fish *Pyrrhulina vittata*. Both rivals swim side by side trying to push each other to the side with the rear half of the body in contact.

On the Galápagos Islands we observed and filmed the ceremonial combats of male marine iguanas (*Amblyrhynchus cristatus*). This large iguana lives along the shore lines, feeding on marine algae at

No warm up petty may

low tide. During the breeding season the males occupy territories which they defend. If a rival intrudes, the territory owner displays by opening his mouth, nodding with the head and stiffed-leggedly walking up and down in front of his opponent, who answers in a similar way. If the intruder does not leave but answers by a similar display, a fight starts. The animals rush toward each other and clash their heads together. Each one tries to push the other away, with the horn-like scales of the heads interlocked. The struggle ends when one of the iguanas assumes a submissive posture by lying flat on his belly. The winner then stops fighting and waits in threat display for the rival to leave. A damaging fight is observed only if the intruder does not perform the ceremonies that signal a tournament: when for example, intruders are suddenly placed in an occupied territory, or if they cross it while fleeing and thus do not show any display. Damaging fights were, furthermore, observed between females during the egg-laying season, when they fought for proper sites. They started in a tournament-like manner, but they soon changed into a damaging fight, biting each other viciously.

Kitzler[13] has described the ceremonial combats of the lizard (*Lacerta agilis*). One male grasps the other at the neck, while the other stands still, waiting for his turn to come. They fight this way, until one is fatigued. Sometimes the one that bit the other suddenly gives up, as if realizing from the size of the other's neck, as well from his standing firm, that he has no chance to win.

Many poisonous snakes wrestle instead of biting the rival. Shaw[27] described the combat between male rattlesnakes (*Crotalus ruber*). The rivals glide along, side by side, each having the front third of its length raised in the air. In this posture they push each other with their head and by hitting the opponent they try to throw him to the ground. This continues until one pins the other to the ground for a short while. Similar ritualized fights have been observed in many other snakes. In the *Bitis*, the rivals climb, in turn, on each other's back and get thrown off by a jerking movement. In this species the origin of the strange mode of fighting can be traced to a sexual fusion gesture.[29]

In birds, highly ritualized fights can also be observed in the ruff (*Philomachus pugnax*),[26] or turkeys.[23] Some of their appeasing postures have been mentioned.

Turning to mammals, ceremonial fights have been studied in cavicornes by Walther.[32] In this group that originated from species with sharp canines, the horns have evolved as special instruments for rival fights, and not, as often assumed, primarily to fight predators. Different species also fight in different, often highly elaborate ways. We have mentioned the tournament of the Oryx antelopes. In the fallow deer the rivals "march" side by side, the head raised, looking at each other out of the corners of their eyes. Suddenly they halt, turn face to face, lower their heads and charge. Their antlers clash and they wrestle for a while and then they continue their "march." Fighting and "marching" alternate until one wins. One notices that the stags attack only when they face each other. Siewert,[28] filmed a fight in which one male accidentally exposed his rear to the opponent who took no advantage of it, but waited for his rival to turn fully until he was facing.

Many other examples of different fighting modes are given by Walther[32] who suggested that the phylogenetic origin is a biting movement which became ritualized to pushing with the snout, from which pushing with the head could well have evolved. Especially interesting are the fights between Nilgau Antelope bulls (*Boselaphus tragocamelus*) The short horned bull, although displaying "head pushing," fights like the tylopods by putting his neck over that of the opponent and pressing him down to the ground.[32]

In man, ritualized ways of fighting have been developed independently in different cultures. No detailed comparative study is available to allow speculation about the common and perhaps inborn features. Ohm[20] studied the submissive praying postures in man, when he makes himself appear physically smaller. Common to man is also the reaction of crying, which releases pity and strong inhibition of attack, analogous to that observed in animals. It does not, however, work in our technical age, as an arrow or a rifle can kill a conspecific before he has any opportunity to appeal to our probably inborn inhibitions.

But altruism is not less deeply rooted in man than aggressiveness, although altruistic reactions in animals, as well as in man, are shown only toward members of the same family or herd. Within this group the individual is as basically "good" as he can be "bad" to the foreigner. In the course of our history man was able to learn that his family has grown, coming first to encompass his clan, then his tribe and his nation. He will eventually learn that his family includes all mankind.

REFERENCES

1. ARDREY, R.: African Genesis. London, Collins, 1962.
2. BACKHAUS, D.: Beobachtungen an Giraffen in zoologischen Gärten und freier Wildbahn. Bruxelles, Institut des Parcs Nationaux du Congo et du Ruanda-Urundi, 1961.
3. BEACH, F. A.: Hormones and Behavior. New York, Cooper Square Publ., 1961.
4. CARPENTER, C. E.: Patterns of social behavior in the desert iguano Dipsosaurus dorsalis. Copeia 4:396-405, 1961.
5. EIBL-EIBESFELDT, I.: Nahrungserwerb und Beuteschema der Erdkröte (Bufo bufo). Behavior 4:1-35, 1951.
6. —: Der Kommentkampf der Meerechse (Amblyrhynchus cristatus Bell.) nebst einigen Notizen zur Biologie dieser Art.Ztschr.Tierpsychol. 12:49-62, 1955.
7. —: Naturschutzprobleme auf den Galapagos Inseln.Acta trop. 17:7-137, 1960a.
8. —:Beobachtungen und Versuche an Anemonenfischen (Amphiprion) der Malediven und Nikobaren. Ztschr. Tierpsychol. 17:1-10, 1960h.
9. —: Rattus Norvegicus Kampf.1.Erfahrene Männchen,E 131. 2.Unerfahrene Männchen,E 132. Göttingen, Wiss.Filme,Inst.wiss.Film, 1961.
10. —: Angeborenes und Erworbenes im Verhalten der Säuger.Ztschr.Tierpsychol. In press, 1963.
11. HEDIGER, H.: Tierpsychologische Beobachtungen aus dem Terrarium des Zürcher Zoos.Rev.Suisse Zool. 69:317-324, 1962.
12. v. HOLST, E., AND SAINT PAUL, U. v.: Vom Wirkungsgefüge der Triebe. Naturwiss. 18:409-422, 1960.
13. KITZLER, G.: Die Paarungsbiologie einiger Eidechsen. Ztschr.Tierpsychol. 4:353-402, 1942.
14. KUO, Z. Y.: Studies on the basic factors in animal fighting. J. Genet. Psychol. 96:201-223, 225-239, 1960; 97:181-195-209, 211-225, 1960.
15. LACK, D.: The Life of the Robin. London, 1943.
16. LORENZ, K.: Die angeborenen Formen möglicher Erfahrung. Ztschr.Tierpsychol. 5:235-409, 1943.
17. McNEIL, E. B.: Psychol. and aggression. J. Conflict Resolution 3:195-239, 1959.
18. NOBLE, G. K., AND BRADLEY, H. T.: The mating behavior of lizards. Ann. N.Y.Acad.Sci. 35:25-1, 1933.
19. OEHLERT, B.: Kampf und Paarbildung bei einigen Cichliden.Ztschr.Tierpsychol. 15:141-174, 1958.
20. OHM, T.: Die Gebetsgebärden der Völker und das Christentum.Leiden, 1948.
21. PEIPONEN, V. A.: Verhaltensstudien am Blaukehlchen.Ornis Fennica 37:69-83, 1960.
22. SCHAPITZ, W.: Das Verhalten von Pyrrhulina vittata (Regan) (Teleostei, Characidae). Ztschr.Tierpsychol. 19:262-275, 1962.
23. SCHLEIDT, W., AND SCHLEIDT, M.: Kampfverhalten beim Wildputer (Meleagris gallapavo silvestris). Göttingen, Wiss.Film,Inst.wiss.Film, 1963.
24. SCOTT, J. P.: Animal behavior. Chicago, Univ. Press, 1958.
25. —: Aggression. Chicago, Univ. Press, 1960.
26. SELOUS, E.: Schaubalz und geschlechtliche Auslese beim Kampfläufer (Philomachus pugnax). J.Ornithol. 77:262-309, 1929.

27. SHAW, C. E.: The male combat "dance" of some crotalid snakes. Herpetologica pp. 137-145, 1948.
28. SIEWERT, H.: Rot-und Damwild in der Brunft.Göttingen,Wiss.Film C 351, Inst.wiss.Film, 1940.
29. THOMAS, E.: Fortpflanzungskämpfe bei Sandottern (Vipera ammodytes). Verh.Dtsch.Zool.Ges.Bonn pp. 502-505, 1960.
30. TINBERGEN, N.: The study of instinct. Oxford, Oxford Univ. Press, 1951.
31. —: Einige Gedanken über Beschwichtigungsgebärden. Ztschr.Tierpsychol. 16:651-665, 1959.
32. WALTHER, F.: Zum Kampf-und Paarungsverhalten einiger. Antilopen.Ztschr. Tierpsychol. 15:340-380, 1958.
33. —: Entwicklungszüge im Kampf-und Paarungsverhalten der Horntiere.Georg-Opel-Freigehege für Tierforschung,Jahrbuch 1960/1961, 3:90-115, 1962.

AGGRESSIVE STIMULI, AGGRESSIVE RESPONSES AND HOSTILITY CATHARSIS

By LEONARD BERKOWITZ

THE INSTIGATION to aggression is usually pictured as an ever-active energy source constantly impelling aggressive responses. Whether these responses appear in overt behavior, however, supposedly depends primarily on the presence of inhibitions or other avenues of expression, and not on the stimulus qualities of the available targets. Hartmann, Kris, and Loewenstein[2] provide an excellent illustration of this type of thinking. Although they do state (almost in passing) that disliked or frustrating objects "invite the discharge" of aggressive energy (energy stemming, supposedly, from some unspecified biological source), the drive object is considered relatively unimportant in aggressive behavior. The object, they maintain (citing Freud), becomes attached to the drive "only in consequence of being peculiarly fitted to provide satisfaction." A particular target is attacked not because it has the stimulus qualities to evoke aggression but because of the satisfactions earned in the course of aggressing against this object.

Many views of aggression assign a very minor role to stimulation from the external environment. For a number of writers such external stimulation theoretically affects only whether the person believes aggression is safe or morally justified. For example, in the usual discussion of the scapegoat theory of prejudice[3] the victim is supposedly attacked primarily because he is a visible and safe target for pent-up hostility within the prejudiced individual. He is a "conveniently chosen outlet," in the words of Hartmann and his colleagues, who is selected largely because the attacker anticipates little or no punishment in return. My own position is somewhat different: basically, I suggest that a target with appropriate stimulus qualities "pulls" (evokes) aggressive responses from a person who is ready to engage in such actions either because he is angry or because particular objects have acquired cue-value for aggressive responses from him.[4, 5]

18

Such a conception has several important implications. For one thing, we do not have to think of a person as being constantly driven to attack someone—anyone—unless his aggressive impulses can be diverted into socially acceptable actions. His likelihood of engaging in hostile behavior can be substantially lowered, theoretically at least, by removing external stimuli capable of evoking aggressive responses.

SIMILAR CONCEPTIONS IN OTHER FIELDS

Anyone familiar with the work of the ethologists in Europe and the United States will recognize the similarity between the position I have just outlined and the ethological concept of *releaser*. A releaser, or sign stimulus, is a cue in the external environment which produces a given reaction from an organism ready to make such a response. To illustrate, Tinbergen[6] has reported that an aroused male stickleback fish reacts with fighting behavior to the red on the belly of a rival male. This red stimulus evoking the attack is highly specific; aggression does not occur if the red is on the rival's back. The evoking stimulus, furthermore, has little if any effect if the organism is not in an appropriate condition. In the aforementioned case the stickleback probably had been aroused by the presence of the rival male. The stimulus *releases* behavior the organism is ready to make. There clearly is an interaction between the organism's internal condition and the external stimulation. Research has shown that a strong releaser is necessary to elicit a reaction if the animal is under low motivation, while a weaker releaser is sufficient if the animal is in a stronger motivational state.[7]

AGGRESSION-EVOKING STIMULI

Elsewhere,[8] I have suggested that an object is capable of evoking aggressive responses to the extent that it is associated with previous anger or aggression instigators. Such a formula, of course, is only an extension of Miller's[9] well known analysis of displacement in terms of stimulus-response generalization. To apply this analysis to aggressive behavior, suppose a man is angered by Person A but cannot attack him because A is absent from the scene. If the man should then encounter other people with varying degrees of similarity to, or association with, Person A, these people will elicit hostile reactions from him in proportion to their association with A.

A recent experiment by Weatherley[10] employing projective test (TAT) responses provides an excellent demonstration of the interaction of cue and emotional state in aggressive behavior. The investigator found that deliberately angered students whose mothers had permitted aggression exhibited reliably more fantasy aggression on the projective test than did a similarly reared but nonprovoked group—but only to cards having strong aggression cues. The formers' aroused hostile inclinations were not revealed, even though their inhibitions were probably fairly weak, unless appropriate cues were present in the environment.

The scenes portrayed on the projective test cards served as aggression-evoking cues to the extent that they depicted situations in which aggression ordinarily occurs. The subject presumably associated the high cue scene with prior situations in which he had been angered and/or had behaved aggressively. Because of this tie, the card could evoke hostile responses from the subject fairly easily if he was angry and ready to make such responses. In the next study the aggression-eliciting stimuli were associated with the immediately preceding arousal condition rather than with common aggressive situations.

In this preliminary experiment[11] male college students were first either angered or not by 1 of the 2 experimenters (Experimenter-1). This particular experimenter had been introduced earlier, depending on the condition, either as (1) a college boxer, or (2) a graduate student in Speech. A few minutes later, the other experimenter showed the subject a 7 minute-long film clip, either a fairly brutal prize fight scene[12] or one dealing with the travels of Marco Polo. At the conclusion of the movie the subject was asked to rate each of the experimenters on special forms. Since these questionnaires supposedly were to go to

TABLE 1.—*Mean Condition Scores on the Hostility Indices, Questionnaire Ratings of Each of the 2 Experimenters.*

	Subjects Angered by Experimenter-1				Nonangered Subjects	
Film	Boxing Movie		Travel Movie		Boxing Movie	
Identification of Experimenter-1	Boxing	Speech	Boxing	Speech	Boxing	Speech
Experimenter-1	21.42_a	15.29_{bcd}	16.00_{bc}	17.43_b	11.00_e	10.71_e
Experimenter-2	12.86_{cde}	9.14_e	10.10_e	11.71_{de}	10.43_e	12.14_{cde}

Note: The ratings of the 2 experimenters were subjected to one "repeated measures" analysis of variance. Cells having a subscript in common are not significantly different at the .05 level. The higher the score the greater the expressed unfriendliness toward the given experimenter. Each mean is based on 7 cases.

the Dean's Office as part of a survey of student reactions to experiments, unfavorable ratings of the graduate student-experimenter could conceivably hurt them and, therefore, are here taken as acts of aggression.

Now, what do we expect? In some cases Experimenter-1 is fairly strongly associated with an aggressive film; he is seen as a "boxer" by some of the men witnessing a movie about boxing. If this aggressive movie tended to arouse previously learned aggressiveness habits,[13] the hostile inclinations aroused by the film should generalize most strongly to external objects bearing the strongest psychological ties to the film, i.e., to the college boxer. The results summarized in table 1 indicate that this expectation was fulfilled. When Experimenter-1 was associated with both arousal sources, the insult and the aggressive film, he apparently had a relatively strong cue value for aggressive responses. He had the stimulus qualities which "pulled" fairly intense hostility from the "primed" subjects.

Much of the experimental research employing notions of the sort described here involves associations based on physical similarities. In the last study, however, Experimenter-1's association with the aggressive film was varied by means of verbal labels applied to him by the experimenter; he was a "boxer" or he was a "Speech student." Our thoughts may also equate different objects. We may regard objectively different people as being similar, for example, because we have learned to apply the same label to them (e.g., "They're all Democrats."), or perhaps because they arouse the same emotional feelings in us.

The hostility displacement involved in the scapegoat theory of prejudice can be readily understood in terms of associations created through the aggressor's thoughts.[14] Our research at Wisconsin indicates that the hostile responses evoked by one frustrater generalize fairly readily to other disliked people. We believe that the thwarted person somehow associates his victims with the immediately frustrating agency. All of these people are disliked, for example, and all may be regarded as essentially alike in being unpleasant. An industrial worker thwarted by his employer may displace his resentment onto Jews, then, because he previously had learned to dislike Jews, and disliking them, subjectively associates Jews with the disliked and frustrating employer. He may also associate Jews with the employer because he thinks of all of these people as "businessmen," and association bonds can summate. Because of such ties, the scapegoat group "pulls" hostile responses from the person who is ready to act aggressively.

HOSTILITY CATHARSIS

Tension reduction through completing aggressive activity. The conception of aggressive behavior outlined so far has some fairly definite implications for the analysis of hostility catharsis. Before going into these implications, however, some basic distinctions must be made, in essence considerably restricting the phenomena included within the scope of the catharsis hypothesis. In the psychological literature at least "catharsis" seems to refer most frequently to a lessening in the strength of the *instigation to aggression* supposedly produced by a hostile act. Such a "drive reduction" is not necessarily involved in the second meaning of the term, *a feeling of pleasure or tension reduction* presumably arising from the performance of an aggressive response. Empirical evidence indicates the thwarted person may obtain some tension release by attacking his frustrater.[15, 16] This can be pleasurable, particularly if the angered person is able to perform the aggressive responses he previously had been unable to make. But the tension reduction does not necessarily mean there is a decreased likelihood of any further aggression against the frustrater. Elsewhere, I have maintained that much of what is commonly meant by the term "catharsis" can be understood as a special case of a "completion tendency." According to research, failure to complete tasks often creates tension leading to the better recall of these tasks and the tendency to resume them.[17] An activity will tend to continue, of course, until the activity-goal is reached. Preventing the organism from reaching this goal, i.e., interrupting the activity, can be a source of disturbance. Several writers have suggested there is an "increase in excited emotion" when a consummatory response—completing the activity sequence—is stimulated but not allowed to occur completely.

Applying this formulation to aggressive behavior, we would say that inflicting injury on the intended target is the goal or consummatory response completing the aggressive response sequence. *As long as a person is instigated to aggress* he does not obtain "completion" until he sees that he has injured his target, or that someone else has done so. Thus, if the aggressive sequence is set into operation, but completion is prevented, internal tension is induced which is channeled into whatever responses happens to be underway at the time.[18-21] Extending the proposition to aggressive behavior, we have the frustration-aggression notion that blocking aggressive reactions increases the instigation to further aggression.

An experiment by Thibaut and Coules[22] provides data supporting this prediction. Male college students were first provoked by an insulting message from a peer and then were permitted to reply to the instigator. However, the men in one group were interrupted for 3 minutes before they could avail themselves of this opportunity. Analysis of the messages sent to the frustrater confirmed the frustration-aggression hypothesis. The people who had had to wait before replying sent a reliably greater volume of aggression to the instigator than did the students responding more rapidly to the provocation even though the instigator was not responsible for the interruption.

Expectations to aggress. Use of the frustration-aggression formula requires a clear specification of the nature of frustration. Preventing a person from satisfying a need *we* think he possesses does not necessarily mean the person is actually frustrated. He is frustrated *when an instigated or ongoing response sequence is blocked.* A writer thoroughly engrossed in his work is not frustrated just because he has been without food for a number of hours. He may not be concerned with getting food. Similarly, an angered person is not frustrated merely because he has no opportunity to attack the thwarting agency; being angry does not necessarily mean there is an instigated or ongoing aggressive response sequence.

This important qualification must be kept in mind in evaluating the results of another study which failed to obtain evidence of a heightened "aggressive drive" in some people not permitted to attack their frustrater.[26] *Unlike the aroused men in the Thibaut-Coules study, the provoked people in the later experiment had not expected to be able to retaliate against their tormenter.* Not anticipating an opportunity to aggress, there conceivably were no ongoing aggressive responses in the latter men. More concretely, since they knew they would not be able to reply to the person who had insulted them, they probably were not thinking of how they were going to tell their tormenter off and, therefore, they conceivably were not disappointed when they could not do so.

A recent experiment from our Wisconsin laboratory was consistent with this analysis.[24] The experimental design is fairly complicated, and can best be spelled out in the following way. First, a male college student was made to be angry with a peer who was working in another room. This latter person had given the student an excessive number of electric shocks as his judgment of the student's performance on a previous problem. In some cases the angered student had been led to believe he would have an opportunity to retaliate—he would have a chance to administer shocks to the anger instigator right away. In other cases, however, the subject was told he would not have this quick socially sanctioned opportunity to get even for the harsh treatment he had received. The subjects were then shown their partner's work.

For the people who had been told they could administer shocks as their "judgment," this was their chance to get even.

However, the expectations were met only half of the time. (The remaining people were told that the experimenter had made a mistake in reading the schedule.) Thus, half of the men in the *Expect to Aggress* group found that they would not be able to give the shocks they had anticipated giving, and half of the subjects in the *Expect Not to Aggress* condition learned that they actually did have an opportunity to "evaluate" their partner via the electric shocks.

Those permitted to administer shocks did so as their supposed judgment of his work. After this a brief questionnaire was administered. Several minutes later the subjects were again shown what was supposedly the partner's performance on yet another problem. This time all subjects had an opportunity to "rate" the performance by giving the partner shocks. A second questionnaire was then administered, after which the experiment was concluded and the deceptions were explained.

In addition to the four conditions created by means of the experimental manipulations described up to this point, a relatively nonangered control group was also established.

Our most important question concerns the effects of the subjects' initial expectations. Would those angered men who had anticipated being able to shock the anger instigator right away, and who then were deprived of this aggressive opportunity, display signs of stronger frustration than the other subjects before the end of the session? The reasoning employed in the present paper suggests that this should be the case. In the words of the more behavioristically inclined psychologists, when we expect to obtain a certain satisfaction we make "fractional anticipatory goal responses." This phrase is a good one for our purposes. First, it suggests that the goal is symbolically present in our thoughts. This symbolic representation, the thought of being able to get even with the anger instigator, is the cue eliciting implicit aggressive responses. Second, the phrase also implies there is an ongoing aggressive response sequence if only in the thoughts of the angered men in the *Expect to Aggress* condition. Those angered people not anticipating an opportunity to aggress against their tormenter should be less likely to have such an aggressive sequence in operation and, consequently, should be less bothered by not being permitted to attack him.

The results with our shock measures are summarized in table 2. The first line of data indicates that the people in each angered condition reported receiving essentially the same number of shocks from their partner. That the excessive punishment was anger-provoking is suggested by the condition differences in shocks given for the partner's first performance (line 2). The 2 presumably angered groups who were permitted to shock their partner at this time gave reliably more shocks to him (when combined) than the nonangered control group. Note, however, that there was no difference between the 2 provoked groups in number of shocks administered at this time; the *Expect to Shock-Able to Shock* men displayed the same level of overt aggression in their first "judgments" as the subjects who had not anticipated being able

TABLE 2.—*Mean Number of Shocks Reported Received and Number Given*

Measure	Angered				Nonangered
	Expect to Shock		Expect Not to Shock		
	Able	Not Able	Able	Not Able	
1. No. shocks reported received by subject on first problem:	6.91	6.81	6.22	6.88	1.00
2. No. shocks given by those permitted to "rate" partner's first problem after arousal:	4.17	—	4.17	—	3.03*
3. No. shocks given as judgment of partner at end of session:	3.72$_b$	4.42$_a$	3.88$_b$	3.64$_b$	3.08$_c$†

Note: Except for measure No. 1, the shock data have been transformed using the $\sqrt{X} + \sqrt{X + 1}$ transformation in order to facilitate statistical analysis. Each mean is based on 16 cases.

*The nonangered group gave significantly fewer shocks to the partner on the first problem than the combined angered groups ($F = 17.40$, $p < .01$).

†Differences among conditions were tested by t test employing the residual mean square from the preliminary analysis of variance in the error term. Cells having a subscript in common are not significantly different at the .05 level of confidence.

to retaliate. The information given the former people that they could shock their partner right away had apparently not "stirred them up" in the short time before aggression was permitted.

The "expect to aggress" information evidently did start an implicit aggressive sequence in operation in the angered subjects, however. As the last line shows, when the anticipated aggressive activity was blocked in the *Expect to Shock-Not Able* condition, a heightened arousal resulted so that at the end of the session the men in this group administered more severe punishment to the anger instigator than did the people in any other group. The thwarting of the instigated aggressive sequence apparently had to persist for some minutes before the increased inclination to aggression could be revealed in stronger overt hostility.

But while there are indications of a frustration-strengthened arousal state, table 2 contains no evidence of a cathartic reduction in aggressive tendencies following the initial display of hostility. The subjects in the *Expect to Shock-Able* group gave just as many shocks to their partner at the end of the session as the people who had neither expected nor been able to shock their peer earlier. .

TABLE 3.—*Mean Scores on Tension Index*

	Angered				Nonangered
	Expect to Shock		Expect Not to Shock		Expect to Shock
	Able	Not Able	Able	Not Able	Able
1. After seeing the partner's first performance:	20.48_{ab}	21.83_a	19.27_{bc}	20.38_{abc}	20.24_{bc}
2 After giving partner the final shocks at end of session:	20.44_{ab}	20.89_{ab}	18.82_c	21.13_{ab}	20.27_{abc}
3. Mean change:	—0.04	—0.94	—0.45	+0.75	+0.03
4. No. in group decreasing in reported tension:	9	11	6	6	7

Note: The tension data were transformed using the $\sqrt{X} + \sqrt{X + 1}$ transformation. The 2 sets of tension scores were subjected to one "repeated measures" analysis of variance with the t tests between condition means employing the residual mean square from this analysis in their error term. Cells having a subscript in common are not significantly different at the .05 level of confidence. Each mean is based on 16 cases. The higher the score the higher the reported tension.

But if the anger reduction version of the catharsis hypothesis receives little support, there is some evidence for the contention that aggressive behavior may lead to a lessening of experienced tension under some conditions. The subjects in the present experiment rated their mood on three separate scales on two separate occasions: (1) early in the session after they had been provoked by the partner and had been given or not given an opportunity to retaliate, and (2) after all subjects had administered shocks to the partner at the end of the session. A combined tension index was established for each occasion by adding the three scale scores. The results are summarized in table 3.

As we would expect, the people in the *Expect to Shock-Not Able* condition on Occasion 1 reported feeling more tense than the men in any of the other groups. These people were the only ones to have a mean tension score significantly higher than that in the nonangered control group. The thwarted ongoing aggressive sequence in the subjects who had anticipated being able to shock their peer but then were unable to do so apparently produced a relatively high level of felt tension within them.

On Occasion 2, after all subjects had been given their final socially sanctioned opportunity to aggress against their partner, the mean tension level in the *Expect to Shock-Able* condition decreased so that it no longer differed from that in the control group. There wasn't a significantly greater tension decrease in this group than that in any other condition, but the general trend is certainly as we would have predicted: the people who had expected to attack the anger instigator earlier but could not do so, and thus, whose implicit aggressive responses were prevented from reaching completion, tended to experience a fairly great tension reduction when they finally were permitted to aggress against their tormenter.

That the tension decrease in this condition is more than a random movement of scores toward the mean (a statistical regression toward the mean) is suggested by the data given in the last line of the table. Comparisons were made of the number of men in each group exhibiting a tension reduction. The results of this analysis again indicate that the "expect to aggress" information had instigated an implicit sequence in the angered subjects which attained at least some degree of completion with the final shocks. Combining the 2 *Expect to Shock* groups and the 2 *Expect Not to Shock* conditions, we find that a reliably greater proportion of the subjects in the former "treatment" decreased in reported tension from Occasion 1 to 2 (Chi-Square=4.00, p.=.05).

What can we conclude from these findings? The results of the present experiment, together with those obtained in the other studies cited here, seem to suggest these conclusions: An angered person does not necessarily make aggressive responses. Among other things, stimuli associated with the anger instigator must be present, whether in the objective situation or in his thoughts, if the hostile activity is to occur. If an angered person is thinking about aggressing against his tormenter and wants to do so—in essence, symbolically giving himself hostility-eliciting cues—an inability to attack his instigator is a frustration and may heighten the person's already aroused aggressive inclinations. Should he then be able to aggress against his anger instigator he may feel better as his internal, frustration-engendered tension is reduced. "Feeling better," however, does not in itself necessarily mean there is a lessened likelihood of attacking the anger instigator again on some future occasion.

REFERENCES

1. The author's research reported here was conducted under grant M1540 from the National Institute of Mental Health, U.S. Public Health Service.
2. HARTMANN, H., KRIS, E., AND LOEWENSTEIN, R. M.: Notes on the theory of aggression. *In* Psychoanalytic Study of the Child, vol. 3-4. New York, Internation Univer. Press, 1949.
3. —, AND WILLIAMS, R. M., JR.: The reduction of intergroup tensions. SSRC Bull. No. 57. New York: Social Sciences Research Council, 1947.
4. BERKOWITZ, L.: Aggression: A Social Psychological Analysis. New York, McGraw-Hill, 1962.
5. —, AND GREEN, J. A.: The stimulus qualities of the scapegoat. J.Abnorm. Soc.Psychol. 64:293-301, 1962.
6. TINBERGEN, N.: The Study of Instinct. Oxford, Clarendon Press, 1951.
7. HESS, E. H.: Ethology. *In* R. Brown, E. Galanter, E. H. Hess, and G. Mandler: New Directions in Psychology. New York, Holt, Rinehart & Winston, 1962.
8. BERKOWITZ, L.: 1962, op cit.
9. MILLER, N. E.: Theory and experiment relating psychoanalytic displacement to stimulus-response generalization. J.Abnorm.Soc.Psychol. 43:155-178, 1948.
10. WEATHERLEY, D.: Maternal permissiveness toward aggression and subsequent TAT aggression. J.Abnorm.Soc.Psychol. 65:1-5, 1962.
11. Conducted by L. Berkowitz, F. DeBoer, and M. Hieronimus.
12. The subjects seeing the prize fight were given a brief story outline which, according to our earlier findings, serves to lower internal restraints against aggression.
13. Cf. Berkowitz, L., 1962, op cit., Chap. 9.
14. —, 1962, op cit.; Berkowitz and Green, op cit.
15. —, 1962, op cit., Chap. 8.

16. —, Green, J. A., and Macaulay, J. R.: Hostility catharsis as the reduction of emotional tension. Psychiatry 25:23-31, 1962.
17. Lewin, K.: A Dynamic Theory of Personality. New York, McGraw-Hill, 1935.
18. Amsel, A.: The role of frustrative nonreward in noncontinuous reward situations. Psychol.Bull. 55:102-119, 1958.
19. Brown, J. S., and Farber, I. E.: Emotions conceptualized as intervening variables—with suggestions toward a theory of frustration. Psychol.Bull. 48:465-495, 1951.
20. Mowrer, O. H.: Learning Theory and Behavior. New York, Wiley, 1960.
21. Sears, R., Whiting, J. W. M., Nowlis, V., and Sears, P. S.: Some child-rearing antecedents of aggression and dependency in young children. Genet.Psychol.Monogr. 47:135-234, 1953.
22. Thibaut, J. W., and Coules, J.: The role of communication in the reduction of interpersonal hostility. J.Abnorm.Soc.Psychol. 47:770-777, 1952.
23. Rosenbaum, M. E., and DeCharms, R.: Direct and vicarious reduction of hostility. J.Abnorm.Soc.Psychol. 60:105-111, 1960.
24. Conducted by L. Berkowitz and R. Luehrig.

VIOLENCE AND THE SOCIAL STRUCTURE

By LEWIS A. COSER

IT HAS been a sociological commonplace ever since Emile Durkheim that deviant behavior is unevenly distributed throughout the social structure. The fact that the rates of such behavior are socially patterned has been the most effective sociological argument against the view that deviance results from biological impulse or idiosyncratic propensity. A great deal of empirical evidence is now available that class position, ethnic belongingness and occupational status are effective indicators for the prediction of rates of deviance. In addition, sociological concepts such as the notion of relative deprivation[1] help to interpret these statistical regularities and afford insights into the ways in which, to quote Merton, "social structures exert a definite pressure upon certain persons in a society to engage in non-conforming rather than in conforming conduct."[2]

Eruptions of illegitimate violence, just as other forms of deviance, are unequally distributed in society. The rates of homicide, for example, vary in the United States in terms of ethnic as well as class belongingness, region, age and sex.[3] An attempt will be made to show that even when the external social controls which normally operate in a society breakdown, the drastically increased incidence of violence is also not random.[4]

THE INCIDENCE OF HOMICIDE

The relation between high degrees of frustration and murderous violence has been discussed at length in the literature. A recent study of the life history of murderers concludes that "the murderers appear to have been terribly frustrated during their early lives . . . the frustration to which each had been subjected seemed much greater than that of the average person."[5] It seems to be the consensus among most students of the subject that high degrees of frustration account for the majority of homicides. Yet, obviously murder is only one

30

among several reactions to frustration. Aggression resulting from frustration may be directed against the self; or it may be repressed or sublimated, i.e., subjected to internalized social control. Hence two related questions must be asked: (1) which categories of persons in a society are likely to suffer structurally induced frustrations greater than those experienced by average members?; and (2) in which social strata are we likely to find that internalized social controls are not strong enough to prevent high rates of homicidal aggression? The first question can be discussed in terms of differential status positions. An answer to the second will focus on processes of socialization in various social strata.

If there is merit in the contention that low status position is a determinant of homicide, one would expect that in the lower class rates of homicide are higher than in the upper class. This is indeed consistently the case. Palmer finds that of the fathers of the 51 New England murderers in his sample, 53 per cent come from the lowest rung of a 5-class scale.[6] Similarly, Porterfield found that the mean annual homicide rates in Fort Worth, Texas was 1.06 per 100,000 population for the lower class but only .26 in the upper class.[7]

There are no nationwide statistics about the relation between class and homicide but there are other indicators of the relative status of categories with high homicide. Homicides are more frequent in the economically underdeveloped areas of the American South than they are in the North. Indeed, these regional differences are startling. The 1961 rates for murder and non-negligent manslaughter were 8.2 in the South Atlantic region as against 1.4 in New England.[8] The Mississippi rate was 10.3 in contrast to the Connecticut rate of 1.0. Generally, as one moves from the economically developed and high-status areas of the North to the low-status and underdeveloped areas of the South, the probability of homicide increases. The regional underdogs in the national status structure have considerably higher homicide rates than the regional top dogs.

It is often said that the higher proportion of Negroes in the South accounts for the higher Southern homicide rates. This is not the case. Even when the effect of race is held constant, homicide rates in the South are still considerably higher than in the North. Yet the high Negro rates of homicide deserve comment in their own right. Negroes are assigned lowest position in all three major dimensions of the status system: ethnicity, class and education. We should expect that the ensuing cumulative frustrations result in extremely high Negro homicide rates. This is indeed the case. Although Negroes comprise only approximately 10.5 per cent of our total population, 2,154, i.e., 60 per cent, of all City arrests for murder and non-negligent manslaughter in 1961 were Negroes and only 1,493 were white.[9] The discrepancy between Negro and white homicide rates exists in all regions of the country. In Birmingham, Alabama, where Negroes account for 40 per cent of the population, they committed 84.9 per cent of the murders between 1937 and 1944. Negroes in Massachusetts constitute only 1 per cent of the population but committed about 10 per cent of the homicides. In up-state New York, the homicide rate in the twenties was 2.8 per 100,000 for Caucasians and 30.4 for Negroes.[10]

These data may suffice to substantiate the view that lower position in the status hierarchy of American society and the frustrations which lower position brings in its wake lead to higher homicide rates. Yet this demonstration still remains incomplete if it is realized that not all low status groups in America show high homicide rates. Females have a lower status than males, yet female homicide rates are considerably lower. The young have a lower status than the middle-aged, yet they commit fewer homicides than their elders. Similarly, there is some evidence that the homicide rates among certain subgroups which occupy a very low status position in America, such as deviant religious sects, is quite low. To elucidate this matter one needs to move from the notion of *absolute deprivation* to a consideration of *relative deprivation*.

The notion of relative deprivation has been developed in recent sociological theorizing to denote the deprivation that arises not so much from the absolute amount of frustration as from the experienced discrepancy between one's lot and that of other persons or groups which serve as standards of reference. Whether or not superordinate groups or persons are taken as standards of reference by subordinate groups or individuals depends, at least in part, on whether the unequal distribution of rights and privileges is considered illegitimate by them. Negatively privileged groups or individuals may not develop the awareness that they are deprived of rights and privileges.[11] In a caste society, for example, members of the lower caste, considering this system justified for religious reasons, may not feel frustrated by it. If the privileges of the superordinate groups are not considered legitimately attainable by their subordinates, lower-status people compare themselves only with each other and not with members of higher status group.

In contrast, in societies such as ours, in which upward social mobility is said to be accessible to all, yet where in fact mobility is blocked for significant sections of the population, the bottom dogs in the status hierarchy compare their lot to that of the top dogs. Persons measure their status and the deprivations which it entails against the superior rights and privileges which they visualize as being enjoyed by the superordinate strata. Thus it stands to reason that, for example, American Negroes are especially frustrated because they contrast the success ideology inculcated by schools and mass media to the reality of continued discrimination. Hence among them, as among other low-status groups discussed so far, relative deprivation is likely to be high. This helps to account for their higher homicide rates more adequately than the notion of absolute deprivation, for it clarifies the fact that in social structures which do not institutionalize social mobility, homicide rates do not necessarily follow the American pattern.

The notion of relative deprivation also helps us understand why other low-status categories, such as women and the young, do not show high homicide rates. To put the matter in a nut shell: the young know that they will grow older, move up in the age hierarchy, and enjoy the perquisites of higher age status in the future; hence their lower relative deprivation. Women similarly do not tend to feel relatively deprived but for opposite reasons: equality with men seems unattainable, and different status among the sexes seems legitimate to both sexes. This accounts for the fact that women experience smaller degrees of relative deprivation. The young tend to accept the higher status of their elders because they know that one day they will be like them. Women accept the higher status of men because they believe that they will never be like them. Thus assurance of success just as assurance of lack of success may equally shield one against a sense of frustration. Similarly, sectarian subgroups who have withdrawn from involvement with the larger society in the name of a set of exclusive values do not compare their lot with that of members of the outside world and hence do not feel deprived.

This reasoning seems to account adequately for the fact that although women occupy lower statuses vis-a-vis men, their homicide rate is distinctly lower. (Of all City arrests for murder and non-negligent manslaughter in 1961, 834 were women and 3,791 were men.) [12] It also explains why the young, although having lower status positions than their elders, still have relatively low homicide rates. (Only 8.3 per cent of the City arrests for murder and non-negligent manslaughter in 1961 were under 18 years of age and only 32.7 per cent under 25 years.) [13]

Having accounted for differential homicide rates in terms of the related notions of frustration and relative deprivation, the second question can now be discussed: Frustrations can be dealt with in many ways other than homicide or other forms of interpersonal violence. They are often responded to with suicide or with successful repression or sublimation. Why do people in lower status positions select more often violent aggression as a way of dealing with their frustrations?

The Effects of Differential Socialization

Psychoanalytic theory seems to be divided on the effects of parental severity on superego formation. Aichhorn and Freud[14] seem to suggest that parental severity leads to inadequate superego formation, while Freud himself taught that "the severity which a child's superego develops in no way corresponds to the severity of the treatment it has itself experienced. It seems to be independent of the latter."[15] However, recent cross-cultural evidence and some experimental work[16] tend to support the view that excessive severity is likely to hinder the formation of a strong superego, whereas permissive child-rearing techniques, which emphasize the loss of love rather than punishment as a means of discipline, are associated wtih a high degree of internalization, a heightened sense of guilt, that is, with a strong superego. Were child-rearing techniques distributed at random throughout the social structure, there would be no reason to expect structured variations in superego formation in the population. But this is not the case. Socialization processes are class patterned, and the bulk of the evidence seems to indicate that working-class and lower-class child-rearing practices are more punitive than middle-class patterns.

In an excellent analytical summary of the many studies of the relation between social class and socialization in America, Bronfenbrenner[17] concludes: "The most consistent finding . . . is the more frequent use of physical punishment by working-class parents. The middle-class, in contrast, resort to reasoning, isolation, and . . . 'love-oriented' discipline techniques." Bronfenbrenner does not only find consistent class differences in child-rearing practices, but he also finds a differential effectiveness of these techniques. Summarizing the results of two large-scale studies in Boston and Detroit, he says: " 'Love-oriented' or 'psychological' techniques are more effective than other methods for bringing about desired behavior. Indeed, both groups of researchers concluded on the basis of their data that physical punishment for aggression tends to increase rather than decrease aggressive behavior . . . these findings mean that middle-class parents, although in one sense more lenient in their discipline techniques, are using methods that are actually more compelling."

Additional evidence comes from a study by Kohn [18] in which parental values and the exercise of parental authority are related to social class position. Kohn finds that "middle-class parents . . . are more likely to ascribe predominant importance to the child's acting in terms of internal standards of conduct, working-class parents to the child's compliance with parental authority." In other words, middle-class parents are mainly concerned with developing internalized control in the child and with enforcing attitudinal conformity;[19] working-class parents, in contrast, are mainly concerned with behavioral conformity, i.e., with external compliance. The working class wishes to instill respectable conduct in its children, the middle class is concerned with inculcating moral standards. The working class focuses attention on the act itself, the middle class on the actor's intention. This different emphasis on types of expected conformity helps to explain why, as Henry and Short[20] have shown, high degrees of frustration tend to lead to different types of deviant behavior in different classes. Where conformity is enforced externally, the agents of frustration remain external to the individual. In contrast, where standards for conformity are internalized, the individual perceives himself as the agent of his own frustrations. These findings make it possible to supplement the results arrived at earlier: not only is aggressive acting out in general and the rate of homicide in particular connected with the relative deprivation of various status categories in the social structure, but also persons in the lower-status categories tend to have lower built-in barriers against the acting out of external aggression.

The Evidence from Extreme Situations

Evidence from situations in which the normal social controls have broken down shows that even in such relatively unpatterned and unpredictable situations the comparative rates of aggressive deviance are predictable. Lower-status categories are disproportionately involved in mob actions and in acts of violence during revolutions.

Competent observers seem to agree that in the eighteenth and nine-teenth centuries—the major revolutionary period in modern Europe —the urban lower classes suffered extremes of poverty and deprivation. They also tend to agree that these classes were hardly considered part of the moral fabric of the society in which they lived. Although it would be hazardous to make dogmatic statements about differences in the internalization of norms in the various strata of the population during this period, it seems probable that the guiding norms and values were most imperfectly internalized in the lower class which was in significant ways excluded from the moral community of the nation. Furthermore, in any class-differentiated society the upper classes tend to have internalized more strongly the guiding normative standards, for these are, to a significant extent, *their* standards. The ruled are always more subject to external constraints than their rulers.

A true sociology of revolutions still remains to be written, yet whatever evidence I have been able to uncover points to the fact that revolutionary crowds were made up in their majority of lower-status persons. The social composition of the participants in revolutionary violence is not related to the social and political character of the revolution. The barricades of the 'bourgeois' revolutions seem to have been manned by roughly similar proportions of lower-class individuals as those of 'proletarian' revolutions. In the French Revolution the extremely poor population was hardly represented among the *Jacobins,* yet the men who actually fought in the streets and stormed the Bastille were drawn in their overwhelming majority from the Parisian *sans-culottes*—from the workshop masters, craftsmen, wage earners, shop keepers and petty traders.[21] In contrast, the political leaders came from the commercial bourgeoisie, the professions, or the liberal aristocracy.

This was not an atypical phenomenon. A student of the city mob in the eighteenth century concludes:[22] "Who, then, were the 'mob'? Its main strength lay in the strata commonly described on the con-tinent as the 'little people,' particularly those of certain cohesive and ancient quarters of the city like the Faubourg St. Antoine in Paris, the Travestevere (sic) in Rome or the Mercato in Naples. It was a combination of wage-earners, small property owners and the unclassi-fiable urban poor." The revolutions of the early nineteenth century did not differ fundamentally from those of the eighteenth.

Students of revolutions have often suggested that revolutionary outbreaks can best be accounted for in terms of what has been called relative deprivation. De Tocqueville, for example, wrote that:[23] ". . . the French found their position insupportable, just where it had become better . . . A people, which has supported without complaint, as if they were not felt, the most oppressive laws, violently throws them off as soon as their weight is lightened. The social order destroyed by a revolution is always better than that which immediately preceded it . . . The evil, which was suffered patiently as inevitable, seems unendurable as soon as the idea of escaping from it is conceived."

In other words, only when hopes have been raised do deprived strata tend to react with revolutionary vigor against a regime which seems to frustrate the achievement of these hopes. Yet this explanation holds for all strata which participated in the revolutions and would not seem to account for the differential rates of participation in revolutionary violence.

From this reasoning one might conclude that the lowest strata of the population, who lived without hope in prerevolutionary days, were therefore predisposed to apathy rather than active revolt. This is indeed so, but one needs to realize that the very outbreak of a revolution is likely to raise the hopes and expectations of the most deprived classes. They now feel that what was an impossible aspiration in the past is such no longer. When the status order is toppling, the absolutely deprived suddenly realize that what seemed impossible yesterday has become possible today. Any revolution is a revolution of rising expectations; it transforms absolute deprivations into relative deprivations. Moreover, since the lower class tends to rely more exclusively on external restraints, their removal through the revolution furnishes a socially sanctioned outlet for aggression.

These is some evidence of the import of relative deprivation in a more recent revolution, the Hungarian Revolution of 1956. A recent analyst of these events writes:[24] "Those who had the amplest ground for complaint were not the most prone to rebel. People who had lost everything tended to be demoralized and passive, whereas revolutionary activity originated with groups who were partly privileged and partly frustrated. . . . In fact, disappointed expectations are particularly likely to result in violent hatreds." I stated previously that the gulf between structurally induced expectations and reality is apt to lead to a high sense of relative deprivation among certain groups in the American cultural setting in which the idea of open channels of mobility is part of the ideology although it is hardly realized in reality. Hungary presented a similar picture. This was predominantly a workers' revolution because the industrial workers had been led to believe that this was 'their' state and that they would hold a dominant position, only to find out that they were actually subject to relentless regimentation and exploitation. Similar considerations also explain the high rates of participation among writers and students in that revolution. Both categories had indeed a somewhat privileged social position, yet suffered acutely from the loss of personal integrity and forced indoctrination. They had been led to expect that intellectual roles would carry highest honor and prestige only to find in practice that they had to submit to the dictates of unintellectual party bureaucrats.

The appraisal of revolutionary violence is broadly in accord with the previous appraisal of homicide rates; yet two significant differences appear. It will be remembered that the homicide rates of the young and of women, although these are lower status categories, nevertheless, are lower than the rates of their superordinates in the respective sex and age hierarchy. But in revolutionary violence, women and the young play a very pronounced role. The active participation of women is noted by all students of the French Revolution. In fact, in certain key revolutionary events, such as the March to Versailles of October 1790, and in later food riots, women were predominant. Writes Rudé: "On the morning of October 5 the revolt started simultaneously in the central markets and the Faubourg Saint-Antoins; in both cases women were the leading spirits."[25]

I know of no detailed breakdowns of the age of participants in violent crowds during the French Revolution. (Rudé gives some data indicating that their 'average age' was in the thirties, but he does not indicate the range.) But, in the case of the Hungarian Revolution the data are unambiguous; here the very young played very active roles so that some observers have talked of a veritable "children's crusade." "To a very considerable extent," says Kecskemeti,[26] the street battles were fought by the young: students, apprentices, school children. A good many older people participated too, but it seems certain that the struggle would not have been sustained as long as it was if it had not been for the death-defying, desperate determination of the very young."

What explains the fact that, at least in certain revolutionary events, women and the young played a considerable role? Here one may suggest that situations of normlessness differ significantly from the normatively structured situations which were discussed when homicide was considered. In the latter case women, having internalized the acceptance of their lower status, tend to experience relatively low relative deprivation. The matter is quite different, however, when normative restraints and traditional expectations have been shattered. It is as if many women were to say to themselves, "If all these extraordinary actions have become possible, then it is perhaps permissible to entertain the extraordinary idea that women need no longer accept their inferior status and can aspire to become like men." In this case, also, the revolution turns absolute deprivation into relative deprivation by raising the hopes of the underdogs in the sex hierarchy. Moreover, and perhaps above all, a revolutionary situation provides the occasion for women to indeed act like men. It offers opportunities for the assertion of equality which were previously unavailable.[27]

The case of the high participation of the young in revolutionary activity can be explained in similar terms. In routinized social situations the young may feel that, although they suffer status deprivations from their elders, the course of time will rectify these felt injustices. But in periods of revolutionary normlessness, or in highly anomic and disorganized situations, normal expectations can no longer be entertained.

The breakdown of tradition creates in the young two seemingly contradictory expectations: the fear that the gradual advancement in the age hierarchy is put into question, and the hope that it is no longer necessary to wait the requisite number of years for the rewards of maturity. Insecurity about the future and hope for the present leads behavior which so far had been future-oriented to be replaced by present-oriented activity. For the young as well as for women, the revolution provides a setting for the triumph of human action over biology.

The composition of the participants in the only major form of mass violence that continue to occur in recent American history, urban race riots, shows a consistently higher rate in the lower-status categories. Participants in race riots, both Negro and white, are of predominantly low status, such as the unemployed, the unskilled or little educated. As in revolutions, here also women as well as the young tend to play a very active part. The composition of the modern rioters is so similar to that of earlier revolutionaries that no special discussion is required.[28]

Relative deprivation accounts for seemingly contradictory findings about two categories of lower status, the women and the young. While in normal periods their rates contrast with the relatively high violence rate among other lower-status categories, this is not the case in revolutionary and mob violence in which participation of the young and of women tends to be remarkably high. This is because revolutions transform the absolute deprivation of the young and of women into relative deprivation so that in these situations all relevant lower-status categories tends to have a disproportionately high rate of participation in violence.

NOTES AND REFERENCES

1. On this concept *cf.* Merton, R. K.: Social Theory and Social Structure. Glencoe, Ill., 1957, The Free Press, pp. 227 ff.
2. Ibid. p. 132. This paper relies heavily on Merton's theoretical guide lines, especially on Chapters IV, V, IX and X, *ibid.* Another major stimulus for this paper came from the seminal work of Henry, A. F., and Short, J. F.: Suicide and Homicide. Glencoe, Ill., The Free Press, 1954.
3. In this paper homicide has been chosen as an indicator of violence. Other indicators, such as aggravated assault, might have been chosen as well. The results would not have differed materially.
4. In the following violence is to be understood in terms of illegitimate violence only. I am not concerned here with the legitimate exercise of violence by agents of the state. In other words, I am not concerned with the violent behavior of a police officer in the pursuit of law enforcement. Only if a police officer exceeds the duties of his office and hence exercises illegitimate violence does he come within the purview of my discussion.
5. PALMER, S.: A Study of Murder, New York, Thomas Y. Crowell, 1960, p. 8.
6. In Hollingshead and Redlich's study of New Haven, the lowest class comprises only 17.8 per cent of the population; in Lloyd Warner's study of Newburyport only 25.4 per cent are found in this class. Only rough approximations between Palmer's New England sample and these two cities are permissible, but the general thesis of class differentials in homicide seems sustained by the date. This is especially so if one realizes that only about one tenth of the fathers of the murderers were in Class I, II, and III. This is significantly lower than the class distribution in the population would make one expect since over three-tenths of the residents of New Haven and over four-tenths of Newburyport were in those 3 higher classes. *See* Palmer, ibid., p. 34, 209.
7. PORTERFIELD, A. L.: Suicide and crime in the social structure of an urban setting. Am. Soc. Rev. 17:341-49, 1952. This refers to the class position of victims, not murderers, but since most homicides are committed by murderers belonging to the same class as their victims, the class differences are meaningful in our contest.
8. Uniform Crime Reports—1961, Washington, D. C.: U. S. Department of Justice, 1961, pp. 34-36.
9. Ibid. p. 97.
10. BLOCH, H. A., AND GEIS, G.: Man, Crime and Society, New York, Random House, 1962, p. 263. The higher rates for homicide among Negroes

relative to whites in various sections of the country does not tell the whole story, however. Negro homicide rates vary in different regions together with white rates so that the Negro rates are highest in the states like Alabama where the white rate is also high (41.1 per 1000,000 for Negroes as against 11.6 for whites), whereas in states where white rates are low the Negro rates are also lower. The Negro rate in Maine (3.2 per 100,000) is considerably lower than the Caucasian rates in Alabama (11.6), although it is considerably higher than the Caucasian rate in Maine (1.9). See ibid. p. 262.

11. Cf. Merton, op. cit. esp. chapters VII and IX. Cf. also Coser, L. A., The Functions of Social Conflict. Glencoe, Ill., The Free Press, 1956, esp. pp. 32-38.

12. Uniform Crime Reports, op. cit., p. 96. It should be noted, furthermore, that to the extent women do achieve a status more nearly equal to that of men, to the extent that they no longer accept their lower status and compete for higher status, to that extent their crime rates approach the male rates. Thus in America the crime rates of females are closer to those of males in cities than in small towns. In Western Europe and the United States these rates are closer to the male rates than in countries like Japan and Algiers where the lower status of females is still clearly and fully institutionalized. Cf. Sutherland, E., and Cressey, D.: Principles of Criminology. New York, Lippincott, 1955, pp. 112-113.

13. Uniform Crime Reports, op. cit., p. 95. It might be objected that our reasoning concerning the relatively low degree of violence among the young is refuted by the extent of juvenile delinquency in the United States. This is, however, not the case. In the first place sensational reportings about juvenile delinquency often distorts the facts in the popular imagination. While persons under 18 do indeed constitute a major proportion of city arrests for certain offenses against property such as larceny and auto theft (49.8 and 61 per cent, respectively) they do not commit a very high proportion of crimes against persons. The homicide figures were already quoted. Similarly, only 13 per cent of all city arrests for aggravated assault were of persons below the age of 18. Even the figure for forcible rape (19.1 per cent), while higher, does not back up the popular misconception that such crimes are mainly committed by juvenile offenders. (Cf. Uniform Crime Reports, op. cit., p. 95.

In addition, juvenile delinquency is in the main limited to specific areas in modern cities in which ethnic and class discriminations have created especially tense situations among especially deprived youngsters amidst an urban middle class culture in which only success meets with applause and defeat invites contempt. These youngsters suffer from particular acute humiliations and frustrations because of their lower class and ethnic status. Low socioeconomic and ethnic status rather than youthfulness per se seems to lie at the bottom of most juvenile delinquency. It would be a major mistake to generalize from these special situations about the younger population.

14. AICHHORN, A.: Wayward Youth. New York, The Viking Press, 1935, pp. 202-203; FREUD, A.: The ego and the mechanisms of Defense. New York, International Universities Press, 1946, Chapter IX.

15. FREUD, S.: Civilization and Its Discontents. (Trans. Riviere, J.) London, The Hogarth Press, 1930, p. 116-17.

16. See Henry and Short, op. cit., Chapter VII. Cf.

17. BRONFENBRENNER, U.: Socialization and social class through time and space. In: Readings in Social Psychology, Eleanor Maccoby, Theodore Newcomb and Eugene Hartley, Eds.: New York, Henry Holt and Co., 1958.

18. KOHN, M. L.: Class and parental values. Am. J. Soc. 64:337-51, 1959; Social class and the exercise of parental authority. Am. Soc. Rev. 24:352-66, 1959.

19. On the distinction between behavioral and attitudinal conformity. Cf. Merton, R. K.: Conformity, deviation and opportunity structure. Am. Soc. Rev. 24:177-88, 1959; Coser, R. L.: Insulation from observability and types of social control. Am. Soc. 24:28-39, 196.

20. Op. cit., passim.

21. RUDÉ, G.: The Crowd in the French Revolution. Oxford, England, Clarendon Press, 1959, esp. pp. 178 ff.

22. HOBSBAWN, E. J.: Social Bandits and Primitive Rebels. Glencoe, Ill., The Free Press, 1959, p. 113.

23. De Tocqueville's L'Ancien Regime, trans. M. W. Patterson, Oxford, England, Basil Blackwell, 1949, p. 186.

24. KECSKEMETI, P.: The Unexpected Revolution. Stanford, Stanford University Press, 1961, p. 117.

25. Rudé, op. cit., p. 73.

26. Kecskemeti, op. cit., pp. 112 ff.

27. Finally, it seems worthwhile mentioning that it was in revolutionary situations impinging more directly on female activities that women took an especially active part. Food riots in response to scarcity or high prices showed an especially high involvement of women in violent and aggressive behavior. GOLD, M.: Suicide, homicide, and the socialization of aggression. Am. J. Soc., 63:651-661, 1958.

28. Cf. GRIMSHAW, A. D.: A Study in Social Violence, Urban Race Riots in the United States. Unpublished doctoral dissertation, Graduate School of Arts and Science, The University of Pennsylvania, 1959, mimeo. This is the best general survey of the subject.

COMMITMENT, CONTRACT, GROUP BOUNDARIES AND CONFLICT*

By DAVID H. MARLOWE

I PROPOSE to deal with organized violence as an aspect of the dialogue of the "we" and the "they" in relationships between groups. This is the dialogue of permissibility and choice that is shaped by the boundary between those who join to slay and those who are lumped together as fit to be slain. Human groups do not fight with each other at random; the choice of war holds profound consequences for the definition and the organization of the social unit that makes it. At the same time, violent conflict is a part of the normative repertoire of human social behavior. It is a mode of action that is sanctioned by most social systems as a necessary concomitant of a vast inventory of transactions a given group can or will have with other groups. The choice of organized violence is regularly available to most men and often represents a preferred form of relationship with other groups. The act of war, the blood feud, the raid, the threat of annihilation, and even the simple assault are all highly pertinent parts of the language of social relations. Each group defines the limits of permissibility. There are those whom one may fight and those whom one may not fight. Conflict is controlled through the invocation of kinship, contracts, alliances, and a myriad of other legal and traditional mechanisms built into each social system.

This paper centers upon the choice of organized violence and its functions within a given social system; one that I believe presents an excellent model for the analysis of violence in intergroup relationships.

*This work was carried out under the auspices of the Washington School of Psychiatry with which the author was a Research Associate during the period 1958-1960. The field research was supported by OTSG U.S.A. through contract AMS-DA-49-007-MD-960 and by Grant 58-177 of the Foundations Fund for Research in Psychiatry.

This is the essentially fluid and decentralized sociopolitical structure known as the segmentary lineage organization. The specific people involved are a semi-nomadic Samaale lineage of the Hawiya clan family of central Somalia. Sunni Moslem in religion and Cushitic in linguistic affiliation, this lineage, the Galjaal Barsana, has a population of about 17,000 and inhabits an area just south of the Webi Shebelli river, about 90 miles west of Mogadishu, the present national capital. The Barsana subsist on a mixed economy combining moderate ranging transhumant pastoralism with the cultivation of Kaffir corn.

The Somali have long been known as a fractious and pugnacious people and a number of commentators have noted that the fundamental basis of Somali sociopolitical relationships is force and the threat of force. Until recently interlineage warfare was a regular aspect of Somali life. Raid and assault were compounded with the need for vengeance and retaliation in a continuous sequence. Today, while an excellent police organization precludes large scale warfare, small clashes and affrays, involving the use of stick, knife, and spear, still occur regularly throughout the year. While police intervention rapidly terminates such conflicts the basic orientation of the participants and their kinsmen to such acts and threats remains much as it has been for generations. Armed force is still, in the Somali system of values, the ultimate and the preferred mode of achieving a solution to any dispute involving corporate rights in land, water, grass, and stock. Violent retaliation remains, as well, the ideal language with which one answers assault, insult, injury or homicide. In many instances the culture demands a violent response from its members. For the young Somali male, the statement, "He who kills my brother, I will kill," denotes the fundamental obligation of a man to those to whom he is affiliated. He views this as the most powerful and enduring of commitments. As one youth put it, "If someone were to kill one of my people and I were not to take back the blood from his people, I would walk in shame for all time. I would not be a man. His blood would cry out in shame in the place where it was taken, because I had not done anything." This commitment is not to one's immediate kinsmen alone, it extends to all those whom the individual sees as standing in a given structural kinship relationship to himself in a series of situations. Equivalently, he is barred from making war or exacting vengeance from anyone who is defined as his structural kinsman.

These fairly rigid views of the needs and uses of violence in inter-group relationships do not, however, complement a rigidly defined structure of social and political groups. Many of the boundaries between the slayer and the slain are relative ones that change dependent upon the relationships of the parties to each act.

The Somali social system is built upon an extensive web of agnatic kin relationships. All groups within it are derived through the joint descent of their members from common ancestors in the patri-genealogy of the people. Each division in the male line has given rise to a new lineage, and each lineage divides into yet more lineages. Each of these divisions represents a segmental order to which each male is born affiliated. Only a few of these segments represent enduring divisions between significant sociopolitical groups. The other segmental orders represent potential groups; groups that serve to orient and position each individual within the full Somali social system, or groups that may be evoked as active organizations of affiliated kinsmen, particularly in the context of war.

To make this clearer it is best to begin at the bottom and work up. Each Somali born is a member of a basic extended family group called the *rer*, usually comprised of an old man, his sons and grandsons, their wives and children. A group of these *rer*, all descended from an ancestor of 3 or 4 generations past, are bound together by their ties of kinship as a "blood responsibility group." This constitutes the primary vengeance group in case of assault from the outside and assumes the largest share of collective responsibility for the acts of its members. A number of these related blood responsibility groups, all the descendants of an ancestor some 6 to 12 generations removed, are again bound together as a single unit, a blood compensation group. Its members jointly pay and receive blood compensation money following war and the representative elders of the group govern relations between the member lineages and act as spokesmen to and negotiators with other lineages. A group of blood compensation segments are further allied into a clan, in an alliance based upon kinship and reinforced by either traditional or written contract, often under the nominal leadership of a political and ritual figurehead. Clans are in turn loosely allied into clan confederacies, and clan confederacies into yet larger units.

Within this ever extending system of affiliations a man's statement of group membership is often a relative one. He defines his own group in terms of its genealogical relationship to the other group with which he is transacting. If he is asked his group's name by the member of a collateral clan, he responds with the name of his clan. When asked the same question by a member of his clan he responds with the name of his blood compensation group, and so forth up and down the scale of possible segmental relationships.

Ideally, within this compounded series of kinship-based alliances specific relationships define specific and reciprocal patterns of behavior for the members of the group so defined. Thus violence is interdicted for members of the same blood compensation segment and war is considered prima-facie negotiable for members of the same clan. These expected patterns of relationships often then come into direct conflict with the statements of the culture at large as to the needs and uses of violence. It is through this conflict of values that the relationship between the group's perception of itself and extent of its membership and the utility of organized violence become clear.

The Galjaal Barsana, the lineage I worked with, was a single blood compensation unit, quasi centralized under the leadership of a Sheik, its ritual leader, and a council of representative elders who held the basic decision making power of the group. The lineage was divided into 5 primary descent groups, each a semi-independent political unit and each in turn highly segmented into numerous blood responsibility segments. The full lineage was in turn part of a large clan, the Galjaal, under the titular leadership of a Sultan who lived several hundred miles away. Like most Somali lineages the Barsana political system, comprised of its Sheik and the councils of elders of the various member segments, was devoted almost in its entirety to conflict control and conflict negotiation.

When disputes take place within the Somali social system, the relationship of the immediate contenders defines the extent of the groups that will ultimately be implicated in any following war or feud. The principle involved is the well enunciated one in social anthropology of structural equivalence and opposability. If members of different clans fight over a water hole, the ultimate parties to the dispute are the full membership of both clans. The matter is one that takes place between the largest equivalent units involved. In this case the members of each group define their primary affiliation at the segmental level of the clan. If one of their number has been killed, he is seen as a brother in the clan who has been assaulted from the outside, and all unite to avenge him. This brotherhood is seen as one that involves a real tie of blood by the other lineages of the clan. It is a brotherhood that exists as a contractual obligation and the act of war that is precipitated represents the fulfillment of the obligations of the alliance.

If, on the other hand, a dispute takes place between 2 member blood compensation segments of the clan, obligatory status brotherhood extends only to the membership of each of the contending segments. Their relationship within the clan is conceptually dissolved during the period of the dispute and each recognizes only those ties that extend to the point of structural equivalence as viable. This process of constant redefinition of the "we" in opposition to any given "they" is capable of operating at all segmental levels within the system, extending from relationships between individual families to relationships between the great clan confederacies, the traditional alliances of clans, that number their memberships in the hundreds of thousands.

With the act of war, a unitary identity is proclaimed for the group and an equivalent unitary identity is defined for the "enemy." This is interestingly illuminated by the different battle cries used in different scale wars. As old Barsana warriors told the tale, when they allied with the full Galjaal clan and other collateral clans of the Gugondubbe Clan confederacy to war with the Daruud Clans of the North in the late nineteenth century, their battle cry was "Gugondubbe gave birth to me." When the Galjaal warred alone, the Barsana warriors cried out "Galjaal gave birth to me." When, however, the Barsana go to war alone they cry out the battle cry of their lineage, "I am a hyena of the Two Barsana, I kill."

It is obvious that in a system such as this, each act that might potentially escalate into organized violence bears profound consequences for the stability of the few enduring groups within the social structure. Thus while organized violence is a highly valued choice, it is one that must be controlled rigorously within the bounded groups of the system. Several factors intensify the need for control. One of the most important of these is the Somali perception of disputes involving the beginning of a zero sum game. The Somali approach to an argument over property or corporate rights is one of "all or none." A water hole is either "mine" or "yours" when its possession is in contention. Each side adheres to its position as a categorical absolute. Each says, "I win and you lose, or we fight." If the dispute is between structurally distant groups, war or absolute concession are the only available alternatives, and each group's constituent segments polarize around their kinsmen. Of equal importance is the need for vengeance when a member of a group has been injured or killed by another. Thus there is, seemingly, a large series of situations for which there is no alternative but violence. In the past, at the higher segmental levels of group relationship, war was the normal choice made in such situations. However, while the culture enunciates its absolutes, its members embroider the negotiatory outs through which they may be circumvented. The Somali have always been embroiled in violence, but at no time has it been anarchic and all inclusive.

The choice of violence in the Somali system depends upon the perceived availability of the other party as a group to which one may or should be violent. In certain relationships between lineages it has been the sole method of communication and transaction available to the contending parties. They speak to each other only in the language of war. The lineage I worked with had conquered its present lands over the course of the past 300 years from a neighboring lineage. Until recently, the sole discourse between them was conflict. The slightest pretext was enough to initiate a major assault and neither lineage was really capable of viewing the other in any other light but enmity. Men would say to me, "Their sole work has been to kill us, and ours to kill them. They are evil people, dangerous people." The full sanctions of the culture in respect to the value and utility of the solution of violence were permanently in force. The groups had classified each other as perpetually available for violence, and each argument and dispute between them was accordingly categorized by both as a cause for hostilities.

With other neighboring groups, however, possible pretexts for war were not dealt with in quite so rigorous a fashion by the Barsana. Good relations were demanded by disparity of strength or the need for the continuance of certain reciprocally granted rights to water or grazing. Therefore, disputes could be compromised by mutual avoidance or mutual withdrawal from a contested well, pasture, or plot of earth, i.e., preventing war by joint withdrawal from the game. With such neighbors, a massive act of hostility was considered the only viable cause for war.

Despite the stated all or nothing basis upon which war is predicated, Somali groups have rarely, if ever, carried on wars of extermination. Each act of violence between large lineage groups is phrased in zero sum terms, but the full series of transactions inevitably involves a mixed and comparatively equal pay-off. If the members of a clan alliance are assaulted by a group from another alliance, they organize for rapid retaliation in order to "get their blood back." The aim of the counter move is to kill or wound more of the other group than one's own casualties numbered. Warfare then falls into a pattern of discrete thrusts and counter thrusts, broken periodically by negotiation and the payment of blood compensation money to the more grievously injured group. Ultimately, the sequence peters out when a respectable balance, one that carries no particular residue of shame for either participating group, is struck. If territory is the cause of the dispute, the weaker lineage finally withdraws once its members recognize that they are faced with overwhelming strength—the ultimate arbiter of the dispute and the ultimate legitimator of possession.

The greatest danger of violence is posed not between groups that normally define themselves as different from each other, such as clans, but between lineages that normally view themselves as members of the same corporate defense group and ritual collectivity. The processes of the social system make the definition of a "we-they" boundary feasible at any point in the order of lineage segmentation since an individual's proclamation of group affiliation is in great degree dependent upon the context in which he speaks. Where group affiliations and identity are shared only in the upper segmental levels, there are no problems. The groups are not collectivities but potential alliances based on symbolic and fictive kinship. If men are far enough separated in the genealogy, usually by at least 8 to 15 generations in the male line, organized violence is an acceptable part of their relationship with each other. It is not, however, perceived as acceptable between lower segmental orders. In these groups, the desire and need for the solution of force and the act of retaliation so strongly enunciated by the value system of the group come into direct conflict with the obligations and posited reciprocal behaviors of kin-committed alliances. Each clash between individuals and families is a breech of the traditional, contractual, and kin-relationship between the groups. In consequence, each such clash and dispute presents an extreme threat to the stability and continued existence of these enduring sociopolitical units within the system. Any fight will polarize large groups of people to that point where the 2 groups would normally meet and fuse under the aegis of a common ancestor. If such polarization takes place a clan divides into 2 clans, or a blood compensation segment into 2 independent blood compensation segments. Any fight between people who stand in the right structural relationship to each other can thus escalate into full scale war and rupture any group. This in turn vitiates and fragments the strength of the groups, since the respective memberships of each are no longer equally kin-committed to each other or contracted together to maintain and defend their land and water resources against the depredations of others. Force is the basis of territorial control and both legitimacy of control and possibility of successful negotiation with others over rights to land, water and other resources decrease with each decrease in force.

Thus while all groups beyond the alliance of the clan are defined as available for conflict, the collateral lineages of the clan are defined to each other as available to each other only for single and short exchanges of violence. If lineage A of the Galjaal attacks the collateral Barsana, the Barsana will retaliate, but the matter is then quickly compromised through negotiation. Even more importantly, the lineages of the blood compensation segment are defined to each other as not available for conflict. If a member of a lineage of Barsana attacks a member of one of the collateral lineages of his group, the collateral lineage must be prevented from retaliating, and the matter must be compromised as it stands.

The escalation of violence and the division of the blood compensation segment into groups bounded against each other is thus prevented through the use of a series of techniques and devices designed to deny the purposiveness of any act and to prevent the assignment of collective responsibility or blame. The language of description and hence the language of classification therefore changes dependent upon the relationship between the parties to a dispute or assault. If a member of a lineage outside the clan assaults an individual within it, the act is invariably referred to as war (*dirrie, dagal*), and men talk of the spot where it occurred as the "place where war stands." If, however, the assailant was a member of the same clan, the event will be viewed as assault or homicide (*dil*), never war. If the assailant was another Barsana, the term of reference is invariably accident (*belaio*), and never either homicide or war. Thus a fight over agricultural land between lineages of the Barsana, which took place while I was with them, that left 8 men seriously wounded was referred to only as an *accident* by the Barsana elders. To have even called it war or assault would have made it almost non-negotiable, and thus possibly non-controllable. On the other hand, a simple assault with a camel stick made by a member of non-Galjaal clan on a Barsana woman, was spoken of as an act of *war*. The difference in terms of reference is the product of deliberate choice on the part of the members of the group. The value system of the group demands retaliation for the act of war, homicide, or deliberate assault. By framing the occurrence in the alternative terms of "accident," the elders hope to prevent the kinsmen of the injured party from constituting themselves as a vengeance group, as the culture demands, and seeking retaliation. Within the Somali system of conflict, this is the sole sure way of preventing a single dispute from escalating into warfare and consequently leading the group to open division. The initial assault simply starts a transaction and opens a potential relationship. Its translation into war lies in the decision of the aggrieved party, the group that has sustained the most injured or dead, to seek retaliation.

The control of conflict through this classification and rephrasing of acts of violence as accidental and nonpurposeful is primarily the role of the elders who must pacify the younger kinsmen of the aggrieved "whose stomachs always burn for war" and dissuade them from retaliation. The vitiation of purposefulness, when assault takes place within the Barsana lineage alliance itself, is achieved through displacing the causal agent. The elders invariably define the act as one that was neither designed nor committed in a state of reason and they assign it an etiology that relieves both the aggressor and the aggrieved of the responsibility to participate in further conflict. In one case when a man severely beat 2 children, who had strayed into his field of grain, the children's father spoke of the aggressor, a moderately distant kinsman of the same blood responsibility group, in the following terms, "I don't know why this was done. They are little children. They did not know any better. But this man Ali, he's a little bit crazy. He sees someone in his field, and his head begins to whirl. It turns and it turns. He doesn't know what he is doing. I should go and beat him, but what is the use of that?" This denial of purpose and thus the consequent denial of the need for vengeance through the allocation of insanity to the aggressor is perhaps the commonest way of circumventing further conflict within the close alliance of agnates in the Somali system. In another case an old woman was gravely assaulted by a young man of her primary descent group but of a different blood responsibility segment. Her sons spent a day seeking the assailant in order to avenge their mother. Failing to find him, they came to the Sheik to request police intervention. The old woman, upon gaining consciousness forbade this act. "This man is of our lineage of the Barsana," she said, "you shall not give him to the police nor shall you seek to kill him. The blood of a brother does not take away my blood." One of the woman's nephews, an immediate kinsman, ideally categorically committed to avenging any assault upon her went into the matter in further detail. "First we cannot go and find one of his people to kill. My cousins would have yesterday, but not today when they have thought about it. They are of our lineage, we are all the children of one father. That is one important reason why the rest of us of our group do not think of fighting even though her sons do. Then, there is the man who did this thing. We know him well. He is married to a good girl who just gave birth to a son. He is a little bit crazy. I think maybe he saw djinn once and it makes him act that way. He doesn't know what he is doing. His head begins to whirl and he sees nothing but red around him. All Somali are like that a little when they get angry, but some people are like that a lot. That man just gets fits that way. He has to be crazy to try to rape an old woman of eighty-six. We are very angry, we want him punished, but it is not a thing we should make war over."

The chief aspect of this allocation of deviance or madness to the individual who initiates conflict within the group is the one that clearly demarcates it from equivalent situations in higher segmental orders. Responsibility is individualized. When a Barsana is assaulted by a member of another equivalent lineage group, the act is perceived as one that is the collective responsibility of all the members of the other group. Reasons are not sought or adduced, and any member of the opposing group may be slain to exact the price of vengeance. Thus the act of assault or homicide is never an absolute; the message conveyed by an assault is governed by the relationship of the parties involved, and is differentially decoded.

The blood compensation group, in this case comprised of 17,000 people, is the broadest possible group within the social system in which such techniques of conflict control can operate. Individualization, and classification of an aggressive act as nonpurposeful, can be permitted by the group members because of their conception of the real strength of their kin ties and the need to maintain them. Both genealogically and structurally they see themselves as the sons of one father, as peer brothers, both committed and traditionally contracted to behave towards each other as brothers. For the group the members of the Barsana lineage are the one enduring "we" of their social universe. Thus blood compensation money is not paid for homicide, assault or delicts within the group since, as the Barsana put it, "A brother cannot pay for the loss of a brother."

Both the aggressor and the aggrieved are considered to have lost in almost equal measure. Therefore, there can be no restitution, only atonement.

Even within the group, however, the threat of violence is ever present, since as we have noted, the language of negotiation is the language of force. If 2 member lineages of the Barsana have a dispute about ownership of land or rights to a water hole, each automatically threatens war in order to legitimate its claim. Here the threat of violence, its simple enunciation as potential behavior within the group, operates to open bargaining and therefore avert violence. The statement of the threat immediately brings the elders of the full Barsana alliance to the disputing parties. The conveyance of the threat thus brings about the union in time and place of the political leaders of all of the scattered groups that make up the Barsana lineages and enables information to flow rapidly between them. The bits of information selected and transmitted in such situations are highly biased ones for the elders, who frame the dispute not in terms of the interests of independently contending lineages, but in terms of the joint interests of all as kinsmen, and the peer brotherhood of the contending parties. Conceptually the contending parties have already split. They speak of the dispute in terms of "our" people as opposed to "their" people. As one man cried out in a dispute over land with a collateral Barsana lineage, "These people are our enemies. They are nothing to us. They are taking the bread from our children. We have every right to kill them. They are not our brothers even if they are yours." Perceptually, even within the social group of maximum unity, absolute division and polarization is probable. It is prevented only when there are elders of nonimplicated lineages who have the moral authority and the desire to serve as a bridge between the contending parties. Their basic leverage lies in their equivalent peer brotherhood with both the contestants, and in the ultimate threat of dissolution of the alliance. If this mediation by collateral elders fails, the Barsana have one final device to force negotiation prior to allowing the lineage to divide into separate and independent groups. The Barsana Sheik enters as mediator.

Possessed of highly potent magico-ritual authority and symbolically viewed as the contemporary father of the lineages, i.e., the one ritual and political leader who has the interests of all lineages at heart, he may use his authority both as Muslim holy man and sorcerer to obviate the dispute. Thus when 2 Barsana lineages disputed the possession of a piece of agricultural land and refused to compromise their differences under the pressures of the elders, the Sheik cursed the land in dispute. One elder noted 3 years later. "For three years now, no one had used this land. The people threatened to fight and the Sheik made a powerful curse. We knew that any crops planted there would die. It does none of us any good. If we cannot make a treaty about it, the land will rot."

Such explicit devices as the above do not exist for the control of conflict involving groups larger than the blood compensation group. If the threat of violence is not acceded to, it must be followed by the actuality of war, and negotiation is really feasible only after conflict has taken place. Most treaties made between the lineages of the clan, for example, are made to control the escalation of an *existing* conflict, not to avoid a future one.

At this point I should like to attempt to draw all of the foregoing together in a kind of general schema. Within a segmentary lineage system where conflict is a common and valued aspect of group relationships, the choice of violence and participation in warfare are governed by a number of different factors. At certain levels of segmentation the many associated family groups view themselves as members of an enduring sociopolitical unit and not only interdict conflict between the constituent lineages of the group but perceive and handle precipitating acts so as to make them amenable to maximal control. Above these levels the group contracted to join together in conflict and the group seen as available for conflict are defined by their over-all genealogical relationship within the social structure. The majority of the lineages that fuse together as a single corporate group for war do so in terms of traditionally defined contractual obligations symbolized in terms of kinship.

Wherever the point of alliance is potential, and does not represent an ongoing collectivity, war is an available choice, both "we and they" are relative constructs that have only small significance outside of the immediate context. At the points where the in-group defines itself as a significant ongoing collectivity, conflict is rigidly controlled, and precipitating acts are translated to serve the cause of group unity.

This leads to a significant question, particularly for a social system like the one under discussion; is organized violence ultimately a dysfunctional or eufunctional factor within the social system? There is, unfortunately, no single or simple answer. There are many, dependent upon the perspective that is being utilized for the analysis. Conflict in the form of war, violence, juridical, or political dispute, is necessary to the ongoing dynamic processes of the segmentary lineage system. The system lives and proceeds upon the fissions that take place within its member segments. Two brothers fight with each other and found

separate descent lines of a new lineage, which in the course of generations becomes a multilineaged clan, and in yet more generations
becomes a clan family comprised of several hundred thousand souls in
many clans. For the segmentary social system as a whole, violent
conflict is the instrument of growth. A number of commentators have
felt that the need for such perpetual division is founded in ecology
and demography. Ultimately, even the bounded blood compensation
group becomes too large to exploit its home territory and must divide
or perish. The final conflicts between the lineages of the bounded unit
then cease to be amenable to control, and the blood compensation
segment splits into independent segments.

While violence may therefore be eufunctional to the life of the
system as a whole, it is certainly seen as dysfunctional within the
segments themselves. Men do not live by the long view of historical
or ecological necessity nor do they consider themselves as subservient
to the inner needs of their social systems. They live and organize their
lives in terms of the givens of a certain time and a specific place.
Whenever real conflict threatens within the Barsana, conflict that could
lead to the reconstitution of the group, the response of most of the
people was one of shock and fear. The fairly comfortable universe of
known and adequately defined social relationships and responsibilities
was seen as threatened with demolition, and the ties of kin which
defined the patterns of this universe subject to reinterpretation. The
normal ritual and social life of the group went into a state of abeyance
and men walked softly, not knowing what to expect next.

Organized violence for the Somali, as for many people, represents
a more than adequate species of behavior, when it is directed towards
someone other than the furthest significant extension of oneself. But
while the identity of the self in the group is widely extensible, it was
never seen as absolutely contractable. There are those enduring others
who are too much a part of each individual to be available to him for
the game of blood and death no matter what its attractions. For the
Barsana the limit involved is that of significant symbolic kinship in
the male line. For others of us, there are other limits that must be
explored and defined.

CONTEMPORARY FORMS OF VIOLENCE

By HAROLD I. LIEF, M.D.

VIOLENCE AND FORCE

VIOLENCE is a generic term, encompassing a number of connotations—such as "the exertion of any physical force so as to injure and abuse . . . intense turbulent or furious action and force or feeling often destructive." Other words used in connection with violence are "unnatural," "undue," "extreme," and "vehement."[1]

Violence is not necessarily identical with *force*. The latter may signify restraint via the threat of violence. When we arrange for four or five attendants to approach an assaultive patient, we use the threat of violence in order to prevent violence. The patient recognizes that resistance is futile, and submits in the face of overwhelming force. This is an instance of successful deterrence. Violence differs from force in that it sooner or later gets out of bounds even, if, at the outset, it had been appropriate to a given goal. It becomes behavior exercised for its own sake, and thus seems capricious, arbitrary, or "needless." Violence is often quite unexpected in its onset and unpredictable in its course, whereas *force* may be controlled, delimited, and appropriately directed toward a goal.

VIOLENCE AND AGGRESSION

There are many psychoanalysts who use the term aggression mistakenly, in a general sense, covering everything from the exploratory drive of the infant and child to the sadistic brutality of the rapist-murderer; in between they include drives such as mastery of self and the environment, self assertion, and dominance. Aggression used in this sweeping way results in endless confusion. Murphy[2] puts it this way:

". . . If we use the term "aggression" to describe both the capacity to move into the environment in an active, discovering, creating, and stimulating way which produces welcome results for other people, small or large, and activity aimed to destroy, depreciate, demote or which in other ways bring discomfort for others, small or large, we create enormous difficulties for our thinking . . . "Aggression" can mean almost anything from hostility to the vigor with which either constructive or destructive acts are carried out."

I will use the word aggression to mean behavior motivated by the wish to injure, remove or destroy a threatening object. In this sense, aggression is a mode of emergency behavior called into play by the blocking of any drive, the inhibition of any function, or the perception of any threat, and it can be utilized by a group as well as by an individual. From this, it follows, that aggression and violence are *motivationally* the same even though there are many different degrees of aggression—violence, ranging from kicking the cat or slamming the door to nuclear warfare. In the words of Scott[3]:

". . . The word aggression is widely used and misused in a variety of contexts. It may describe either an act of war by a nation or the behavior of an overenthusiastic salesman. Used precisely, 'aggression' refers to fighting and means the act of initiating an attack."

Buss[4] has defined aggression in similar terms:

". . . The term aggression subsumes a large number of responses that vary in topography, energy expenditure, and consequences. All aggressive responses share two characteristics: (1) the delivery of noxious stimuli, and (2) an interpersonal context. Thus aggression is defined as *a response that delivers noxious stimuli to another organism;* the term *attack* will be used as a synonym."

Although Buss defines aggression as an attack, he, paradoxically, (as do many other experimental psychologists) refuses to define it in motivational terms, because "intent . . . implies teleology, a purposive act directed toward a future goal" and because "intent is a private event that may or may not be capable of verbalization, may or may not be accurately reflected in a verbal statement."

Psychoanalysts think and observe in a motivational context; if they did not they could not make use of introspective methods. Indeed, even the analysis of inspective behavioral data usually depends on the interpretation of motivation. It would be unnecessary to explain my defining aggression in motivational terms if this were not an interdisciplinary meeting, where matters, taken for granted by one discipline, may be sharply disputed by members of another.

Violence is thus an end-point on a continuum of aggressive behavior. It is characterized by extreme force, often physical, as well as by its irrational nature, so that its original goal-orientation may be lost as it becomes an end-in-itself.

The origins of aggression are considered to be either instinctive or reactive. I believe aggression to be reactive, but in any case, the *capacity* for violence is innate in man. The emotion that usually fuels this behavior pattern is rage, and this affect seems to be widespread in the animal kingdom. Fighting occurs from the arthropods on up.

> Fighting occurs so widely in the animal kingdom that it cannot be dismissed as accidental or abnormal in occurrence. In reality, aggressive behavior is a common and apparently useful part of the daily lives of many animals, and only exceptionally does it become destructive or harmful.[5]

Most individual acts of human violence are rage-driven, as are most group-centered violent actions, such as race riots or political revolutions.

On the other hand, there are violent acts which appear to be carried out without any anger behind them. An example was the 1957 "senseless" gang killing of a 15 year old boy, partially crippled by polio— the so-called "Egyptian King" homicide. In the same attack, another boy was critically injured, being stabbed a number of times with a bread knife. As Yablonsky[6] puts it:

> The motives for this crime fit no simple category. No money was taken. No direct personal revenge was involved. According to all reports, the victims did not personally know their assailants, nor did the youths who committed the homicide know their victims.

This is almost a "pure culture" example of violence for the sake of violence. Indeed, the more unconcerned, the more unfeeling, the more "cool" the killer acts, the greater are the plaudits of his fellow gang members. It is the violent act itself which is prized as an "easy, quick, almost magical way of achieving power and prestige. In a single act of unpremeditated intensity he establishes a sense of his own existence and impresses this existence on others."

Another type of violence without rage is a detached, depersonalized, goal-oriented act, namely, that of electronically controlled, push button nuclear war. The emotions of the men pushing the buttons are irrelevant unless the act is impulsive or accidental. Rage would not be instrumental, but, in fact, would be an obstacle in contemporary scientific warfare.

I am able to discern at least three types of violence: (1) The type driven by rage, (2) a detached type in which the significant aspect is the violent act rather than the object of the attack, and (3) a detached type in which the destruction of the object is the significant aspect, and the violence is an instrumental act required for the attainment of the goal.

I will examine these three types of violence in relation to some of the violent types and types of violence familiar to twentieth century man: the gangster, the Western gunman, the youth who is a member of a violent gang, genocide, and nuclear war.

SOME GENERAL ASPECTS

Anthropologists, historians, and political scientists tell us that violence has been present in every society and in every age. With the coming of the nation-state in the seventeenth century, violence came into the hands of national leaders with increasing power. Yet that power was limited, both technically and politically. Technically, the gas chamber and the atom bomb had not been invented and politically the wielders of power were usually held accountable despite the lip service given to the doctrine of the Divine Right of Kings. In contemporary life, accountability for violence has been generally a postmortem affair, with the trials and judgments of Hitler and Stalin occurring after their deaths. Even the culpability and accountability of their lieutenants necessitated unusual charges as exemplified in the Nuremburg and Eichmann trials. Few people raise the question of accountability for the Hiroshima and Nagasaki bombings, for we were the victors. If the United States and her allies had lost the war, we might have witnessed a trial similar to the Nuremburg trials, in which the guilt of our national leaders would have been adjudged. I am not suggesting the equal culpability of these acts of violence—genocide and atom bombing—but I am suggesting that accountability for violent acts causing mass deaths does not follow automatically; it is rather a question of who has won and who has lost.

Our modern world has witnessed technological changes permitting mass murder to be carried out on an unprecedented scale. At the very same time, as Wolin[7] has stated, we have developed increasing concern for the poor, weak, and sick members of society, developing institutions and financial assistance for their care also on a huge scale. This is a *paradoxical* social attitude in which people can actually analyze detachedly whether the United States can tolerate 60 million or 100 million dead, but become intensely aroused over the multiple postponements of the death of Caryl Chessman. Seemingly, we must have increasing concern for individual life as a necessary *defense against the total detachment* involved in contemplating millions of dead. The mind cannot grasp the enormity, the immensity of the casualties in a nuclear war. Szent-Gyorgyi[8] graphically points out that the concept of nuclear disaster is intellectual and detached because it is outside immediate experience:

> Here we stand in the middle of this new world with our primitive brain at-
> tuned to the simple cave life, terrific forces at our disposal, which we are
> clever enough to release, but whose consequences we cannot comprehend.
> Their dimensions are too far beyond our human dimensions. When my wife
> tells me, "the water is hot," I am careful. . . . But if I hear that an atomic ex-
> plosion has 15 million degrees of heat, it means nothing to me. I am deeply
> moved if I see a man suffering and would even risk my life for him. But
> then I talk impersonally about the possible pulverization of our big cities,
> with a hundred million dead. I am unable to multiply one man's suffering by
> a hundred million.

As a consequence of this social split, have we become inured to mass violence? It appears as if we can contemplate non-nuclear war, such as the Korean, Indo-Chinese, or Algerian conflicts, with greater equanimity than did past generations. The very term we use to de-scribe some of these conflicts, "brush-fire warfare" indicates the en-larging scale of violence to which we have grown accustomed.

Other aspects of modern life such as automation and the growth of huge corporations, which may house 30,000 employees in one build-ing, contribute to the dehumanization growing more prevalent day by day, which we desperately try to counter by our search for the mean-ing of individual existence. But it is the fact that the "world annihila-tion" fantasies of the schizophrenic have now become a reality that increase the pace of this emotional detachment while the detachment, in turn, becomes an obstacle to more energetic efforts to find non-violent solutions to international conflicts.

Special Types of Violence

Cannibalism

Cannibalism reflects the 3 categories of violence to which I re-ferred earlier. Often motivated by revenge and "consumed" with anger against neighboring tribes who trespassed on their land, stole property, particularly wives, and exerted magical influence against them, can-nibals also used aggression as an instrumental act, for capture of their neighbors added to their food supply. Yet, raids against their enemies designed for revenge as well as to increase their protein in-take were often a sort of tribal gamesmanship and were carried out as ritualistic exercises as part of puberty or other religious rites. In the latter instance, the violent act becomes all important, rather than the emotions behind it, or the object of its execution. In one of our "refined" civilizations, an impersonal and gigantic mouth, the crematorium, replaced the inefficient mechanisms of the savage.

The Gangster and the Western Gunman

Although there are certainly gangsters and, in the past, there were Western gunmen, one can truthfully say that most Americans have never seen either. Why then, do they appear so significant, in our consciousness? Warshow[9] in an illuminating essay on American movies, says that "What matters is that the experience of the gangster" (and of the Western gunman) *"as an experience of art* is universal to Americans." Since violence plays a dominant and central theme in these art forms, it stands to reason that gangster and Western movies and TV shows have had an important bearing on our concept of and attitude towards violence.

The gangster has to be viewed against the background of the dominant values in American life, equality and achievement. Lipset[10] has traced the development of these two values since the beginning of the nineteenth century, and in his view, these values have had a great deal to do with the extreme emphasis on success found in our society. To paraphrase Lipset, Americans are led to feel that the game must be won no matter what methods are employed to win it. The worst thing that can happen is to lose, and to be perceived as being a failure. This places a great deal of stress on the ends rather than on the means of attaining those ends. In contrast to the ethos of the more rigidly stratified societies, where the stress falls on the value of playing the game well, rather than on its result, in America there is a constant push to achieve, to get on, to get ahead; and with the emphasis on equality comes the feeling that one is as good as anyone else, and that one has the right to success no matter how it is achieved.

Sociologists have suggested that the much greater prevalence of organized vice and racketeering in America as compared with England and other affluent countries in northern Europe reflects the greater pressure on those with deprived social backgrounds to find illegal ways of succeeding when the more legitimate fields are closed to them. It has been suggested that the rackets must be seen as one of the principal ladders of social mobility among members of minority ethnic groups.

In the case of the film gangster the path to success, irrational brutality, becomes itself the mark or symbol of success. The more sadistic he is, the more successful, thus providing one more example of violence becoming an end in itself. As Warshow states the case, "Thus brutality itself becomes at once the means to success and the content of success —a success that is defined in its most general terms, not as accomplishment or specific gain, but simply as the unlimited possibility of aggression."

Warshow demonstrates how the gangster portrays the competitive dilemma of our society in which failure is the worst thing that can happen and success becomes impossible because of the guilty fear it evokes. "Failure is a kind of death and success is evil and dangerous, is—ultimately—impossible." Our enormous attraction to the gangster film is not based alone on the vicarious acting out of our violent aggressive impulses, but because the dilemma is resolved by the death of the gangster—it is his failure, not ours, his guilt is punished, not ours. Wertham may be right in his contention that the cultural emphasis on violence has a deleterious influence on our youth, but I submit that it is not violence in a total, abstract, or generic sense that is deleterious for violence is a fact of life, some say even more of human than of animal life, and we had better find ways of facing and controlling it before it is too late) but it is the confusion of means and ends, the extolling of the violent act as a value in itself, or as a passionless instrument of gain, that is false, misleading, and perhaps ultimately disastrous.

The differences between this type of senseless or depersonalized violence and an act of passion is sharply etched by a comparison of the gangster film and the Western. In contrast to the gangster, the Westerner is a man of honor, with a code, and a style of life that is inner-directed. The Westerner's autonomy dictates the "when" and "how" of violence—it is hardly ever needless, capricious, or sadistic. While the violent act may be the high point of the drama, it is the Westerner's honor which is at stake and which is the reason for the violence in the first place. His violence is marked by control and self-restraint. In this sense it comes close to the concept of force with its use of violence or threat of violence to restrain, control, and ultimately prevent greater violence.

The Western movie has such a great hold on our imagination, says Warshow, "because it offers a serious orientation to the problem of violence such as can be found almost nowhere else in our culture." We train ourselves to deny the possibilities of violence (a recent survey I made of the reactions to the Cuban crisis found among the patients of 60 New Orleans psychiatrists amply confirms this, or to be shocked or bored by actual or by symbolic images of violence, leading to or viewing violence quite unrealistically. Through hypocrisy or fear we tend to delegate our responsibilities for the control of violence to others—generally the more irresponsible or morally vulnerable. The Western movie gives us an example, which we still cherish, of a hero whose violence makes sense, in a world where senseless violence is a daily occurrence.

Gang Violence

As indicated earlier, teen-age gang violence is characterized by the value attached to the violent act itself, "coolly" carried out with little regard to the victim or to the purpose of the act. It is the violence itself that gives the gang member a sense of his own existence, as well as a sense of belonging to a group. A conformist, whose greatest fear is to be left alone, ignored, or rejected by his gang, he has no sense of autonomy, of being able to influence or manipulate his environment in any constructive fashion.

The relationship of the rewarding effects of environmental feedback to the growth of such ego functions as exploration, attention and perception, language and thinking, manipulating the surroundings, and producing effective changes in his environment, have been extremely well described by White.[11] He has chosen the word "competence" to signify those processes by which the animal or child learns to interact effectively with its environment. This occurs through a continuous chain of transactional events which include stimulation, cognition, action, effect on the environment, new stimulation, etc., in a series of spiraling processes. As I see it, the basic defect in the member of a violent gang is the failure to achieve this sense of competence. He is unable to change his environment effectively, and he gradually loses his desire to attempt constructive changes. Although White does not talk about the delinquent youth, his words are, nonetheless, appropriate in this context:

". . . Interest wanes when action begins to have less effect; effectance motivation (here White is referring to the motivation to effect meaningful changes in one's environment) subsides when a situation has been explored to the point that it no longer presents new possibilities."

Unable to believe in the generally held values of happiness and achievement, the gang member turns to violence as an existential act. In an interesting essay, the playwright, Miller,[12] presents a similar thesis—that the mainspring of action in the juvenile delinquent is boredom:

The delinquent is stuck with his boredom, stuck inside it, stuck to it, until for two or three minutes he "lives"; he goes on a raid around the corner and feels the thrill of risking his skin or his life as he smashes a bottle filled with gasoline on some other kid's head. In a sense, it is his trip to Miami. It makes his day. It is his shopping tour. It gives him something to talk about for a week. It is *life*. Standing around with nothing coming up is as close to dying as you can get. Unless one grasps the power of boredom, the threat of it to one's existence, it is impossible to "place" the delinquent as a member of the human race.

If an act of violence can give the youth a feeling of existing, it can also, if carried to its ultimate limits, symbolize, par excellence, the purposelessness of life. Miller illustrates this by referring to a story of Andre Gide's:

Gide wrote a story about a man who wanted to get on a train and shoot a passenger. Any train, any passenger. It would be a totally gratuitous act, an act devoid of any purpose whatever, an act of "freedom" from love, without love at all, with nothing in his heart but the sheerly physical contemplation of the gun barrel and the target. In doing this one would partake of death's irreproachable identity and commit an act in revolt against meaning itself, just as death is, in the last analysis, beyond analysis.

In similar fashion the "New Wave" movies of France and Italy often depict senseless, brutal acts of cruelty, in which the violence gives the perpetrator a measure of meaningfulness, while simultaneously revealing the alleged utter futility of life.

The aggressive play of a normal child is quite different from the sadistic "play" of the adolescent gang member. In the child, the emphasis is not on the violent act itself, but on its meaning for the identity of the child. He is the hero, sometimes the victim, or even the villain—but the act has meaning, because it is the role-playing of a child experimenting with different identities. The gang member has foreclosed on his future role identifications; the future is closed to him except in terms of the consequences of violence directed against society or (as in drug addiction) against himself.

Genocide

The ultimate in dehumanized violence was the extermination of millions of Jews and other prisoners of the Nazis in the gas chambers of Auschwitz and the other concentration camps. The efficiency with which Eichmann ran the transportation system bringing the victims to the camps, the business methods used to make a profit of the prisoner's bodies and personal effects, "including dental gold, and the utilization of his body after his death—hair sold to make cloth, fat for soap, bones and ashes for glue and fertilizer (less 2 marks for the cost of cremation)" denote the nadir in the history of human degradation.

Alvarez[13] has recently described what Bettelheim[14] described earlier —the process of regression and personality disintegration until all spontaneity and will cease—until the prisoners become indifferent to all stimuli except food and even that response disappeared before the end.

The inability to influence the environment developed into the inability to perceive stimuli because of the extreme danger of doing so. The SS deliberately fostered this complete loss of autonomy by calculated, passionless acts of violence. When the prisoners became walking corpses, or entered the "moslem stage," they would walk indifferently to the gas chamber. At first people's identities were replaced by numbers, but in the last stages the crowds on the way to the concentration camps were never even registered, "and oblivion took over."

If we were certain that the people who ran these chambers of death so efficiently were sadists, who in another society would have been placed in institutions, we would be able to discuss this sickening chapter of history as proving only that our most sadistic fantasies can be acted out. But, in fact, it is quite certain that they were not sadists, but that they were efficient, dispassionate destroyers of personality and will. Given a certain combination of societal factors, especially those which promote automatic obedience, it "could happen here" or anywhere. If the process of dehumanization continues unchecked, given man's inventiveness, it is only a matter of which type of mass violence he will decide to use. At this point in time, the odds are in favor of nuclear extermination.

Nuclear Warfare

The process of detached, depersonalized violence which I have traced through some contemporary forms of violent activity—the gangster, the juvenile gang member, and the violence of the concentration camp —reaches its apogee in nuclear warfare. Even in the concentration camp where malevolence was at its greatest, even though the prisoner was deprived of his autonomy, his will, and his personality under the impact of the violent acts of his guards, there was still *personal* contact with his oppressors. Not so in nuclear war, where a button pushed will explode a missile thousands of miles away, killing millions of people who are faceless and completely unknown to the man pushing the button. What act of violence could be more dehumanized than that, except, perhaps, blowing up one's own countrymen? Rage or any other passion plays no part at all in such a process. In this act the executive functions of the ego—the action self if you prefer—are completely separated from the emotions. A form of *dissociation,* it is an act which could be, and in a special sense, is performed by a mechanical robot—a computer.

It is this view of human beings as numbers, statistics, interchangeable pieces in a vast numbers game, that brings with it a sense of noninvolvement and indifference to the actual or potential suffering of others and permits people to tolerate the implications of mass destruction in a nuclear war. Slowly and imperceptibly this attitude grows and permits us to view an irrational world situation as if it were rational, and permits us to make decisions based on an inner logic which seems sensible, just the way the paranoid's inner logic seems airtight once one accepts the original delusional premise.

While violence is universal, not all types of violence are. War is not. There is no evidence that there is anything in the nature of man which needs warfare as its outlet—and certainly not nuclear war, a type of violence which is completely irrelevant to man's emotional life. (This is not true of irrational, rageful, or guilt-laden acts which may trigger off a nuclear detonation, which in turn may accidentally touch off a world-wide holocaust—hence the need for the Human Reliability Program[15] of our nuclear forces, currently in operation.) In William James'[16] day, there may have been a need for the moral equivalent of war, but what is the moral equivalent of nuclear war?

Psychological factors, however, do play an important role in all aspects of international relations, and are intimately involved in the processes which may lead to war. Aside from the probabilities of human error, and irrational reactions by subordinates with nuclear command decisions, there are ethnocentric misperceptions leading to mistrust while mistrust leads to further perceptual distortions in a vicious circle, increasing the difficulties of an already difficult political situation. Tension further increases the rigidity and stereotypy of responses. As Van Atta[17] has stated:

> ". . . Control of the arms race is not a problem of hardware design nor of technical schemes for carefully balanced disarmament, detection of weapons tests or evaluation of war-making capabilities . . . It is a problem of human understanding and human control."

Yes, man's basic emotions, rage and pride, are certainly at the root of international conflict, but nuclear war is not a sane solution for mankind's perennial struggle for possessions, power, or belief systems.

We have paradoxically reached a point in our development as a species where the act of nuclear global devastation, the most violent act of all, is best done by computers, machines which cannot feel the brute emotions which have led us to the brink of disaster.

But I will make the assumption that there will always be something in the nature of man (at least for many generations to come) that requires violent solution. Every society has need of "hate satisfaction." I think, however, that if we can find ways of preventing the dissociation of emotions from the act of violence, we can probably prevent mass violence such as genocide and nuclear annihilation, while we find better ways of sublimating aggression, not only through international games, but through nonviolent international competition.

There are two possible programs we can initiate to deal with the threat of detached violence. We can no longer return to the violence of Medea or even of the Borgias, but we can and must find societal controls which prevent detached, dehumanized violence from being carried out. As one possibility, deterrence is most effective, not in the 2 group situation, as between the US and USSR, but when there is a third party wielding the power of deterrence. Certainly, this is the function of the police and judicial systems in civilized countries. Beatrice Whiting pointed out many years ago that those preliterate societies having superordinate institutions had recourse to much less magic and supernatural means of violent retaliation than did those societies lacking such institutions. By analogy, a superordinate institution, such as a greatly strengthened UN, should have the power of deterrence. This demands a sweeping change in political attitude in all the countries of the world, not only in ours. But the need is urgent and the times demand it.

A second program, ultimately more far-reaching in its consequences, is a revolutionary approach to education in which the realities of emotional life are taught to our children from the nursery on, in terms appropriate to each age group. Among others, Rado and Bettelheim have been advocates of such a program. It is only through such an intense educational effort over many generations that our cave-man emotions can be modified and brought into appropriate resonance with our technical genius.

REFERENCES

1. Webster's Third New International Dictionary, Springfield, Mass., G. & C. Merriam, 1961, p. 2554.

2. Murphy, L. B. et al: The Widening World of Childhood. New York, Basic Books, 1962, p. 350-351.
3. Scott, J. P.: Aggression. Chicago, The University of Chicago Press, 1958, p. 1.
4. Buss, A. H.: The Psychology of Aggression. New York, John Wiley, 1961, p. 1.
5. Scott, J. P.: *op. cit.*, p. 6.
6. Yablonsky, L.: The Violent Gang. New York, McMillan, 1962, p. 9.
7. Wolin, S. S.: The theme of violence in western political thought. Paper delivered at the 39th Annual Meeting of the American Orthopsychiatric Association, Los Angeles, March 21-24, 1962.
8. Szent-Gyorgyi, A.: The persistence of the cave man. Saturday Rev. of Literature, July 7, 1962, p. 11.
9. Warshow, R.: The Immediate Experience. New York, Doubleday, 1962. Quotations from "The Gangster as Tragic Hero" and "Movie Chronicle: The Westerner."
10. *a.* Lipset, S. M.: Equal or better in America. Columbia University Forum 4:17-21, 1961.
    b. ——: A changing American character? *In:* Culture and Social Character, Chapter 7. Edited by S. M. Lipset and Leo Lowenthal, Glencoe, The Free Press of Glencoe, 1961.
11. White, R. W.: Motivation reconsidered: The concept of competence. Psychol. Rev. 66:297-333, 1959.
12. Miller, A.: The bored and the violent. Harper's 225:50-56, 1962.
13. Alvarez, A.: The concentration camps. The Atlantic 210:69-72, 1962.
14. Bettelheim, B.: The Informed Heart. Glencoe, Ill., The Free Press, 1960.
15. Department of the Air Force, Guidance For Implementing the Human Reliability Program. AFM 160-55, U. S. Printing Office, Washington, D. C.
16. James, W.: The moral equivalent of war. *In:* Memoirs and Studies. New York: Longmans, Green, 1911, p. 267-296.
17. Van Atta, L. C.: Arms control: Human control. Am. Psychol. In press.

THE FUNCTIONS OF WAR

By ANTHONY LEEDS

IN THIS presentation I shall approach war as if it were merely another social phenomenon to be understood with the same armamentarium of concepts, the same weaponry of analysis, the same strategy of sociocultural explanation as any other social phenomenon. At the same time, this approach, at least as far as analysis is concerned, has attempted to avoid *a priori* value positions as being irrelevant to analysis, however, much the analyst may personally derogate war. This approach has tended, however, to be used mostly in the analysis of an individual case or of classes of cases as in the works of Blackett,[4] Newcomb,[24] Turney-High,[25] and Vayda.[26] War, as such, is understood as a social institution with sociocultural functions and linkings with the rest of the "parts" of the society and culture.

The content of values is cultural and derives from, or is related to, the social and technical forms extant at a given time and place, but the *exercise* of value is an individual and subjective matter. This is true even when a complete or near consensus of values exists. The value-orientation of the analyst often tends to be transformed into a psychologistic world-view, particularly among Americans, and especially American psychologists, although it has also affected numerous American anthropologists when they deal with contemporary or even primitive war (Cf. Allport,[2] e.g., p. 53; Kluckhohn,[16] pp. 224, 278; Turney-High,[25] pp. 141-152). Psychological forces, like aggression and frustration are then thought to cause wars.[2,9]

This is not the place to attack the psychologistic fallacies. That has been done by White[29] (*passim*, esp. 132ff) and Newcomb[24] (pp. 321-326), among others, who, albeit largely correct, state the case poorly and in a sterile dogma, failing to see that psychological variables *are* relevant in defined ways, certainly as significant dependent variables, and possibly, in a few quite limited spheres, as independent variables. But psychologistic value approaches do not explain the incidence or

regularities in the occurrence of wars in typologically and evolutionarily different societies; nor the prevalence of warfare; nor the moments of outbreak of war; nor the alleged transference of aggression
from "normal channels" to "war channels" and vice versa back to
"peace channels"; nor the causes of the intensification of aggression
to warlike levels, *assuming* that aggression levels are indeed higher in
wartime, for which I have seen no evidence; nor the organization of
war; nor, especially in the warfare of large-scale, complex societies,
the selection of combatants; nor the reasons for peacefulness or "non-
aggression," unless one assumes that peaceableness is the Natural State
of Man. That none of these is explained, is a reflection of the view
of war as an "aberration" and as a psychological phenomenon rather
than as a social institution probably possessing a lawfulness of occurrence.

Conditions of War and Peace

I shall not attempt any rigorous definition of warfare other than to
refer to armed and organized conflict between two or more recognized
political entities and, in certain instances, between two or more recognized political subdivisions. Conflict, in a definition modified from
Coser, may refer to struggles over values and claims to any cultural
resources, whether economic, political, or (dubiously) intellectual.
By "recognized," I wish to indicate recognition on the part of the
entities in conflict, which may or may not be recognized as entities
by an observer. With respect to such recognition, interests are defined
and action taken as against other entities. Minimally, I think it necessary to consider three phases in the state or institution called war:
war prelude, war proper, and war cadence. In a large sense, war
prelude comprises all sociocultural process and war cadence, in the
long run, interdigitates with war prelude. One might look at the total
process as a kind of pulsating progression of increasing and decreasing
dissonances and harmonies.

Conversely, peace, like war, must also be understood as a particular
state of a larger process. Peace may also be considered as having at
least three phases: prelude, peace proper, and cadence, the first and
last overlapping inversely with the last and first phases of war. Peace
of course might also be looked at as a pulsation of waxing and waning
harmonies and dissonances. The considerations of the functions of
peace and its phases must be left for another time, although this
creates an artificiality of abstraction.

In an over-all view, *"normal"* total social process may indeed consist of oscillations between war and peace. The limitations to war would be precisely those functions of peace whose too-long continued abolition by, or too-drastic abrogation through the instituting of, the state of war destroy the possibility of satisfying the so-called "functional prerequisites" of society.[1,21] On the other hand, the limitations to peace would be exactly those major functions that war so markedly displays, which, if not accomplished, in turn produce a host of consequences that militate against the possibility of satisfying the same basic "functional prerequisites" mentioned. The phase of war proper has characteristic attributes which are of the highest significance. One of these is the drastic and sudden shift from one set of interaction norms, both among and within recognized entities, which we may call the "rules of peace," to another set of norms, perhaps minimal but normative nonetheless, which we may call the "rules of war."

Lest it be forgotten, the rules of war include such items as the defined rights and guarantees in the treatment of prisoners (notice the special depravity and immorality attributed to those who depart from these conventions); defined procedures for surrender, for what may be considered targets, for the treatment of civilians and enemy soldiers (e.g., capturing, enslaving, killing, as possibilities), for establishing and observing truces, for conferring in the field, for the treatment of spies, for the maintenance of buffer areas (e.g., Switzerland), even for the conduct of battle itself.

Another of the attributes of war proper is a shift from legal relations through networks of juridically defined statuses to extra-legal relationships through networks of customarily or informally defined roles which provide continuing means of communication and interaction between or among parties to the war.

A third attribute is the shift from a distribution of relationships over a wide variety of forms of interaction in the state of peace to a concentration of relationships primarily in a single form of interaction, the military encounter, in war proper. Ideally, this would involve the total elimination of other than war-like forms of interaction. This ideal, however, is not reached because of the necessity, in some degree, to maintain minimal role networks for important functional reasons, such as reestablishing the conditions for achieving the functions of peace.

The maximum dissociation achieved during warfare among recognized entities removes them from the equilibria, the checks and balances, of the internal and external rules of peace. With respect to most significant institutions, it opens a period in which the rules are not defined, a period which may be short, perhaps days or weeks, as after Pearl Harbor, during which are instituted the new rules that are to obtain during the armed encounter, and, even more importantly, in some degree *after* the war.

FUNCTION AND THE SELF-REGULATION OF SYSTEMS

Before turning to the functions of war, it is vital to discuss briefly the conception of function as used here. "Function" refers to the feedback effects of observed consequences of the behavior through time of a structure or process upon one or more of the variables relevant to the operation of the structure or process in such a way as to contribute to the maintenance of old equilibria or to the rapid establishment of new ones when the old are irrevocably disturbed (cf. Collins[6]; Hammer[13]; Hempel,[14] esp. pp. 277-281; Levy,[18] pp. 56, 77; Nagel,[22] p. 525, etc.). It may be noted that *no* notion of consciousness, awareness, intention, or purpose is necessarily implied by this definition, although any of these *may* contribute in the case of war, for example, to achieving its functions. In most of the functions I shall discuss, they seem not to contribute, or at least not to play any significant parts.

Central to this conception of function is that, at given times and places, some significant variable may be limited to a certain range of states (e.g., size of population) by the operation of other significant variables (e.g., periods of minimum food supply; institutions for reducing birth rates, etc.), in turn, limited by still other variables (such as the techno-ecological conditions of food procurement) which may once again be limited to a certain range of states by other variables, and even the original variable considered (e.g., the food production volume being kept in a given range by the size of population). Where such a circularity of effects is observed, one may speak of a stable equilibrium, such as so often occurs in primitive economies.[17,27]

Other types of equilibria may also be defined in terms of relationships among variables. Where circularity does not obtain but the system departs from and returns to a given state periodically, one may speak of unstable equilibrium. A gradual, incremental and irreversible change in the ranges of variables throughout the system, where no increment occurs at any one time which falls beyond the defined range, may be called a directional equilibrium. A change in a variable such that the increment, in one leap, goes beyond the defined range so that the system cannot tolerate the shift without compensatory drastic shifts in the other variables of the system may be referred to simply as a new equilibrium state.

Stable equilibrium functions tend to be most characteristic in extremest forms of total peace, whereas new equilibrium functions tend most to typify the extremes of total war, with lesser degrees of states of peace and war tending to be characterized by unstable and directional equilibrium functions.

THE FUNCTIONS OF WAR

We may arrange the functions of war, according to a set of five ways of looking at socio-cultural systems formulated by Nelson[23]:

1. Where culture is regarded as an adaptive system, warfare may be understood as an adaptive institution as regards its functions. We turn first to the internal adaptive functions of warfare, that is, the effects which occur and feed back into the recognized sociocultural entity which has entered into war.

In any of the three phases of war, and perhaps especially in the cadence, consolidation of internal power may occur as an effect of the abrogation of the rules of peace and the necessity, real or alleged, for organizing the "war effort." Probably universally, some degree of focussing of the entire entity about the effort of the war, about its operations, occurs, and with it, some centralization of power. Plainly, as power distribution and redistribution evolutionarily become more important in society, this consequence of warfare is likely to take on greater significance. It may or may not be anticipated by the participants and it may or may not provide motivation for individuals.

Another internal adaptation or adjustive consequence may be the consolidation of trends already present in the society, especially in societies in states of directional equilibrium most characteristic, perhaps, in modern societies and observed in such processes as industrialization, administrative centralization, militarism, etc. The functioning of war to consolidate and advance these trends has been excellently shown for Japan and for several Western powers.[5]

Again, the abrogation of the rules of peace and instituting of the rules of war may produce as consequences the establishment of institutions of community coordination and control and the creation of community consensus. The war and war-cadence events in the United States appear to have been of this sort. I refer to the various post-World War II laws and agencies created to control labor, "subversives," and foreigners which, severally and jointly, have brought the community into a coordinated consensus or apathy, have exercised increasing control over the populace at large, and have thoroughly demolished most opposition organizations in the country. All these effects are, incidentally, consolidations of trends clearly present in the war prelude. Examples of at least temporary community coordination, control, and consensus can be found in the literature on primitive societies, as, for example, regarding Plains Indian warfare. The postwar continuity of such effects has even been argued as a possible or partial origin of the State.

The initiation and operation of the rules of war create a break with prior conditions, so that the sloughing off of antiquated or rigidified norms or structures, with or without replacement by new ones, can be accomplished, deliberately or unintentionally. The Japanese warmakers in the latter part of the last century apparently foresaw such effects of war and deliberately fostered wars so as to bring about the consequences, and, with them, new functional relations.[5]

A related effect, mentioned by Coser[7] (p. 154) may be the revitalization of existing norms and values. The effect may be more vigorously to secure the maintenance of an equilibrium by intensifying the ideological variables of the system. Thus the world becomes "safe for democracy"; becomes a place where countries are "free to choose their own forms of government"; where people who are "democratic," who have fought for "self-determination," who ostensibly have the right to private property are "free," that is, are at liberty to operate within defined ranges of behavior, and only within these ranges. Similarly revitalizations may be observed in primitive societies at various levels of complexity.

Moreover, consequences of the war condition may elicit innovational consequences, especially in technology and, to some extent, in institutions. The innovational aspects were strikingly clear in World War II and are drastically changing human life today. Such innovations may contribute to directional equilibria or new equilibrium states through the feedback of the innovations into the system. In this sense, the innovational functions of war contribute to change, reorganization, and evolution, and may, because of the special conditions of war discussed before, increase the rate of development and adaptation to new circumstances.

Finally, war may lead to the resolution or intensification of old social conflicts within the society (cf. Coser,[7] Chapt. IX). With respect to different contexts, both effects have been observed in the case of Negro-White relationships in the United States. The organization for World War II to some extent undermined existent social institutions of Negro-White conflict, thereby permitting the intensification of that conflict in other arenas.

It may be noted that many of the functions I have been discussing contribute in the short and long runs to shifts of sociocultural equilibria in irreversible ways. War, then, may be seen as an evolutionary agent, and one which facilitates internal and external adaptations to crucial old or to important new internal circumstances.

Next, we may turn to the external adaptive functions of war, that is, to the effects which feed back into the internal systems of the parties to war and into the systemic relationships between them. These effects would seem particularly important where the relative autonomy of one or both of the parties extensively changed, but where the barriers to such change had ben especially great. In a general evolutionary perspective, the trend appears to have been towards intensification of the intersystemic relationships—that is, in the direction of creating ever-larger supersystems—despite local occurrences of rarifactions. Both intensification and rarifaction represent new equilibria.

Again, ossified rules of peace may, by war, suddenly be redefined in terms of current internal and new external conditions. Put another way, war may serve as the tool for reordering intersystemic relationships more or less regularly where peaceful change cannot be accomplished at all or only at a rate too deliberate to meet the new exigencies.[15] Territorial hegemonies, trade routes, exchangeable goods, mutual rights and obligations, and so on, may be reallocated in terms of new exigencies. This function can be observed both in primitive and advanced societies.

A further function is the consolidation of slowly developing trends present in the intersystemic relationship, or super-system, such as the tendency to develop economic or administrative institutions across the boundaries of recognized entities, as in the consolidation of ecological areas suited to modern productive technology. I believe the various common markets and free trade movements of recent years are phenomena of this sort. The opposite effect, that of the retrogression of such trends, is also possible. In long-term evolutionary perspective, the latter possibility appears to be relatively local in time and place. Related to this are the effects of the establishment or fragmentation of super-communities through war.

We may consider, here, too, some ecological effects of war between recognized entities. One such effect is the creating of no man's lands or buffer zones which are utilized by neither party regularly, but, by virtue of the absence of permanent and fixed exploitation, supply a fallow area for possible later use or a resource pool for emergency use, as, for example, in equilibrating internal food balances. Buffer zones also provide areas where role network transactions between warring parties can take place or where personnel of the warring parties may selectively remove themselves from the arena of combat (e.g., Switzerland or embassies as asylums). Existence of such buffer zones may stabilize both internal and intersystemic equilibria over long periods of time, whereas direct juxtaposition of the two parties would contribute to heightened disequilibrium.

Ecologically, the effects of war may be to augment the resources accessible, as is clearly the case in territorial aggrandizement.[26] Augmentation may also occur as a consequence of war by the elaboration of intersystemic institutions such as tribute and trade.

Again, resources may be used more intensively during and after wars, as in the bringing of so-called "marginal" lands under cultivation and in the World War II Victory Garden development. Such intensifications of use may be permanent when accompanied by changes in variables throughout the system. The use of apparently "marginal" resource areas as a result of war may have been of extensive importance in the evolution of culture as in the case of the development of agriculture based on seed uses in the "marginal" foot-hill hunting-and-gathering areas of Mesopotamia.

Finally, warfare may lead to the exploitation of new resources or of old resources in new ways, a special case of war innovation as mentioned.

It is not to be overlooked that warfare may also have as consequence the destruction of resources with functional repercussions throughout societies party to the war or to the super-system itself. The degree of such destruction is itself a functional limitation to the continuance of the rules of war, to that equilibrium state which we call armed conflict. Obviously, depending on the severity of destruction, the effects may continue well into or beyond the cadence period and even contribute to a new war prelude.

2. Where culture is regarded as an allocation of symbols and values, warfare may be understood as a distributional institution.

We may consider first the internal distributional effects brought about by the war activities of parties to wars.

Warfare as a rule substantially reorders the allocation of rewards within the society, at least during the war proper. Since the rules of war require a reorganization of the entire populace for longer or shorter periods, the equilibrated patterns of peacetime distribution must be realigned. Although in the course of evolution, the importance of this reallocation of rewards appears to increase greatly, yet it can be shown that reordering of rewards occurs also in primitive societies. Whether rewards consist in ownership or use of land or other resources, or in prestige, or in additional spouses or laborers, or in changed conventional role attributions, etc., some rearrangement is found in the case of every war and every kind of war, even when the war is of a ritualized sort. Some of this rearrangement persists after the war.[26,27] Examples, although varied, are as universal as warfare. I think it may be argued again that many of such shifts brought about suddenly and quickly through the agency of war represent shifts whose preliminary phases or trends were already present in the peace period but were inhibited from developing by the rules of peace. This is especially so where innovations have appeared in the society which are, in some respect, contradictory to existent patterns.

The feedback from war activities may serve to confirm, validate, or implement the operation of the statuses and roles of the internal reward system. This is, of course, the complement of the reordering mentioned. It is, for example aptly exemplified by Aztec warfare.

Another important function may be the redistribution of labor both quantitatively among old uses and qualitatively among new labor uses. The latter case may be extremely significant where rigidified labor distributions impede the development of labor-using innovations present in the society prior to the state of war. Much of this labor redistribution is likely to be permanent.

Warfare also functions to redistribute values externally to any given system, and, in some respects, super-systemically between or among the warring parties.

Most important, of course, is the immediate or delayed movement of resources: goods, services, money, or people, through war in any of the phases of war: e.g., Lend Lease, the Marshall Plan, the disposal abroad of war surplus goods, or in the form of Fulbright scholarships serving to disseminate knowledge and technical training. The institutions for such redistributive movements have been legion. We need only mention tribute-paying, ransoming, indemnification, looting, and so on.

Another functional consequence of almost all warfare has been cultural diffusion, producing, in the long run, an ever larger trait content in warring entities from which to select responses. Virtually anything may be diffused: material traits, techniques, behaviors, tastes, knowledge, etc. A great number of mechanisms of diffusion are specifically fostered by the rules of war. For example, combatants display markedly greater physical mobility than under the rules of peace, a mobility which may cause them to encounter opposing combatants directly or indirectly. A mutual transference of cultural content between them may occur. Spying is, of course, deliberately directed at expediting "involuntary" diffusion. Capturing things (such as utilizable weapons) and persons (who are, of course, culture bearers) and, often, incorporating them also contributes effectively to the diffusion of culture. Finally in the war cadence and subsequent peace phases, subjugation and acculturation provide social channels for the back-and-forth movement of cultural content.

It must be recalled that diffused culture content presents expanded repertories from which individuals and societies may select new and more varied behavioral adaptations. Either immediately or in the long run, cumulations of new behavioral inventories effect changes in equilibrium, ultimately of an irreversible and evolutionary sort.

Two other major redistributive functions of war may be mentioned here, although they are not properly redistributions of cultural values and symbols. First is genetic redistribution, a tendency towards panmixia and the elimination of local breeding populations. It is conceivable that there is a degree of selectivity, by virtue of the constitution of the military, for the stronger and healthier members of at least one party to a war to enter into genetic redistribution and to increase genetic variety. Other mechanisms of genetic redistribution include fraternization, capture (including incorporation as slaves or as spouses), population displacement, rape, etc.

Again, the degree and, especially, the nonselectivity of the destructiveness of war, as in the cases of total bombing with conventional bombs or atom bombing, may contribute to the loss of some genes or, in extreme instances, of all genes. The destructiveness ultimately defines parameters for the functions of war—that is, beyond some point of destructiveness, no viable equilibrium or no equilibrium at all can be established by the functional feedback of war activities; in other words, feedback ceases.

Second, war tends to bring about demographic changes by death, capture, exile, and modified procreative habits. The age and sex structure, particularly of the USSR, was drastically affected in World War II by the enormous slaughter of men who would today be between about 35 and 60 years of age. Functional responses to this have appeared throughout Soviet society, perhaps most notably in the composition of the labor force in general and especially of the professional group, so extensively composed of women.

Another common effect of war is the dispersion of population, its spacing out for wider resource use and greater exposure to variant ecological niches. The evolutionary import of this function is very great in that it tends to contribute to the generating of cultural variation and diffusion, from which selection may occur.

CONCLUSIONS

What has been said is sufficient to give a broad view of the variety of functions of war, their enormous complexity severally and especially jointly, as they *concomitantly* relate to a single institution, war.

It should also be noted about almost all the functions that they are essentially social and that assertions regarding the motivational states of individuals would not merely be hazardous guesswork, but probably also erroneous in most cases. The motivations would quite possibly be almost as varied as the number of people affected by each function. The motivations demanded are institutional and conventionalized ones ("fight for freedom!"), the responses largely institutionalized (fighting); but motivational states are exceedingly diverse (fighting with or out of fear, anger, hate, love, apathy, etc.) and not determined by social "motivations." The institutional demands and the institutionalized responses are sociocultural phenomena, sometimes themselves functions of war, while motivational states are phenomena of individuals, irrelevant to the sociocultural demands and responses, the social "motivations."

Some words respecting the control or elimination of war are appropriate in view of this discussion. If, from some value stance, war is declared undesirable and to be eradicated, especially in the presence of an assertedly qualitatively new kind of war, nuclear war, then the total range of functions which have been discussed and remain to be discussed must be accounted to in the most economic fashion possible. I say "economic" because I believe that in the evolution of human culture and society, it can be shown that institutions which carry on multiple functions are much more likely to be selected and to persist than those with single or few functions. The latter tend to disappear or to persist peripherally in the sociocultural structure. Such multifunctional institutions are the family, the state, the church, the voluntary association.

Warfare is another such multifunctional institution, cross-cutting the others, and possibly more labile and flexible because not as narrowly tied to a particular form of organization as are the others. As a highly multifunctional institution, we may infer that it would have a high probability of persistence, a proposition readily observable in fact, to our subjective sorrow.

The eradication of war, if at all possible, would most likely be by means of an as yet unknown equivalent multifunctional institution. Football games or international contests will not do; changing infancy experiences or revolutions in the education of children to achieve new motivations are irrelevant, as are virtually all the multitudes of such suggestions appearing with ever-increasing frequency even from professional scientists. They are largely irrelevant to the functions of war and hence inevitably ineffectual.

A second, but I think only ancillary, road to eradication, if such a road exists, is in the deliberate social surgical transference, all at one time, of a multiplicity of war's functions from war to other social institutions. I think that this possibility is limited partly because the technical problem would prove insuperable—most functions in the sense defined here are not legislatable and we do not know how to make such transferences—and partly because of the "problem" of ossification of the receiving institutions, a "problem" which war is peculiarly adapted to "solve." The most likely institutions for the purpose are, of course, the other multifunctional institutions, the family, the state, the church, the association, and so forth.

A third, but again only ancillary possibility, might be the deliberate manipulation of the different phases of war. I think that more detailed examination would reveal differential functions for war prelude, war proper, and the other war and peace phases. These phases, as I have suggested before, may comprise a self-regulatory system in the sense defined. The extreme parameters controlling the oscillations between peace and war are "total" ossification in peace and "total" destruction in war. An approach to either parameter increases the tendency to oscillate in the opposite direction. It is therefore conceivable that in extreme war, functions for war may be carried out not by war proper but by the activities of the war prelude, that is, the functions are shoved back to an earlier stage of the oscillation. Since the functions are performed in this phase, say by threats of war, limited war-like activities, or even by ceremonial expressions of war, the oscillation need not fulfill its swing to war proper but may return to the peace phases or hover in war prelude more or less continuously. Possibly the 1962 "Cuban crisis," the Sino-Indian "war," and "deterrence" are examples. It is conceivable that the adroit political-and-scientific manipulation of war prelude conditions might contribute to inhibiting war.

ACKNOWLEDGMENT

This paper is part of a larger collaborative endeavour in the study of war being undertaken by Dr. A. P. Vayda and myself. Much of what appears here would have been impossible without his insights and hard work. Although he is in no wise responsible for the present formulation, credit is by rights due him as co-author, a role he cannot now fulfill as he is studying aspects of warfare in the New Guinea highlands.

REFERENCES

1. ABERLE, D. et al.: The functional prerequisites of a society. Ethics 9:100-111, 1950.
2. ALLPORT, G.: The role of expectancy. In: H. Cantril, (ed.) : Tensions that Cause Wars. Urbana, University of Illinois Press, 1950, pp. 43-78.
3. BERNARD, J. et al.: The nature of conflict: Studies of the sociological aspects of international tensions. Paris, UNESCO, 1957.
4. BLACKETT, P. M. S.: Studies of War, Nuclear and Conventional. New York, Hill and Wang, 1962.
5. CLARKSON, J., AND COCHRAN, T.: War as a Social Institution: the Historian's Perspective. New York, Columbia University Press, 1941.
6. COLLINS, P.: The nature of a functional system, Ms. 1962.
7. COSER, L. A.: The Functions of Social Conflict. Glencoe, Free Press, 1956.
8. DAHRENDORF, R.: Toward a theory of social conflict. J. Conflict Resolution 2:170-183, 1958.
9. DEUTSCH, M.: Psychological alternatives to war. J. Soc. Issues 18:97-119,1962.
10. ETZIONI, A.: The Hard Way to Peace: A New Strategy. New York, Collier Books, 1962.
11. GLUCKMAN, M.: Rituals of Rebellion in South East Africa. Manchester: The University Press, 1952.
12. ———: Custom and Conflict in Africa. Oxford, Blackwell's, 1955.
13. HAMMER, M.: An Analysis of Social Networks as Factors Influencing Hospitalization of Mental Patients. Ph.D. Thesis, Columbia University, New York, 1961.

14. HEMPEL, C. G.: The logic of functional analysis. *In:* L. Gross (ed.) Symposium on Sociological Theory. Evanston, Row Peterson, 1959.

15. HUNT, G. T.: The Wars of the Iroquois. Madison, University of Wisconsin Press (reprinted 1960 in paperback), 1940.

16. KLUCKHOHN, C.: Mirror for Man. New York, Whittlesey House, McGraw-Hill, 1949.

17. LEEDS, A.: Yaruro incipient tropical forest horticulture—possibilities and limits. *In:* J. Wilbert (ed.): The Evolution of Horticultural Systems in Native South America: Causes and Consequences—a Symposium, pp. 13-46. Caracas, Editorial Sucre, for the Sociedad de Ciencias Naturales La Salle, 1961.

18. LEVY, M. J.: The Structure of Society. Princeton, Princeton University Press, 1952.

19. MALINOWSKI, B.: An anthropological study of war. Am. J. Soc. 46:521-550, 1941a.

20. ——: War—past, present, and future. *In:* Clarkson and Cochran: cf. *supra.*, 1941b.

21. MARX, K., AND ENGELS, F.: The German Ideology. New York, International Publishers (1947), 1846.

22. NAGEL, E.: The Structure of Science: Problems in the Logic of Science. New York, Harcourt Brace, 1961.

23. NELSON, B.: Meaning systems and crises of identity: Paradigms. Paper read at the Annual Meeting of the American Association for the Advancement of Science, 1962 in the Symposium on Structural Approaches to Meaning Systems, Philadelphia.

24. NEWCOMB, W. W., JR.: Towards an understanding of war. *In:* G. E. Dole and R. L. Carneiro (eds.): Essays in the Science of Culture, New York, Crowell, 1960, pp. 317-334.

25. TURNEY-HIGH, H .H.: Primitive War. Columbia, S.C., University of South Carolina Press, 1949.

26. VAYDA, A. P.: Expansion and warfare among swidden agriculturalists. Am. Anthropologist 63:346-358, 1961.

27. ——: A reexamination of north west coast economic systems. Tr. New York Acad. Sci. Ser. II, 23:618-624, 1961a.

28. ——, AND LEEDS, A.: Anthropology and the study of war. Anthropologica, n. s. 3:131-133, 1961.

29. WHITE, L. A: The Science of Culture. New York, Farrar Straus, 1949.

30. WORSLEY, P.: Rebellion and revolution in social anthropology. Science & Society, 25:26-37, 1961.

THE PLACE OF HOSTILITY AND CONFLICT IN A DISARMED WORLD

By ARTHUR I. WASKOW

MANY Americans, looking back on World War II, now realize the absurdity of thinking that "surrender" was an end in itself. But many of them today think of "disarmament" as if it were an end in itself, in a sense the unconditional surrender of the military in all countries. What we now realize about "surrender" we must remind ourselves applies also to "disarmament": there are many imaginable worlds in which disarmament would happen, and many imaginable different kinds of worlds that the process of disarming might create. In these different worlds there are many imaginable ways in which present conflicts and present hostilities would be pursued, resolved, and transformed.

In examining these various possible changes in the place of hostility and conflict, it would be useful to construct several possible models of what a disarmed world might look like.

It may be said parenthetically that the making of such models is not only a necessary act of scholarship in order to think about disarmament effectively, it may also be a political act of considerable importance in making disarmament more likely. For probably even a government that wants disarmament and that believes the problems of adequate inspection and enforcement have been solved will not be interested in disarmament if it has no idea of how its conflicts with other states might be handled and the hostilities of its own citizens dealt with. We do not know the ways in which various governments use images of a radically different future world in assessing present policies—and, in fact, this is a question on which research is badly needed. But we can at least suspect that building alternative models of a disarmed world will allow governments to consider disarmament more seriously.

In any case, our study of the role of violence in human behavior will be advanced if we examine some ways in which eliminating international violence through various techniques might change the patterns of international conflict and hostility. I should therefore like to sketch two polar models of what a disarmed world might look like.

One such model is that of "world order under law." There might be a kind of disarmament in which the controls were vested in a world government and all nations agreed that their disputes would be resolved peaceably under agreed principles of law or by agreed legal-political institutions. World courts, a world parliament, a world executive to control the peace police, all would be essential components of the disarmament arrangements.

The difficulty that seems to arise from this model is that the existing conflicts between states are too basic and too intense. The consensus necessary to underlie agreed legal codes or political assemblies seems not to exist. The provisions of present "international law," for example, were developed mostly by Western experience and owe little to Communist notions of law or to the developing codes and interests of the underdeveloped nations. What legal institution could be agreed on beforehand, for example, to deal with a dispute over uncompensated expropriation of private property? In one state and in present international law, the possession of such property may be regarded as a legitimate right that can only be withdrawn upon payment of just compensation. In another state, large corporate properties may be looked on as a species of theft and expropriation be regarded as a return of property to its rightful owners. What court could adjudicate or commission arbitrate a dispute on such a point?

Yet if an appeal to arms and an appeal in court are both impossible, what techniques can settle such a dispute? The alternative model of a disarmed world suggests a "disarmed disorder," in which each nation could attempt to advance its interests and defend its ideology without restraints, so long as it did not use violence. The United States might attempt to free Hungary by appealing to hopes of political liberty, by offering economic inducements, and by judiciously managing educational exchanges. The Soviet Union might attempt to communize Mexico by arousing unrest in the peasantry, by demonstrating scientific superiority in the race for Mars, and by offering to direct a quick industrial-development program. Some colonial power might use a combination of bribes, control of the schools, and manipulation of the price of key products to continue its domination of a colony. A former colonial nation might use nonviolent Gandhian techniques to infiltrate a neighboring area still under colonial rule. And so the conflicts of states might be settled through economic, political, and psychological "wars" that did not involve arms or killing. No state would be subjected to a "world government" that might control its social system.

The main objection to this model of "disorder and disarmament" is that it would not stay disarmed very long. It is argued that once conflicts were "fought out" by means so threatening, even though initially nonviolent, one or another nation would, in anger, rearm in order to further its ends. The hostility of its populace would be raised to such a pitch that war would become inevitable.

The dilemma then is between so much emphasis on preserving order in a disarmed world that no nation agrees to disarm, and having so little machinery to keep order that the world cannot be kept disarmed. It is this dilemma that requires more study than any other aspect of disarmament.

Purely for heuristic reasons, I should like to propose one possible means of dealing with this dilemma, a means that might be acceptable to major nations and that might be able to keep the world disarmed. It is possible to imagine a world institution for enforcing disarmament that would not have the physical power or the legal authority to change the social systems of nations or of the world. We might call such an institution a "world state," borrowing Weber's definition of the state as an institution with a monopoly of legitimate violence, but not a world "government," in the sense that a government focuses shared values and shared interests to decide the outcome of political disputes. Such a world "state" may have been foreshadowed, for example, by the joint action of the Soviet Union and the United States in 1956 to force the abandonment of international violence as a means of carrying on political conflict in the Middle East. It should be noted that the Soviet-American joint action was not based on any shared values of the two powers except the desire to prevent war, nor did it resolve the political conflicts of the parties. In fact, the Middle East settlement permitted the continuation of all sorts of political and economic pressures by all the states involved, except for international violence.

Let us imagine, then, that this approach were carried forward and institutionalized in a "world state" that had only such weapons and force levels as were necessary to punish violators of a disarmament agreement, and to secure its own monopoly over the legitimate use of international violence. Such an institution might well be small and deliberately made powerless to coerce a whole nation to change its social system. What effects would the creation of such an institution have on international conflicts and hostility?

Let me hasten to say that I do not regard this particular kind of disarmed world as the only possible sort. I should like to explore its implications rather than that of others for several reasons. First, I regard neither the "world order under law" nor the "disarmed disorder" model as probable of achievement in the next generation. Second, we know much more about situations analogous to those two polar models than we do about the model of a world state plus intense conflict. The "disarmed disorder" model is analogous to the situation obtaining, say, in Latin America between the end of the Spanish Empire there and the intervention of the United States to keep order. Arms were at a comparatively low level, but no institution existed that could prevent war; and the result was a series of desultory arms build-ups, wars, revolutions, and so on. Total international anarchy seems not to stay disarmed very long, even when there is a broad sharing of basic values between the various nations. On the other side, such histories as that of the United Kingdom, the United States, Switzerland, the Union of South Africa, and the Empire, Dominion, and Republic of India suggest what we might expect from an attempted merging of sovereignties in the model of "world order under law." From these histories we can learn what we might on the basis of analogy expect in the way of resolution of conflicts through law, the failure of resolution and the occurrence of civil wars, the transfer of hostilities, and so on. The study of these analogues to possible models of a disarmed world is important. But for today, I should like to address myself to the problems of studying the implications of a world "state" as I have defined it.

First let me distinguish between what I am calling "hostility"—the direct and personal feelings of hatred and fear that citizens of one state may hold toward the people, ideas, government, and society of another—and "conflict"—the disagreement of national governments over how to resolve sociopolitical problems and in what directions the world should change. It is the place of international conflict that is perhaps easier to examine.

There are in existence a number of techniques for carrying on conflict without violence, and indeed during the last decade it has become clearer and clearer that it is extremely hard to use or threaten nuclear war in order to accomplish political ends. In short, we are already in the process of having war expropriated from us, and the invention of substitutes for traditional war has therefore already begun. We have seen the democratization of competitive bribery, in the form of some kinds of economic aid. We have watched the revival of guerrilla tactics as a means of overthrowing weak governments, and an increase in the sophistication of commando tactics as a support for those same governments. We have seen nations resort to the space race as a nonlethal way of demonstrating superiority in weapons technology. We have even seen the testing of nuclear weapons over oceans replace their use as bombs on populations. (In this fashion, outright war is avoided because fewer people are killed by the bombs, the deaths are spread over a longer period of time—and those killed are confined to no one nation—but at the same time, the nations that test the bombs are able to demonstrate and compare their national power and sophistication almost as well as if we were using the bombs on cities.) Of these comparatively new techniques for carrying coercive pressures to the enemy without fighting him outright, some obviously would be unavailable in a disarmed world. Others might have to be invented.

The conditions under which substitutes for war can most easily be invented are amenable to research. For example, we have the way in which the characteristic American race riot of the early twentieth century was recently replaced by the sit-in, the bus boycott, and the freedom ride as means of carrying on racial conflict. A close study of the conditions that allowed these social inventions to flourish as substitutes for the riot might suggest hypotheses on how to create analogous conditions in the field of war. Such hypotheses could be tested by small-group experiments similar to the famous Robber's Cave study. In that experiment, induced conflict was successfuly replaced with co-operation. Might we not try analogous experiments to see under what conditions juvenile gangs, for instance, would replace outright violence with new forms of trickery, bribery and competition?

As for the substance of new means of nonmilitary conflict, a systematic examination of the historical evidence would be useful. The richness of city-state conflict in Renaissance Italy, baronial conflict in medieval France, princely conflict in ancient India, need to be examined if we are to understand the possibilities.

We also need to have political scientists, anthropologists, and sociologists reexamine the structure of such different societies as a highly developed Communist state like the Soviet Union, underdeveloped

Communist countries like China, and developing tribal societies like Nigeria, in order to see what nonmilitary means of carrying on conflict would seem appropriate to their different histories and social strengths. For while military competition presses nations toward strategic symmetry—most look longingly toward nuclear weapons, all equip their armies with machine guns, and so on—nonmilitary techniques are likely to be more idiosyncratic, more asymmetrical and to require more imagination from one society to defend itself, against the unfamiliar means of attack used by another. This new asymmetry will result from the fact that while the technology of killing operates on genetically similar human bodies and has a restricted line of development, the technology of nonlethal coercion operates out of and onto a multiplicity of human cultures and psychologies. Thus the RAND Corporations of a disarmed world will have a far more subtle and complex task to carry out.

On the question of international conflict, let me say finally that we shall need to know more from the behavioral sciences about how an unprecedented institution like the "world state" could deal with the internation conflicts that would be manifested within its own structure. We know how full-fledged governments go about resolving conflicts between internal groups and quasi-sovereign provinces. But we do not know how an institution based on the narrowest imaginable agreement —a covenant against killing—can deal with attempts at internal *coups d'etat,* with struggles over the definition of weapons permissible for nations to keep, with international disagreements over what sort of violence is internal and domestic and what sort is international and to be suppressed. Means of insulating the small and fragile world state from national conflicts, of keeping it "impartial" in problems of re-armament regardless of whether its members are "neutral" in politics, will be developed only after more research on the organization of conflicting groups into institutions that attempt to accomplish only one job, but are effective at that one. The organizational experiences of monastic orders in transnational churches, of the French Foreign Legion and of the World Health Organization would be useful grist for research on this problem.

Now let us turn to the problem of personal hostility in a disarmed world, a problem in which both the social-political probabilities and the research possibilities are far less clear than they are on the question of conflict. It is necessary first to point out that just as thermonuclear weapons have begun to expropriate our ability to fight wars, they have also begun to expropriate our ability to express any direct and personal hostility against an enemy. No man who is stationed deep in a Polaris submarine with his finger on the button can meet face to face with his enemy Khrushchev, nor even with Khrushchev's minion Ivan. He may press the button that kills 5 million people, but he is not present to see their death, to express his fear and hatred of them, to triumph in their annihilation. If he presses the button, it will be coolly and bureaucratically, on orders from a capital thousands of miles away to destroy another capital still other thousands of miles away. He may never know what has caused the order to be given, anymore than he knows the effects or the quality of his own act.

Compare such an act with the hereditary human necessity of standing in full sight of the man to be killed, of killing him in full knowledge of the reasons, the time, the blood. The comparison makes a mockery of the argument that war is necessary as a means of expressing hostility, since the kind of war now contemplated will not allow the expression of hostility. Indeed coolness, gamesmanship, the strategist's distant scorn for both righteous wrath and fearful cowardice—these are the correct qualifications for the modern warrior.

In fact, one might conceivably hail disarmament as a way to restore human hostility to the world. There have been several suggestions that bear on this possibility. It has been proposed that in a disarmed world, national security and independence might be protected against any possible would-be violator by the training of whole populations in the techniques of hand-to-hand guerrilla resistance or face-to-face non-violent resistance.* Such an arrangement would certainly restore the opportunity for an individual citizen to take up the defense of his own life and liberty, to express with his own body his hostility to an invading soldier and to any system the invader would impose. But such training in the effective expression of hostility would probably not be frequently used against invaders, on the assumption that the world state was doing its job of enforcing disarmament. Might the training be turned to use against other citizens of the trainee's own country?

That question is really a special case of a more general problem of hostility in a disarmed world: will feelings of hostility that are now turned against foreigners and foreign nations be redirected into hostilities at home? It is sometimes argued that hatred directed overseas

*Arthur I. Waskow, The Limits of Defense; Stephen King-Hall, Defense in the Nuclear Age.

is a convenient means of displacing anger that is aroused within every nation by the racial, economic, and family clashes that occur between citizens every day. Because it is generally dangerous to hate the man down the street, the tax collector, or your wife, it is comparatively safe to hate "the enemy" out there—especially a nation with H-bombs. Will the displacement of hostility break down if the enemy loses his H-bombs, and if so what will happen to the hostility? Will it be redirected into domestic channels, even if these are dangerous?

First, it should be pointed out that this "hydraulic" theory of hostility may not apply to the international situation. Hostility to foreign nations may rise legitimately from their threats to strongly held values, from their obstinacy as constant obstacles to one's own country's pursuit of its world policy, and from the danger they pose to continued life; and if these threats are reduced, the hostility may be reduced instead of being redirected from home consumption. In other words, there may not be any fairly constant amount of hostility which has to flow somewhere.

There is, however, some evidence, both historical and experimental, that tends to support the displacement theory of international hostility feelings. For example, there is the response to the disappearance of a foreign enemy that came from the United States after the defeat of Germany in 1918. By 1919, a horde of domestic conflicts that has been temporarily subdued for reasons of national defense—hostilities perhaps, that had first been displaced into foreign hatreds and then were redirected into domestic channels—were boiling over in a series of race riots, political bombings, and violent strikes. Again, there may be some evidence of disparity between the threat that particular foreign nations seem to be in the daily lives of most people and the hostility that most people feel toward the same nations. If there is such a disparity, the higher level of hostility might be most easily explained by postulating a process of displacement.

But when I say there is "some evidence" of such a disparity, I should hasten to add that we need more research on this question. We do know that most people do not report "the Russians" as one of their immediate daily worries; a guess from simple observation would be that most people are, however, intensely hostile toward "the Russians." Careful study of the people who seem not to worry over world problems and the people who seem most hostile to the world outside may give us more information on the connection or lack of connection between day-to-day conflict and hostility displaced onto the international scene. We need this information before we can estimate the effects of disarmament upon hostility processes.

We also need to know whether hostility to a foreign power is based mostly on distaste for its social system and opposition to the spread of that system, or on fear of its weapons. Do Americans hate the Soviet Union because it may kill us, or because it may make our grandchildren Communists? And what do Americans feel about the possibility that French, or Indian, or Brazilian grandchildren may be Communists? We have little knowledge of who in our society feels which aspects of the Cold War most intensely, and we need to know the bases of present hostilities more accurately before we can estimate the probable changes that will take place in a disarming and disarmed world.

This last question raises the point that the kinds of hostility we feel in the Cold War will have much to do with the kinds of conflict that are carried on in the disarmed world. If Americans have no direct interest in the social system of Brazil or India, and are now giving economic aid to those countries only in mortal fear of the Soviets' nuclear capability, then in a disarmed world where the Soviet nuclear capability is gone, Americans are not likely to pursue conflict with the Communists in some of the ways I have mentioned. On the other hand, the existence or elimination of intense nonmilitary conflict in a disarmed world will have much to do with whether international enmities remain sufficiently salient to focus hostility feelings that are displaced from daily conflicts—if displacement is indeed the mechanism at work.

In short, the persistence of personal feelings of hostility toward other nations and the persistence of conflicts between nations will have much to do with each other in a disarmed world, even as now. Before going very far in predicting the possibilities, we need to know a great deal more than we do now about what sorts of conflict have been and are being carried on between nations and about what sorts of hostility are felt by individuals. The research is possible, and it is needed; it remains for us to do it.

VIOLENCE IN THE PERSPECTIVE
OF CULTURE HISTORY

By MARGARET MEAD

THIS symposium has concentrated heavily upon violence as destructive behavior—behavior intended to injure, destroy, or eliminate other human beings. This particular emphasis is almost inevitable, given the special competence of psychoanalysts in dealing with the breakdown of the enculturation process in individuals, a breakdown which is frequently accompanied by manifestations, overt or covert, of ungovernable rage, hostility, and destructiveness. But it is necessary to place aggression, on the one hand, and violence, on the other into a wider context. This emphasis is also a consequence of our present preoccupation with nuclear warfare and the new capabilities man has acquired by means of which not only rivals—the members of a rival state, the aggressor at the doorstep, or the feared aggressor at a distance—can be eliminated, but even the whole population of this planet. The close association of violence and warfare is reflected in the fact that many of the discussions in this symposium have moved directly from a consideration of rage and hostility in childhood, through manifestations of frustration and identity loss characteristic of dispossessed adolescents and minority groups, to a consideration of war itself, as if we were here dealing with a single sequence, only moving from simpler to more complex and more dangerous expressions of the same impulse structure in man.

In his paper and film, "Aggressive Behavior and Ritualized Fighting among Animals," Eibl-Eibesfeldt made distinctions between several types of species-characteristic fighting behavior observed in Galapagos Island iguanas: the ritualized fighting of males, behavior directed toward aggressors of other species, and the nonritualized, deadly fighting of females at egg sites. Later, Rado raised the question of whether we expect to substitute ritual fighting—football games on an

92

international scale—for warfare, and so settle the problem of war. His question focused our attention both on the importance of ritual fighting as a form of behavior between conspecifics, with its built-in devices for terminating conflict before it becomes lethal, and on the ritual avoidance of the more deadly equipment designed to ward off predators or to subdue prey successfully. Behavior of this kind is well documented for vertebrates, but it cannot be regarded as a direct analogue of man's behavior nor can it be treated as a single thread which might lead through culturally elaborated biological behavior to Olympic games (seen as peaceful rather than as conflict-exacerbating activities).

Man himself is a domestic animal—in some sense, an animal in a cage. However, man is confined not only by mountains, rivers, and oceans, within which population pressure occurs, but also by the symbolic system which, technically, is called culture. Men have the choice, which creatures in the wild do not have, of viewing other men as conspecifics, predators, or prey. To emphasize only the ritual fighting of conspecific males or the deadly fighting of conspecific females is to select but one part of our biological inheritance, a part which has been enormously overlaid by culture. Man is not protected, as are creatures in the wild, by a set of instinctive responses, which make it possible to terminate a ritual battle; instead, man's ability to symbolize makes it possible for him to think of those who are absent from the scene—dead, not yet born, feared but never seen—and place them in various biologically based but culturally elaborated categories.

Significantly, man is a *domesticated* caged animal. Calhoun's experiments with rats are particularly relevant to this aspect of man's existence. For example, he altered the conditions of life by removing all the young from the cage for a period of time; in this situation, the caged adults developed new patterns of accommodation to each other. Later, when a group of same-aged young were reintroduced into the cage, the adult rats turned violent; in fact, they killed conspecifics. Ritual combat was replaced by destructive, lethal violence.

It is crucial to recognize that man himself has constructed the cage in which he lives, through the meshes of which he views the world, often in far greater security than creatures in the wild but always with intervening symbolic variables between his instinctive equipment and its expression in fighting, defending, attacking, and so on. Otherwise, we may easily be misled by analogies based on observations on wild creatures, such as those by Eibl-Eibesfeldt, Calhoun, or by Zuck-

erman in his classic study of Monkey Hill.[1] Man has species-characteristic types of behavior, but from the moment of birth these behaviors are modified in historically distinct ways in each society. No
creature in the wild, for example, displays the kinds of savagery that
man, time and again in the course of his history, has elaborated in
feuds, blood vengeance, head hunting, systems of torture, and so on. We
can build ingenious and beautiful models to explore specific biological
possibilities of limited space (Calhoun) or a limited food supply,[2]
but in interpreting the results, we must realize that the conditions in
which new manifestations of behavior occur (e.g., the bloody fighting
among the rats which ensued when Calhoun interfered with the normal
balance of generations) are man made—and can be altered by man.
And, in thinking about man, we must distinguish between the intract-
ibles in man's biological inheritance and those capabilities which can
be enormously modified by learning. The cultural cage which man
has built for himself, being man made, can be altered by man.

It has been the purpose of this symposium to combine the insights
from ethology, experimental animal behavior, social and cultural
studies with the delicate, detailed, intensive insights into psychodynamics provided by psychoanalysis. I want now to stress one part
of the total picture which has been little touched upon here. If, instead of starting our discussion with biological given propensities to
violence, we begin with culturally patterned forms of violent behavior
that end in the injury, death, or destruction of individuals or groups,
we find that human warfare can be separated into several different
strands.

In one kind of warfare the emphasis is on destruction—killing—for
its own sake. In various ways, head hunting, cannibalism (a somewhat exaggerated and oversimplified picture of which Lief presented
here), blood feud, and war games for the attainment of honors
(as among the North American Plains Indians) exemplify warfare of
this kind. In contrast, there is the kind of warfare which is primarily
protective of the life of the group—protective of the group's territory
and means of livelihood, the lives of its members (especially infants
and females), and the values cherished by the group. In both kinds
of warfare, the end results may be much the same. Men killing in behalf of their women and children may be caught up in the lust of
battle. Modern leaders of states mobilize hatred as well as protectiveness. So we continually confuse these two essentially different types

of warfare and, in doing so, assume that the same set of motivations are involved in fighting a world war, in the behavior of a child who tries to tear his younger sibling from his mother's breast, a deprived street urchin who joins a looting gang, a head hunting party in a New Guinea tribe, and Hitler's Luftwaffe and England's RAF.

Eibl-Eibesfeldt gave us an illustration of ritual fighting. Other types of observed animal behavior, not stressed in this symposium, could have been brought in to illustrate the enormous importance of fighting for the protection of conspecifics (especially the young and females) against predators. Looking at the two types, it would have been apparent that protective fighting is at least as important an element in the behavior of many vertebrates as is the ritual fighting of male conspecifics. A characteristic feature of protective behavior is reckless self-disregard, as the mature animal risks its life—the bird to decoy the predator away from the nest, or the male baboon, baring its teeth, to distract the giant feline predator while the females and juveniles move ahead toward safety. This element of self-sacrifice, when the safety of those who need protection is at stake, may also be related to the conspicuous rarity of ritual fighting between females, who, typically, only fight (but then may fight to the death) when their nests or their young are attacked. In the fierce battle for an egg-laying site between the 2 female iguanas, it was possible to detect a fragmentary bit of ritualized iguana fighting behavior; similarly, the fierce, unrelenting female type of fighting may be represented within the male's equipment for display aggression.

In some forms of warfare one finds a number of blocks on all-out aggression, resembling those described by Eibl-Eibesfeldt. This is the case where ritual fighting—designed to demonstrate manhood, impress females, and establish identity—has been elaborated into a kind of warfare in which some other group, another clan or village or tribe, is defined as a legitimate object of destruction (as among head hunters in Oceania). The head hunter is not self-sacrificing. He does not fight to the death, although he tries to kill and may be killed. Typically, he prefers ambush to open fighting, and odds of 20-1 delight him. Fighting according to the rules of chivalry can be seen as an elaboration of the ritual dance of 2 males in the rutting season, but head-hunting, raiding, and cannibalism know no chivalry. In head hunting, the object is a head; the head of a lonely old woman or a frightened child will do. In warfare of this kind, conspecifics have been transformed into prey, symbolically indicative of manly valor, and the result is bloody, unrelenting, socially disruptive fighting and a perenially low level of social organization.

But human beings also have the capability of extending to every person whom they identify as a member of their own group—a totemic group, a territorial group, a religious group, an occupational group, a national group—the kind of self-immolating protectiveness which characterizes the male animal defending its young. Generally speaking, defense of own group and defense of own territory are combined, but territory—in actual spatial terms—need not be involved. In the Admiralty Islands, members of a totemic group living in different places could make claims on one another for safe-conduct and protection even when the different village or tribal groups to which they belonged were at war.* Marlowe, in his discussion, gave us a wealth of examples of the way in which the blood feud, intrinsically a disruptive factor in the relations of groups linked by real or fictive kinship, had been extended and modified to make possible a wider social organization. Despite this, his material from Somaliland demonstrated the disruptive characteristics of the blood feud where other types of social integration also were occurring. In contrast, Matthiessen, in his recent book, *Under the Mountain Wall*,[3] gives a vivid natural history account of feud running riot through New Guinea tribal society and taking precedent over most forms of socially integrative behavior.

Throughout history, the willingness of human beings to fight protectively for whatever they have valued—living human beings, the grace of the ancestors, the future of the group, their gods, their political ideals—has played an important role in the building of larger social units within which men define one another as conspecifics and owe one another protection. Through their abilities to transform conspecifics into enemies—prey or predators—human beings have involved themselves in endless petty warfare and disruptive fighting; but they have been able to use the same processes of imaginative transformation to treat individuals whom they have never seen as, in effect, blood brothers for whom they would lay down their lives.

---

*It is not without significance that the right to nonbelligerent status, accorded by special groups—scientists, for example, broke down only under the conditions of modern warfare; nor is it without significance that the right to free communication, particularly in the scholarly community, is a critical issue in the modern world.

With the development of great nation states and widespread networks of communication, human beings are now able to define as members of their own group, to be protected and defended and never to be injured or killed, millions of individuals whom they have never met and never will meet, with whom they would perhaps have in common only the one point of identity as Americans, Frenchmen, Christians, Buddhists, Members of the Free World, and so on. The extension of this type of protection to ever larger groups within a political system (and even between political systems in periods of truce) may be seen as the triumphant extension of the original protectiveness found in the small face-to-face group. This is an achievement which has been possible only to man, with his capacity to think about the absent, the past, the event still to come. In discussing the integrative effects of warfare, Leeds discussed, in effect, ways in which man has succeeded in building larger, more varied, and more complex socioeconomic systems on the basis of this willingness to accept an ever larger number of fellowmen as fellows who deserve care and forebearance and protection against human aggressive impulses.

In the past, protective warfare, whether it was pursued actively or responsively, was an integrative mechanism to the extent that it was conceived of as being in the interests of the group and was not undertaken primarily for the mere accumulation of trophies or the relentless pursuit of plunder or blood feuding. The mobilization of men's protective impulses called forth a cluster of associated behaviors: genuine bravery, heroic effort and endurance, a spirit of brotherhood and solidarity with other males, an ardent reassertion of values—religious belief, love of country, defense of freedom, respect for the heritage from the past, responsibility for the future. Between wars, men grew fat and slack, greed and corruption were institutionalized, and many ardent moralists yearned for the purification of the spirit which a just war might provide. In this setting, almost all wars *were* just. (It is a peculiarity of the last century, during which men have come increasingly to repudiate war as a means of settling national differences, that men have fought badly in wars they have not conceived of as just and good—the Russians fighting in Finland or the Americans fighting in Korea, as compared to the Russians fighting in World War II or the Americans fighting in World War I and World War II.)

But in the past, the population of the planet was divided into a large number of relatively independent, sometimes intercommunica-

Regulatory Treatment of Sex Drive

ting but often isolated groups. With the application of nuclear energy and other discoveries of modern science and technology to warfare and with the full exploration of the earth's surface and the establishment of worldwide communication systems, with all the attendant dangers of the spread of disease, involvement in war, and exposure to radiation, the situation has radically changed. Today, throughout the world, man is faced with the need to extend the behavior appropriate to conspecifics to every people, every race and nation on this planet.

In this same period, the findings of scientific biological research have confirmed the hypothesis that man is, indeed, one species—that all men are not only symbolically but in fact conspecifics. Based as they are partly on the fossil record, partly on our knowledge of speciation among living creatures, partly on observations on living human beings and their capacities to learn whatever human beings anywhere have invented and practiced, these findings are new and not wholly comprehended. As yet, this new understanding has not become part of man's unchallengeable assumptions—as the abhorrence of incest has; not a part of the central core of man's sacred concepts, it does not yet give men a basis for continuing group action. Up to the present, human beings have used their capacity to transform experience in the ingenious selection of traits—birth on other soil, different pigmentation, a different style in ritual or in the interpretation of dogma, a preference for or an antipathy to frogs or snakes, cattle or horses or pigs as food—by which to differentiate between groups and in terms of which to define other groups as possible predators and the legitimate objects of protective-destructive behavior. Today, the knowledge that human beings are conspecifics, the knowledge that there are no other human-like creatures (now that the Abominable Snowman has been disposed of[4]), inferior to or superior to ourselves, provides us with a sure basis for establishing worldwide acceptance of the idea that all men are entitled to conspecific protection.

The potential destructiveness of nuclear weapons is such that we cannot speak of nuclear *warfare*. A war, by definition, can be fought and won, as well as fought and lost; explicitly, in the past, wars were fought to benefit individuals and to further the interests of a group. Today, all men might perish in a nuclear catastrophe, and all life on earth would be endangered and might well be destroyed. The recognition of interdependence, which is the basis of human society, was once confined to small clusters of families. Now it must be extended to include the planet's population.*

The cultural and social aspects of the problems attendant on group integration and intergroup hostility are crucially important and could be elaborated on, but to do so here would lead me away from the problems of this symposium: man's inborn, biologically-given capacities and potentialities which can lead to various kinds of violence and socially disruptive behavior. The biologically based impulse to protect has been neglected; the biologically based impulse to destroy—in the interests of autonomy, or the achievement of goals, or the establishment of identity—has perhaps been over-stressed. But the problem remains of how man's age old types of biologically-given behavior are to be integrated in each developing child, in each human group, in the behavior patterns of those who are in a position to lead and to determine the future of mankind. This is the area in which cooperation among ethologists, experimentalists, psychoanalysts, and students of human culture and society can have great significance.

We have had a rather full discussion of the ways in which rage and aggression, resulting from the learning experiences individuals have had in the society in which they were born, are rooted in individual frustration and biologically-given patterns of maturation. And the discussion has been extended by Coser to include the behavior that can be expected of groups whose members have been reared and who live under conditions of conspicuous deprivation. Calhoun has suggested the significance of individual tolerance of group size and contacts with intimates and strangers with its implications for the difficulties of living, without further cultural learning, under density conditions like those of New York City. Recent studies on the effects of crowding have shown that the deleterious effects persist for several

---

*In this discussion I have focused on cross-species behavior only to the extent that potentially violent behavior is involved, i.e., to the extent members of one species are related to those of another as predators or prey. In a more comprehensive discussion it would be necessary to include, also, symbiotic relationships (and the analogies to these in human groups). However, it is necessary to point out here that man's capacity to destroy all life on earth has effected a decisive change not only in the interdependence of human beings but also in the interdependence of man, as a species, and all other living species. We need, therefore, to take into account symbiotic relations, as we did not do before, both as part of our total responsibility and as part of our symbolic use of other living species in the formation of human character structure.

generations. In fact, we know a great deal about the consequences of parental hostility and social deprivation, as these are manifested in the lives of human beings, making them prone to individual or small group violence and responsive to propaganda which, covertly or overtly, plays heavily on the desire to destroy individuals and groups because they seem to threaten one's own security or continued existence.

Other aspects of individual psychodynamics in cultural settings have been less fully explored. One of these is the particular means by which nonviolent behavior is enjoined upon the learning individual in any society. It may be that the educational means—taking the word education in its widest sense to include not only formal education but also child rearing and all the social practices to which the child is exposed —are more significant than the avowed objectives, i.e., the cultivation of manliness and bravery, the attainment of a pacific, nonviolent, law-abiding character structure, etc. Recent material on homicide[5] suggests the importance of the devices that are used in a modern society to teach a child the difference between murder (the killing of a member of one's own society or of another society, except under the peculiar circumstances of war), justifiable homicide (killing in self-defense against an attacker, etc.), and war. Normally, in modern societies, children do not come face-to-face with killing; instead, they are taught indirectly, through prohibitions about the killing of animals. Where this learning goes wrong, when a child is overpunished or underpunished for inappropriate violence against an animal, the groundwork may be laid for later uncontrollable murderous violence. At another level, the extreme limitations set on the mobility of deprived city boys, who are confined to a small area of a few blocks—in a world in which the socially privileged range over hundreds, even thousands of miles—may result in the development, in these boys, of a narrow sense of territoriality that is reminiscent of early tribal life.[6] In their eyes, the inhabitants of the next block may be inappropriately transformed into enemies against whom their own small world, with its open borders, must be defended.

Deeply entrenched and apparently satisfactory methods of inducing the control of aggressive impulses within a whole society may operate successfully for a long time, yet they may carry within them the seeds of dangerous transformations. Gorer[7] has described how, in nineteenth century England, the formation of a national police force around a core of big, gentle, unarmed men played an important role in the transformation of English society from one in which open violence and open enjoyment of sadism (e.g., in the witnessing of public hang-ings[8]) were common to one which was essentially law abiding and peaceful. In recent years, however, there has been an increase in crime in England, and the police are less incorruptible. On the one hand, there has been an upsurge of violent antiviolence (as in recent anti-fascist demonstrations or in the attacks on the United States embassy during the Cuban crisis); and on the other hand, there has been an increasing public search for violence.[9] The English method of obtain-ing law abiding and gentle behavior—with its basic postulate that man is naturally cruel and violent but can be taught to control his passions by the right, powerful mentors—produced outstanding results; how-ever, the type of character structure developed was one in which the possibility of violence and cruelty was fostered by the very counter-measures taken against it.

The recent history of Bali is another case in point. In the late 1930's, Bali was one of the least violent spots on the face of the earth. Murder was exceedingly rare and warfare had completely vanished. At the beginning of the century, the Balinese had accepted the final victory of the Netherlands troops by a spectacular mass suicide. Dressed in full regalia, they had marched out to meet the advancing Netherlands forces. When the European soldiers recoiled before the prospect of butchery, the Balinese turned their krisses against them-selves. Occasionally, in 1936-39, there was a case of apparently un-motivated violence, in the ethnically distinct form of amok; or a thief, caught red handed, was beaten to death by a whole community. But such occurrences were rare.

Children never showed violence in their behavior toward one an-other. If 2 creeping babies reached for the same toy, they were im-mediately separated. Angry 6 year olds did not fight; instead, they declared a mutual ceremonial silence. I never saw a real fight between children or adolescents, and I was given only one account of a fight. My informant, a young man, described how he had fought with one of his cousins, while they were both so young that their frontal locks of hair had not yet been cut (roughly, under 5 or 6 years of age). His father had taken both of them and had tied their hair locks together, and he had made them sit side by side, in uncomfortably close con-tact, from sunrise to sunset. Children in Bali were stimulated by con-ventional patterns of parental and adult playfulness to express anger and jealousy toward surrogate siblings, but they were expected to behave carefully and responsibly toward actual siblings. These theatrical replications of jealousy and rage were carried over into the ubiquitous public theatrical performances where, before an audience which included the young children and with a cast which included many members of the community, the hostilities of older and younger siblings and of mother and child were endlessly reenacted.

In the 1930's, it could be said that the Balinese had achieved a peaceful, law abiding character structure, somewhat withdrawn and schizoid in tone, but effective in a small society which, under the complete control of the Netherlands government, flourished, multiplied, and devoted itself to the cultivation of the arts. A writer like Covarrubias could picture Bali as an almost ideal society;[10] even in 1955, Huxley could still cite its balance and harmony.[11] But actually, in World War II, with the coming of the Japanese, and later, during the war for liberation, the Balinese willingly and with gusto took to burning villages and slaughtering the people in neighboring villages. Since the establishment of the Indonesian Republic, they have not returned to the nonviolence of the past. The balance between aroused hostility, jealousy, and aggression and their expression in art forms—so completely realized in the art forms of the early part of the century —was an unstable one; the individual personality was left with a resource of violence which was none the less real because it was tapped only through theatrical representations.[12]

The violent conflicts between Moslems and Hindus which broke out during the partition of India are another example of a situation in which a population (the Hindu Indians) with a long history of passivity and nonviolence responded to change by erupting into riot and massacre.

The opposite situation, in which a population with a high standard of personal bravery and self-control, combined with violence, deteriorated into low-level characterological corruption, is described by Djilas in his book, *Land without Justice*.[13]

These instances from recent history suggest that our knowledge of the psychodynamics of human maturation, as illuminated by psychoanalysis and studies in culture and personality, can make an important contribution to planning for world order and for the transformation of different populations into willing participants in a world order. But in planning for education in changing societies, our own and all others, we must take into account as much of the history of a type of character structure, over as many generations, as we can; and we need to be able to make comparisons. In England, the possibility of violence is

kept alive by the nature of the steps taken to control violence. In
middle-class American upbringing, in contrast, the child is confronted
by his mother's fear that he will not be aggressive enough; this
provides, on the one hand, for the typical American display of the
"ability to take it."[14] and, on the other, for our "chip on the shoulder"
behavior.[15] Both of these attitudes, the display of the refusal to yield
to sadism and the display of compensatory aggressive behavior,
contain dangerous potentialities for violence. No less dangerous is
the attitude of those who would be willing to consider the destruction
of three-fourths of the United States population, providing only that
the enemy was completely destroyed; this attitude is rooted in a type
of identity, characteristic of a portion of Americans, which is intolerant
of any kind of difference.[16]

I now wish to turn to another aspect of the problem, one which was
highlighted by the film on ritual fighting presented by Eibl-Eibesfeldt
and by material on the American astronauts presented at another
symposium at this same meeting.[17] Essentially, the astronauts were
presented as men who were called upon to act under extreme stress and
under conditions of enormously highlighted personal competition.

Ritual fighting, as it was displayed by the iguanas, can be regarded
as an exercise in male courage and skill. This is even more con-
spicuously the case when it occurs among the young males of a species,
who must defend themselves against predators, for here the playful
fighting serves the double function of resolving male competition for
females and of preparing males for defense against predators and for
attack against prey. This theme, the exercise of male bravery and
skill, is recurrent in human history; the astronaut is but the most contemporary version of the hero with whom boys and men can identify.

The symposium discussion of the astronauts emphasized their
normalcy and the adequacy of their performance. Certain highly
relevant points, however, were not mentioned. There was a discussion
of the astronauts' need to trust the other technical members of the
whole, larger launching team as technicians, each of whom knew his
job, and it was suggested that this order of rationalized trust took
precedence over deeper trust. Technical skill was emphasized somewhat
at the expense of body discipline. I believe, however, that it is
important to stress that, in addition to high technical competence, it
was necessary for the astronauts to have a tremendously disciplined
relationship to their own bodies and to their ability to transcend a
dangerous situation. That this was significant to the American public,

who were achieving vicarious satisfaction from their feats, is fully attested to by the savagery of the press treatment of Carpenter's error in handling his flight. The primary response to the astronaut is not to the trained engineer, but to the man who has already mastered a tremendously exacting and dangerous craft, that of test pilot, and who now has the bodily endurance, the precision, the skill, and the courage to take the extraordinary risks involved in space flight.

The speakers treated competition among the astronauts as no more than ordinary competition, and they failed to mention a unique feature of the 7 astronauts' training. During the period of preparation, the men divided up the tasks so that each of them became a specialist in one part of the whole operation. This meant that, in the end, the man who went up first, whichever of them it was, would be dependent on the other 6. This interdependence was dramatized by the location of the other astronauts during Glenn's flight and by the power of protection and decision which each of them had.

The selection and training of these first 7 Americans for space flight does, in fact, provide us with one model for a world of the future, in which men can be trained so to handle and trust their bodies that they are completely reassured about their own capacity for effort and bravery and, at the same time, are protected from destructive competition by a mutually supportive social organization. I believe that we shall only at our own peril rob young males of their biological need to prove their manhood—to themselves. And this they cannot accomplish satisfactorily in purely symbolic ways that do not involve the body. In a world in which warfare is no longer a possibility and in which a willingness to die in war—some time in the future—cannot be substituted for a contemporary self-reassurance of adequacy and bravery, we shall need better, not less good, forms of rigorous and precise physical activity for young men. The problem here is not one of providing substitutes for the destructive violence of war; instead, the problem is that of providing young men with the sense of mastery over and trust in their own bodies which is such an important component in their achievement of identity—of which war was once a supreme test (or, for which it was sometimes, a substitute). At the same time we shall need complex social inventions to build a world of such overlapping and interlocking divisions of labor that each man will become (as each astronaut was) technically and socially his brother's keeper, wherever his brother may be on the face of the planet.

Finally, I should like to comment on Rado's suggestion that we need to replace the symbol of divine authority, which brings out our childishness and our dependence, with a new symbol, which would evoke the drive to autonomy and self-sufficiency. Rado suggested *the child* as a suitable symbol—the child protected and cared for by the peaceful exploitation of atomic energy. I realize that Rado was speaking as a psychoanalyst and that he was dealing with the possible roots of useful symbolism, and I agree that we need some over-riding and compelling new symbols around which men can build their hopes and loyalties and in terms of which they can exercise protective-aggressive behavior. But I should like to suggest an amendment. It is not enough for us simply to have *the child* in this symbolic position; this could all too easily feed into and exacerbate the problem of population pressure. Instead, we should take as our symbol *all living children*— our children, the children of our allies, the children of uncommitted countries, the children of those whom we (or any people) regard as our enemies. For only by protecting all of them can we protect any of them. And this symbol, *all living children,* can come to stand for the unity of man.

Today, our new scientific knowledge of man and our new scientific capacities for wholesale destruction, taken together, have placed in our hands, for the first time in human history, the possibility of realizing, at the highest level of man's symbolic relationship to himself, his history, his future, and the universe, the idea—of which in the past we had only intimations—that we are indeed one species and that all men are our conspecifics.

REFERENCES

1. ZUCKERMAN, S.: The Social Life of Monkeys and Apes. London, Kegan Paul, Trench, Trubner, 1932.
2. EMLEN, J. T.:
3. MATTHIESSEN, P.: Under the Mountain Wall. New York, Viking, 1962.
4. BISHOP, B. C.: Wintering on the Roof of the World, Annual Illustrated Lecture of the National Geographic Society, presented at the Annual Meeting of the AAAS, Philadelphia, December 30, 1962.
5. MEAD, M.: Cultural factors in the cause and prevention of pathological homicide. In press.
6. LAURENTS, A.: West Side Story: A Musical Based on a Conception of Jerome Robbins. New York, Random House, 1958. SALISBURY, H.: The Shook-up Generation. New York, Harper, 1958.
7. GORER, G.: Exploring English Character. London, Cresset, 1955.
8. KOESTLER, A.: Reflections on Hanging. New York, Macmillan, 1957.

9. GORER, G.: Personal communication.
10. COVARRUBIAS, M.: Island of Bali, New York, Knopf, 1942.
11. HUXLEY, J. S.: Cultural process and evolution. *In:* Behavior and Evolution, Anne Roe and G. C. Simpson (eds.) New Haven, Yale University Press, 1958, pp. 437-454.
12. MEAD, M.: Field work, 1936-39; 1957-58.
13. DJILAS, M.: Land without Justice. New York, Harcourt, 1958. GORER, G.: Pride, Shame, and Guilt: Notes on a Montenegrin Memoir, Land without Justice, by Milovan Djilas, Encounter, 67:28-34, 1959.
14. MAILER, N.: The Naked and the Dead. New York, Rinehart, 1948.
15. MEAD, M.: And Keep Your Powder Dry. New York, Morrow, 1942.
16. ADORNO, T. W., et al.: The Authoritarian Personality. New York, Harper, 1950.
17. KORCHIN, S. J., AND RUFF, G. E.: Personality characteristics of the Mercury astronauts. Symposium on Human Reactions to the Threat of Impending Disaster, Part III. Annual Meeting of the AAAS, Philadelphia, December 28, 1962.
18. RUFF, G. E., AND KORCHIN, S.: Psychological responses of Mercury astronauts to stress. Symposium and Human Reactions to the Threat of Impending Disaster, Part III. Annual Meeting of the AAAS, Philadelphia, December 28, 1962.

HUMAN VIOLENCE: CRITIQUE
AND INTEGRATION

By JULES H. MASSERMAN, M.D.

BY WAY of self-introduction, I rate myself as a moderately competent sailor, just a fair musician, but only a so-so prophet of fundamental scientific advances—and I regulate my adventures correspondingly. Operationally speaking, then, I can generally trim a jib sheet fairly well on first try, but I have learned that I cannot appreciate the worth of a musical composition or the significance of a scientific paper on first hearing; indeed, the value of either, as judged by my apparently more perceptive friends, sometimes permanently eludes me. In the present instance, therefore, I shall make extended comments only on those essays the authors of which were kind enough to let me read at least a few hours before I heard them presented publicly; fortunately, the papers by Drs. Eibl-Eibesfeldt, Coser, Berkowitz and Waskow are also fairly representative of the biologic, social and humanitarian concerns of this Conference.

In his ethological preface to the symposium Dr. Eibl-Eibesfeldt ably demonstrated that various agonistic patterns—all called "aggressive" —actually differ greatly with many contingencies: e.g., the species of the animal, its conspecific friendships or rivalries, its modes of extra-species preying or defense, and, most of all, the unique past and current experiences of each individual. This analysis furnished a most welcome corrective to previous overgeneralizations about a mythical absolute called "aggression"—a term that constituted another instance of what Alfred Whitehead, Susan Langer and others have so often warned us against: the misleading reification of an abstraction. A human being is no more motivated to go toward (L.*a-gresso*) his myriad objectives by a postulated "force" called aggression than an airplane is activated to fly by an English part of speech spelled "flying." But it is pleasant to play with pleomorphic participles; indeed, to change the alliteration, they sometimes seem to be the *sine qua non* of social science seminars.

Dr. Coser's contribution is on the whole likewise clear, reminescent and evocative. For example, his concept of "relative (social) deprivation" recalls Adolf Meyer's arithmetical formula for contentment: i.e., the seemingly simple ratio of *what I've got* divided by *what I want.* The reciprocal of this [(I have learned to want) much but have (what I consider) little] is, of course a measure of dissatisfaction, which in turn might lead to pre-emptive violence. However, the term "what I have" is a personally unique appraisal of values held rather than an inventory of material assets, whereas what one "wants" depends greatly on comparing one's lot with that of others. This contrast is a far more disconcerting experience to the hopelessly frustrated adult Negro than to the recalcitrant middle-class adolescent, who not only demands but expects gratification; hence, as Dr. Coser infers, the rates of frustration and crime would be expectedly higher in the first of these two "lower status groups."

From here on, however, I find it difficult to correlate my own clinical experiences, which range on economic parameters from clinics for the indigent to couches for the cohorts of Croesus, with Dr. Coser's more sweeping class distinctions. For example, he states: "In the lower classes the highly frustrated individual will tend to act outward toward persons . . . who seem to constrain him; whereas in the upper classes the highly frustrated individual will tend to blame the self rather than others." Actually, the differences appear to lie more in elocution than execution; the rich patient, who as Dr. Leeds points out, is far more protected from frustration by our social and juridical systems than is the poor one, nevertheless, also beats his own breast far less than he does a spate of alleged malfactors ranging in time and space from parents who, so he insists, long ago victimized him forever by staging a primal scene too traumatic for his delicate childhood innocence, to a society that now doesn't permit him to achieve his "true identity"— even when the "identity" striven for is still that of an omnipotently preemptive child. It is true that the "lower-class" laborer, angry over debts, demands and deprivations, may occasionally assault his friends and beat his wife and children, but so also does the executive—with the difference that the latter, although withholding physical violence, usually finds more subtle ways to make everyone within reach suffer longer and more excruciatingly. True, a person's tendencies toward crude expressions of hostility may in itself relegate him to, and keep him socially immobilized in, the so-called "lower-classes," but the fact remains that money, intelligence, education and social power do not really "internalize" violence but only make its external expressions—

including destructively intended suicidal gestures—all the more versatile and devastating. For that matter, I may also enter a demurrer about Dr. Coser's repeated implications that women are really in a sub-dominant position in our society; as part of their many and versatile manipulative ploys, a few women may profess to agree with this self-reassuring male fiction, but as an analyst as well as a husband I have yet to know any woman who really believes it, let alone practices it. Regrettably, then, some of the facile social stratifications found in sociology texts and mentioned by Dr. Coser, seem to blur or evaporate under clinical scrutiny—although, of course, they may continue to be of heuristic value at other levels of generalization.

On the other hand, Dr. Berkowitz calls attention to another definition of aggression which highlights our currently atavistic tendencies to equate aggression not with *initiative* but with *destruction.* In this sense, the adjectival form is a euphemism for the furious hostility beneath the well-tailored gray flannel of the "aggressive business man." Perhaps in some future civilized society, aggression will again mean what it is supposed to say: "I go to meet" rather than "I go to destroy." I was also a bit puzzled as to why Dr. Berkowitz thought it necessary to immerse himself once again in Freud's hydrostatic postu- late of a "pressure of aggressive libido," however, redirected through the fluid trivalve of the ever-flowing Hartmann, Kris, and Lowenstein. Nor is Dr. Berkowitz' similar concept of aggression as an easily triggered form of *elan vitale* altogether supported by the ethologic or other evidence he cites. It is true that Tinbergen's famous male stickle-back attacked any rival with a red belly—or, for that matter, a moving red marble—but this happened only when the attacking fish considered its territory *violated* and its reactive *violence* was likely to be success-ful; if the latter was in doubt and neither attack nor escape seemed feasible, the poor fish summoned another of its relatively few talents and, of all things, proceeded to build a nest. So also, in my own experiments, conduct with obviously destructive intent occurred in cats and monkeys only when they were physically frustrated in some accustomed activity (e.g., by a mechanical barrier) or by a social rival* (e.g., a more dominant animal) but only rarely when the

---

*Conversely, a high degree of "social cooperation" could also evolve: for example, some paired animals would alternate in working an electric switch which delivered food to their cage-partners. An example of "violence" which illustrated the relativity of this term occurred when two feline genuises in 14 pairs studied learned that by vigorous action they could jam the switch into a corner of the cage so as to keep it permanently in a closed position; the mechanism then operated continuously and both partners could feed at leisure.

destructive behavior had no chance of success; under the latter circumstances, the animal ate more, sought coitus, licked its fur, or indulged in other available gratifications. We can, of course, call these alternatives "displaced" or "substitutive" aggression, but in doing so we would again be assuming that "aggression" is basic, and furnishing another example of the type of circular reasoning that has occasioned more vacuous vertigo than conceptual closure in the behavioral sciences.

The same reservations, unfortunately, apply to Weatherly's personal-questionnaire data as cited by Berkowitz. How did Dr. Weatherly know, without having had microphones and TV cameras secreted in his subject's homes for the preceding two decades, that the mothers of some of his coeds had "permitted aggression" whereas others had not? Could it be merely that what Weatherly called his "aggressive" young ladies were precisely those most likely to blame their troubles on their families in retrospect and the rest of the world in prospect—thus again introducing a similar circular error? Even Freud had to admit that he had overlong confused personal history with wishful fantasy. For that matter, did the subjects labeled by themselves or by Weatherly as "aggressive" actually behave so: i.e., did *any* of them tear up the cue-card, invite the experimenter to combat, or bring suit for invasion of personal privacy? Perhaps because of such considerations, Dr. Berkowitz properly called the results of his own insulting experiments "tentative"; indeed, I would suggest the term tenuous. Laboratory transactions so vaguely defined, so palpably staged and so nearly infinitely multifactorial, when performed on a small roomful of complex human subjects are, as Dr. Berkowitz correctly implies, of casual anectodal rather than heuristic utility; to hold otherwise would be a scientific contempt of court. Nor can we gain greater assurance from Skinnerian circularities such as "An activity will tend to continue until the activity goal is reached." Operationally analyzed, how do we know when the goal is reached? Simple: when the activity is discontinued. And when does that happen? When the goal is reached. Q.E.D.—but in this instance meaning *quod erat duplicandem*. Nor can we evade the difficulties of a multifactorial analysis of our complicated, variable and contingent human transactions by attributing our behavior to improbable imps oddly named Narcissism, Libido, Superego, Masculine Protest, Thanatos—or, for that matter, "Aggression"—all panchrestic terms which never have the same operational connotations to any two persons—or to the same person in two successive transactions. To abandon these shibboleths does not mean conceptual, methodological or expositional chaos in our thinking, doing and writing, but it necessitates a far greater relativity of thought, broader contextualization of observation, and operational specificity of expression than we usually essay in the present embryonic state of the behavioral sciences.

Harold Lief next presented us with vivid examples of how outrageous violence may gain prestige for an adolescent member of a delinquent gang, security for the hoodlum with a reputation for operating with cold cruelty, renown for the quick-shooting fast-triggered Western gunslinger, or the supposed advantages of deterrent nuclear *schreck-lichkeịt* in international maneuvering. Yet, while citing these implicitly meaningful illustrations, Dr. Lief played the contrapuntal theme that violence can be, and very often is an "unmotivated" experience sought only for its suigeneric existential intensity. Once again, to sound a chord from my introduction: my perhaps over-traditional musical training makes it difficult to follow this form of fugal writing, but I shall look forward to further expositions.

I had a similar difficulty with what seemed to be Dr. Rado's occasionally conflicting thesis. I agree with him that the illusion of omnipotence is one of the 3 Ur-defenses of man, the other 2 being his faith in his fellows (or at least, as David Marlowe points out, those of close kin) and his belief in philosophic or theologic systems. But the first of these illusions denies death outright, the second circumvents it through progeny and good works, and the third invokes resurrection and immortality—despite which Dr. Rado also stated "You cannot fight death with illusion!" And as to his proposal that we reunite all of humanity through the supposedly universal love of the child: it may be true that we no longer, as the Vikings did, make a game of throwing children in the air and catching them on swords, and that only a few tribes still serve roast infant for dessert—yet this is also the age of the world-wide population explosion, and it may be that the infant is *not* the happiest symbol available for Dr. Rado's cause. Parenthetically, as Dr. Mead points out in the current Reader's Digest, it is certainly not a welcome symbol of college sexuality.

We may next turn with Arthur Waskow to broader perspectives. Although wars have long since been largely shorn of "personal hostilities" (Alexander respected the third Darius, and Alexander's soldiers slew far more for supposed gain and glory than in personal anger against their unknown antagonists in far countries), Waskow poses the problem "in a disarmed world, will feelings of hostility that are now turned against foreigners . . . be redirected into hostilities at home?" On the whole, Waskow questions the hydraulic theory of hostility, yet qualifies this by pointing to postwar "race riots, political bombings and violent strikes." But these also occur after any widespread and prolonged stresses, from earthquakes through crop failures or economic panics, and may therefore be more generally described as frenetic social upheavals rather than specific resultants of "aggression."

Waskow next poses what to him is the inevitable dilemma in a world with nuclear arms but without world law: i.e., "an appeal to arms and an appeal in court are both impossible." Parenthetically, in a recent address, Justice William O. Douglas of our Supreme Court dealt with this impasse by pointing out that international tribunals (e.g., the Hague Court, the European Court of Human Rights, self-regulating Economic Unions, etc.) operating with the consent of the parties or litigants concerned, may still be effective without either a World Constitution or an international police force to enforce their decisions. Perhaps the active development of such increasingly salutory substitutes for mutual destruction would be preferable to a "world state" of nebulous organization and power.

In this connection, Dr. Leeds did so thorough a job of demolishing various ramshackle and labyrinthine slums in our thinking about war that he had little time left to submit plans for the more attractive architecture of the palatial familial residences, the universities and the cathedrals he proposes to erect on the cleared ground—or how to protect them in turn from new encroachments and destruction. But since at least some of the world's inhabitants look to us for guidance, we ourselves must grow in comprehension if we can but avoid stumbling over our lethal toys. It is in this last relevance that I may make a brief contribution to this symposium in the City of Brotherly Love about an attempt to apply such putative wisdom to world affairs.

In September 1961, an International Conference on World Order and Freedom was assembled in Athens, Greece, under the auspices of the Fund for the Republic. At this meeting Justice Douglas discussed the current deficiencies in international law; Denis Healey of the British Cabinet predicted rapidly mounting conflicts among world leaders (and offered to refer them to me for psychotherapy); David Horowitz of the World Bank reviewed the current economic disparities that must lead to more national revolutions, and Ramanohar Lohia of India foresaw that these upheavals would involve his own subcontinent. In other discussions, some of the world's leading authorities in history, economics, law, communication and military science agreed that unless every effort were made immediately to decrease world tensions—particularly those arising from the almost irreversible suspicion, truculence and belligerence between the United States and the U.S.S.R.—unavoidable border of influence wars would soon involve tactical atomic weapons and quickly lead to a nuclear Armageddon that would inevitably destroy not only democracy, but civilization and humanity itself. In my own address I admitted that we psychiatrists seemed at times as wishfully dereistic and escapist as our patients in picking pebbles under a breaking tidal wave. Nevertheless, we were in no position to deal with people who do not consult us, and the best we could do was to advise that any plan for rapprochement with Russia must have the following psychological characteristics: (1) It must be made with complete sincerity and credibility; (2) it must not pose an economic or military threat to either nation. (3) it must be politically and administratively practicable; within the immediate future; and (4) it must have instant and universal appeal.

I then proposed:

". . . That we offer to send to Russia, as soon as possible, large numbers of students, mostly from the ages of 17 to 20 (*not* to serve as 'hostages'!) but for the purpose of broadening their education and promoting new and mutually advantageous understandings. At the same time we shall invite the Soviet Union to send comparable numbers of their students to live in our homes and attend our schools for a year or two for similar purposes . . . This would certify unmistakably to all the civilized world that we had no intention of unleashing nuclear destruction on a nation that was playing host to our own sons and daughters; simultaneously, we would be inviting the Russians to show the same sincerity and humanity in the open and compelling court of world opinion. If the Soviets refused we would have at least expressed our own good will; if they accepted, one path to world peace would be opened."

The proposal, of course, entailed many problems: financing, organization, selection and supervision of students, bilingual preparation, coordination of educational levels, etc., but careful surveys indicated that none of these presented great difficulties. As a national movement called Youth for Tomorrow, the plan was endorsed by the presidents of the American Association for the Advancement of Science, the American Psychiatric Association, the American Psychological Association, and by various leaders in American education, science, religion, arts, labor, industry and statesmanship. It was also sanctioned in principle by the State Department, the White House staff and by the Soviet Embassy and, at the local level, by the Mayor of Chicago. All seemed promising until the Cuban Crisis, when the Directors of the plan thought it best to suspend operations to a more favorable time. If and when, heaven grant, this arrives, physicians, psychologists and educators may be asked to serve in the following capacities:

1. To interview and examine our young ambassadors of good will as to their physical status, scholastic excellence and adherence to American ideals of human justice and freedom.

2. To offer foster homes to Russian youngsters with, we hope, similar qualities during their stay here.

3. To enlist their own family in the plan if they so desire.

Perhaps in this, we can again help waken the world out of its current nightmare of violence into a happier day of welfare through sanity.

Part II. Clinical Research

PRESIDENTIAL ADDRESS:
A DYNAMIC STORY OF THE "HOMOCLITE"

By ROY R. GRINKER, SR., M.D.

HAVE YOU ever come in contact with a *group* of "mentally healthy" young males? Well, I did—accidentally while interviewing volunteers for one of our psychosomatic experiments. Only recently I found that Murray[1] had written: "Were an analyst to be confronted by that much-heralded but still missing specimen—the normal man— he would be struck dumb, for once, through lack of appropriate ideas."

I was startled by meeting people whom I never encountered in my role as a psychiatrist—patients or colleagues—and rarely in my social contacts. At least on the surface they were free from psychotic, neurotic, or disabling traits or symptoms. The absence of these criteria of illness and the startle effect on a psychiatrist may constitute a rough first-order definition of health. Startled though I was, I was not "struck dumb." To the contrary, I spent several years studying these subjects, thinking about them, and discussing them with anyone who would listen to me.

I soon found that it is impossible to communicate sensibly and objectively with anyone when such terms as "normal" or "healthy" are employed, since they are so heavily loaded with values. A neologism was needed, one that nobody understood. I therefore sought help in finding a name for these ordinary, conforming, noncreative, goal-seeking people. Percival Bailey finally came to my rescue after discovering that "heteroclite," meaning "a person deviating from the common

From the Institute for Psychosomatic and Psychiatric Research and Training of Michael Reese Hospital and Medical Center, Chicago, Illinois. Supported by State of Illinois Mental Health Fund No. 1711.

rule," is in Webster's dictionary. He then suggested coining the word "homoclite" to apply to my group of healthy conformists.

The essential descriptive data derived from interviews, tests, and questionnaires and my basic conclusions are presented in another publication.[2] However, as a psychoanalyst I am interested in the dynamic processes involved in the development and functioning of this group and presume now to give my presidential address on this subject. This presumption is compounded by the fact that I have not psychoanalyzed a single homoclite and, therefore, present only inferences and hypotheses within the framework of some aspects of general psychoanalytic theory or what is called metapsychology. However, I do not limit my considerations to psychodynamics alone, but include a discussion of the homoclite from other frames of reference as well.

BRIEF DESCRIPTION OF THE SUBJECTS

In 1958 and 1959 I studied a number of students originating from all over the United States and Canada (thereby representing millions of people) attending a small local Protestant college engaged in occupational training rather than general education, for specialization in (1) group work and recreation and (2) health and physical education. In 1958 I interviewed 31 subjects and in 1959 gave a 700-item questionnaire to 80 subjects, of whom 34 were later interviewed. Thus, in addition to interviews with 65 male college students, extensive data covering 18 major categories regarding self, parents, and social, cultural, religious, work and other experiences, were available for various types of ratings and statistical analyses. The techniques and raw data are all presented in the previous publication.

An outline of the current characteristics and past conditions of the homoclites which I am about to enumerate does not give the living feeling—the flesh and blood of these subjects. They look like fine young men, in fact are derided by students and teachers at a nearby university as "upright young men." Yet they are not conscious of their differences or their supposed liabilities in contrast to others. To the contrary, they are naively unselfconscious, clear-eyed, ordinary young men who speak the language of their peers. They are on average extremely likeable to me, a bias which I have tried to overcome by using various techniques to tease out their possible psychopathology. Their life-plan is startling, refreshing, and unbelievable until one encounters it repeatedly and is convinced of its sincerity through depth interviews.

The characteristic traits of this sample population at the time of the study are summarized as follows:

CURRENT CHARACTERISTICS

Physically healthy.

Average intelligence (I.Q. 110).

Self-image fair and realistic.

Mild affective response of anxiety, depression, and anger evoked by external stimuli, rarely "spontaneous."

Rapidly stimulated and effective coping devices against affective arousal by muscular action, denial, or withdrawal.

Interest in physical activities, athletics.

Little introspective capacity or "communication with self" and low degrees of fantasy, regression, or creativity.

Fairly strong impulse control.

Moderate anxiety concerning failure in competitive sports and school examinations.

High degree of ethics, morality, and honesty.

Few cultural interests.

Little heterosexual experimentation for average age (18-20 years) and social class.

Moderate dependency on current idealized figures or symbols.

Good capacity for warm human relationships.

Minimal psychopathology.

An outline of the past experiences and influences bearing on the subjects' development is as follows:

PAST CONDITIONS

Constitutionally sound physical health from birth.

Relatively low socioeconomic status of biological family.

Satisfactory positive affectionate relationships with both parents.

Parental agreement and cooperation in child-rearing.

Definite and known limitations and boundaries placed on behavior.

Parental emphasis on control.

Punishment reasonable and consistent.

Strict early religious training.

Early work history.

Moderate adolescent rebellion.

Model of real world calls for action—one does something about problems.

Model of life-plan: contentment, sociability, and doing good; goal-seeking, rather than goal-changing, behavior leading to concern for success at what one chooses to do rather than ambition for prestige, social advancement, or wealth.

Father suitable as model for masculine identification.

Easy stages of progression from home, church, YMCA, high school, and college; environments whose value systems were relatively similar and stable.

Although the 80 subjects who answered the 700-item questionnaire constituted a fairly homogeneous group, it was soon apparent from a study of those who came for interviews and those who did not that differences existed, sufficient for the study of subgroups. The differences between these groups reflect differences in basic orientation toward life-goals. The interview group is more socially oriented, verbal, and aesthetic. The noninterview group is more rugged, sports- and activity-directed and more anxious regarding school work, reciting, and examinations.

Using rating scales which assessed adjustment, it was also possible to isolate 3 groups according to degrees of adjustment to the current environment. The differences among family background, childhood experiences, and current traits were essentially quantitative.

In the families of the subjects certain patterned structures may be extrapolated. Mother was lovingly concerned about her child yet expected independence and early work and later education. Father loved, disciplined, and established firm boundaries. These points of view were complementary rather than antagonistic, father furnishing the instrumental patterns of ideals and goals of masculinity while mother furnished the expressive content of expectations involving education, goals, and ideals. The healthy balance of both influences resulted in the average subject I am describing under the term homoclite. The polarities of mild psychopathology can also be discerned in the passive dependent character (when maternal concern was excessive), the paranoid character (when paternal strictures were excessive). Since the average of innate factors, including intelligence, and the socioeconomic-cultural environments are the same, differences between adjustment groups are probably determined by early experiences within the nuclear family.

LITERATURE

Psychoanalysts have not been vitally interested in concepts of "normality" or "health," yet they use these terms freely. Their writings are pretty monotonous, so that I shall quote only 3 distinguished authors.

To begin as usual with Freud,[3] he states: "Every normal person is only approximately normal. His ego resembles that of the psychotic in one point or another in a greater or lesser degree." In the same paper he states that it is impossible to determine how the instincts are tamed to be in harmony with the ego without summoning help "from the witch metapsychology."

Jones,[4] after admitting that no absolute normality is ever achieved, indicates that it consists of: first, happiness or the capacity for enjoyment and self-content; second, efficiency in mental functioning including relationship with fellow-men; and, third, a positive social feeling determined primarily by a degree of internal freedom for such feelings.

These quotations immediately demonstrate the repetitive polarities found in the psychoanalytic literature. On the one hand are those authors who consider that mental health is only definable in terms of a balance of internal psychological forces and, on the other hand, those who base their concepts of normality on types of behavior.

One of the most balanced and sensible discussions of normality from a psychoanalyst stems from Glover,[5] who points out that little is known about the normal individual because he is inaccessible to the psychoanalytic method, which requires motivation and will to recover from suffering. He also cautions us that we do not worship or idealize an absolute concept of normality, since inevitably it is a state conforming to social standards of adequate adaptation with at the same time the quality of elasticity and the capacity for anxiety tolerance. Glover points out that normality in descriptive psychology is a continuum depending on the end products of its instinctual origins. He states that the normal person is symptom-free, unhampered by mental conflict, has a satisfactory working capacity, and is able to love another person. Structurally the psychic organs are in successful function and balance, and the resulting characterological reactions are not noisy. From the economic point of view the normal individual must have the capacity for the exploitation of earlier pleasure systems. Thus there is an harmonious and simultaneous function of mechanisms which controls instincts and secures direct or substitute instinct gratification.

Glover, in addition, speculates that in normality there is an harmonious confluence of the reality and pleasure principles with an overlapping psychotic and objective reality testing. He believes that the state of normality cannot be attained without an infantile psychosis and a subsequent adolescent psychosis. Then normality is a state in which the subject's psychotic estimate of the world around him coincides with an objective estimate in two respects: the amount of love that can be satisfied and the amount of danger to the ego that is present. Normality is, then, a form of "madness" which goes unrecognized because it happens to be good adaptation to reality and has the capacity for elasticity and anxiety tolerance.

PSYCHODYNAMICS

When we attempt to explain behavior from the psychoanalytic point of view, we try to establish causal relationships based on theoretical concepts of processes, whether they be forces, energy, information, etc. Psychoanalytic metapsychology usually utilizes several frames of reference such as "genetic", "economic", "dynamic," and "structural". The term *behavior* is used as a focus of description and explanation referring not only to total action or specific motoric behavior in an external environment, but also including feelings, thoughts, or what Rapaport terms "latent behavior." In any given and designated span of time, one may examine various aspects of behavior, not necessarily as specific and differentiated behaviors but as the same time-defined behavior viewed from several frames of reference.

On the basis of the cluster of characteristics which I have observed and described for the young male adults whom I have called homoclites and from the memory-images of their developmental experiences, I shall attempt explanations from the various frames of reference characteristic of psychoanalytic metapsychology.

Genetic: This frame of reference views those series of chronological experiences that establish form and determine content of intrapsychic functions and which are difficult to validate. It matters not whether the technique consists of psychoanalytic reconstruction or interviews or questionnaires directed to conscious and preconscious recall. There are so many facts which are unavailable either from the subject or the people surrounding him during his crucial years of growth that we can get only a general picture of experiences that are subjectively meaningful to the patient.

However, with these precautions in mind, we are able to reconstruct the general influences which impinged on our subjects in their developmental periods. They had positive affectionate relationships and communications with both parents and expressly denoted their mothers as warm, giving, and close to them. It seems that the mother-child relationship was relatively satisfactory without indications of coldness, rejection, frustration, and other negative aspects that are characteristic of subjects revealing varying degrees of psychopathology. It is only when we classify our subjects into degrees of adjustment that we find indications that those who are marginal within our sample population had less satisfactory relationships with the maternal object.

Probably even more important is the universal statement from our subjects that their relationship to father was warm, close, and satisfactory. There seemed to have been parental communication, agreement, and coöperation in child-raising, and the father constituted in many ways an ideal with whom strong identifications could be made. This is evidenced in the attitudes concerning future goals: the economic and social life which father provided for his family is conceived of as suitable for his son.

In terms of developmental influences, it seems that not the mother *or* father was most essential or beneficial, but that an early positive relationship with mother *followed by* a positive relationship with father enabled the child to make those masculine identifications which lead to the capacity to behave and function adequately as a man. Thus, subsequent identifications were possible and could utilize available and constructive figures such as YMCA secretaries.

Bruner[6] in discussing degrees of sensory deprivation in early life points out that it results in the absence of a model of expectations of probable variable happenings in later life, lack of differentiation of spheres of activity, and deficient use of cues. Bruner's interesting suggestions can be applied to a continuum of experience and effects. An inadequate model of the environment because of sensory deprivation, and no experience with trial and error may result in deficient strategies for evaluating information. On the other hand, overloading with sensory experiences produces too much information, too many choices, and contradictory or unconfirmed trial and error experiences. The resulting personality disorders can be hypothesized to range from the dull or pseudo-imbecile to the excitable, hypomanic neurotic with the homoclite somewhere in the middle area.

Economic: From the economic point of view, psychoanalytic metapsychology considers so-called psychic energies derived from drive pressures and expressed in intensities of instinctual representatives. I would like to make it clear that I cannot utilize such notions as psychic energy of drive origin and prefer to speak in a different language, but I shall discuss the concept of energy from the usual psychoanalytic point of view.

It is apparent from the current psychological position and the past experiences of our subjects that their drive or total energies are expressed more directly in motor action than in psychological processes. They deal with problems and conflicts by direct action. Whatever energies are concerned in this process are, therefore, not inhibited or long-circuited or indirectly expressed in psychological symbolic processes. To the contrary, these are people who fix things and who use as their defenses, muscular action expressed in their frequent cliche, "Kick it off."

This by no means indicates that our subjects are muscularly highly developed or skilled. They are not giants or muscle-men from a physical point of view. Nevertheless, they very early came into contact with the YMCA through their interest in swimming and other sports, and very early in their lives they began a consistent career of work from delivering groceries, etc., caddying, camp counseling, etc. On the other hand, these subjects have little interest in introspection; they rarely ask the question, "Why do I feel this way?" or "Why did I do this?"; and are not particularly interested in finding the sources of their affects when aroused. Rather, they attempt to deny, withdraw, or work them off. Thus the world is conceived as being external and calling for action. There is little introspection of an internal world—one does something about problems.

A similar example of drive fate which these subjects demonstrate is their relative lack of ambition for upward mobility; they are not intellectually ambitious but settle for a C grade in school. They seek goals which more or less directly satisfy their drive needs rather than searching for stimuli which would evoke goal-changing behavior. Finally, their vocabularies are limited, and a direct proof of limitation of thinking is their deficient syntax and spelling. Some of the subjects are more verbal than others, and these have more problems since they were the ones who, after being questionnaired, came for subsequent interviews.

Dynamic: In considering the behavior of our subjects from the dynamic point of view, I am well aware of the deficiency in my information. Nevertheless, in my own work with the subjects whom I have described, I ascertained little that could be called serious psychopathology.

An harmonious interplay among the allocated functions of the psychic apparatus seems to be generally present. The unrepressed id drives derive more direct satisfaction through the relatively free and nonconflictful functions of the ego. There seem to be little anxiety, depression, or anger which cannot be handled easily by ego functions in action.

The absence of any great degree of intellectual competence, since most of the subjects have only average intelligence, indicates that there is little striving for the unusual or difficult. The self-evaluation of my subjects is accurate; their appraisal of their abilities is almost exact. It seems, then, that they have the capacity for self-evaluation and acceptance of self and the ability to find the environment in which their capacities can be expressed with success and achieve their ego ideals.

These ideals involve contentment, sociability, doing good, and making friends. Thus, their ego functions in dealing with inner psychic reality and external problems seem relatively free from conflict. Their ideals are appropriate to their capacities, and thus there is little tension because of failure or lack of success. Yet they strive to obtain the positions toward which they are oriented, which means passing their examinations and being graduated. This incites a certain degree of fear of failure evidenced in anxiety before examinations and depressions when their grades are not good enough. Thus, they have the capacity for understanding, feeling, and acting in response to their true capacities.

In terms of their superego functions dealing with the expected and prohibited, there is some evidence that in early life some tension occurred between their drive needs and what had been permitted. There had been some rigidity in their parents as evidenced by the frequency of concern about growing phases of independence. As a result, there is a degree of compulsivity in our subjects' behavior indicating superego functions that are firm. One can only conjecture that this type of superego is related to their need to achieve and to the defenses which they have adopted in avoidance of behaviors which would produce anxiety and depression. They are considerably more reality-oriented and free from fantasy than might be considered entirely healthy. In that sense their early religious training and their incorporation of the prevailing Protestant ethic may also have some significance.

The homoclites as a whole report relatively little adolescent turbulence. Some increase of conflict with the parents and greater reaction to discipline were experienced during adolescence. Only 4 had *acted out* rebelliously and had come in contact with the law, but these all were enuretic, tending to confirm Michael's[7] hypothesis of a common root (constitutional?) for lack of sphincter and social controls. Some talk about experiences of "coming to terms with myself." Only 2 turned bitter and paranoid, and a like number became "angry young men," and 1 turned into a shy quiet person full of damped-down explosive rage.

In general, the transitions during development were smooth and not sharply phase-demarcated. There was a gradual progression toward distant goals. Social space superseding bodily contact was accepted quietly in the processes of maturation. Freud in 1937 had said that phases do not succeed each other suddenly, but gradually. Later Erikson[8] developed his theory of phase-stage progression inevitably associated with critical conflicts and crises. Anna Freud[9] believes that a steady equilibrium during adolescence is abnormal, and Joselyn[10] states that adult normality is not possible in the absence of an identity crisis.

Are psychological crises part of the maturation process, or do they occur in development because of pressures and external crises-stimulating conditions? For the homoclite the cultural and family background was conducive to growth and change without many difficulties or serious conflict. They have reached an "identity" without crisis and with little ego diffusion. From home, church, YMCA, high school, and college the value systems of their environments remained relatively constant. Whatever changes took place in their personal worlds were gradual and could be absorbed without too much strain. This I believe is a general phenomenon among the mass of people but not those seen by psychiatrists. It is an antidote to severe neurosis-making; whether it is likewise antagonistic to creativity is an open question.

Structural: It is clear that these subjects who function realistically and in action have little access to their unconscious or preconscious processes. Their capacity for "regression in the service of the ego" is minimal. They rarely engage in fantasy and in introspection. Thus, they have moved slowly and fatefully from an early position to their present state with aspirations for the future on the basis of forces about which they are naive. They know what they want to do, and they know how to do it. This has little symbolic value to them and is only interpreted as a real achievement of their ideals.

That they have moved upward by going to college seems somewhat contradictory. Yet their patterns of behavior and their goals as expressed consciously and realistically are no different from their fathers' except for the means by which they are achieved. It must be remembered that their college is an occupational school rather than an institution of higher learning in which they probably would be unsuccessful.

The homoclite has a moderate degree of structural or character-ological compulsivity for which parents' "concerns" were sufficient precursors. We now ask how much autonomy of the ego from the id[11] or dominantly unconscious alliance exists and what are the handicaps? The homoclite is not creative in the sense of Kubie,[12] nor is he similar to Stein's[13] creative chemists. But he is not repetitive, obligatory, insatiable, or stereotyped. In fact, despite his characterological defenses, his coping devices against external stress consisting of motoric activity indicate an adequate, interested, and efficient situational cathexis. He transcends his characterological binds and views reality and himself accurately and behaves accordingly.

From the structural point of view, the persistence of patterns of behavior maintained over a fairly long period of time indicates a slow rate of change. The structural components seem to be crystallized rather early. In that sense, their position in training for a specific occupation has prevented them from getting into conflict which would have developed if they had attended a university where a multiplicity of goals and objectives were constantly dangled before the students. Yet there is a certain degree of change and, in fact, a simple creativity in the way in which they are able to handle groups in activities, physical play, and recreation. They are adept at manipulating groups into cohesive and reality-adapted behavior. They develop new devices which fit the particular groups with which they are working. Thus, although the rate of change is slow, one can make no prediction as to how far change will occur or whether creativity will be expressed later in a more dramatic manner than at present.

I believe that greater emphasis should be placed on the structural frame of reference in the psychoanalytic study of all individuals and certainly the homoclite. The structural or patterned processes of the ego are the end result of a vast number of genetic and dynamic factors whose integration is expressed in adaptation. Dull though he may be in school, the homoclite reveals his "normality" by productive action, satisfactory relationships, and rewarding emotional experiences.

Obviously his drive tensions are reduced by the necessary repressions; hence he seems to have less quantities of "drive energy." His motor activities used in the process of nonspecific discharge of affects minimize his symbolic functions. Homosexuality, if at all present is sublimated in social action for which his choice of occupation is conducive. Finally, the integrative and adaptive functions of his ego are manifested by the fact that, left to his own devices, the homoclite chooses the kind of life for which he is suited.

DISCUSSION

We have now reviewed the behavior of our subjects from the various frames of reference laid down as constituting the metapsychology of psychoanalysis. Sketchy to be sure, this has led to several hypotheses for future testing. Yet there is an incompleteness in the frames of reference which psychoanalytic theory utilizes. Despite Rapaport's[14] statement that borrowing from other sciences indicates a lack of self-confidence, it would seem that the concept of mental health requires the use of other theoretical frames of reference, particularly the constitutional or genic and the adaptive or psychosocial points of view.

Constitutional: It seems from both a survey of the present state of our subjects and the historical data elicited from them, that as children and adolescents they displayed sound physical health. At birth their feeding, sleeping, and other functions were without noteworthy deviation from normal. They grew up in environments where it was expected that everything possible should be accomplished for the children's health. It is not possible for us to measure or demarcate the degree of health present beginning at birth, but the general conclusions can be made that they had little or no difficulty in their physical developmental processes. It has been repeatedly stated that no behavior stands in isolation, and certainly there has been enough evidence to indicate how physical defects, physical trauma, infections, and other illnesses have a profound effect in the growing child on ego development. No such catastrophes happened to our subjects.

Probably of equal importance constitutionally, should be the hereditary differences in drives, energies, and the so-called autonomous psychological functions which show a wide range of difference at birth. Freud, for example, discusses congenital variations of the ego leading to the selection of specific defenses. Glover talks about instinct or drive quantities, sensitivity to frustration, and anxiety or hate tolerances as constitutional forces. Indeed, to include the concept of constitution and at the same time avoid admitting its importance psychoanalytic theorists now speak of psychological "givens," a truly vitalistic notion for a deterministic discipline. To explain the homoclite it is necessary to include the motoric constitutional processes as Escalona and Heider[15] did in their predictive studies. What other more subtle enzymatic, metabolic, or physiological factors need to be included I do not know.

Psychosocial: Although it is true that psychoanalysis has lately included as one of its dimensions what is known as the adaptive point of view first stressed by Rado[16] indicating that some behavior is determined by realities and serves an adaptive function, there are many who object to this intrusion. In looking over the backgrounds of our subjects we can see that the reality of their early lives was oriented towards the adaptational point of view. The social and cultural aspects of their families indicated that the goal-seeking behavior which involved the Protestant ethics had a great deal to do with the content and intensity of their ego ideals and superegos. Without the information concerning the social and cultural determinants, one certainly would be limited in explaining the type of mental health demonstrated by our subjects.

Freud recognized the environmental (social, cultural) component of health, even postanalytically. "If the patient who has made such a good recovery never produces any more symptoms calling for analysis, it still, of course, remains an open question how much of the immunity is due to a benevolent fate which spares him too searching a test." And again from Freud: "Health depends on the dynamic relations between the agencies of the psychic apparatus the existence of which psychoanalysis has discovered, deduced or conjectured." But a solution of the instinctual conflict depending on a particular relation between strength of the instinct and strength of the ego may be unbalanced when the latter is weakened by shocks, overwork, illness, etc. Freud added that he did not know if psychoanalyzed persons are equal to heavier strains than those who have not been analyzed.

The relative neglect of social and cultural parameters in psychoanalytic theory resulted in a vacuum which has attracted the theories of sociologists, anthropologists, and the so-called neo-Freudians. The latter have transcended the determinism of instinctual theory by stressing adaptive processes to society and the influence of society and culture on personality. Birnbach's[17] recent review of the neo-Freudian social philosophy, while indicating its emphasis on man's proclivity for growth by means of his transactions within his social environment, also raises the problem of overemphasizing man's psychopathology. Eckardt[18] questions: "Is conformity only a symptom defeating self-development, or is it also a force that tries to stabilize and structure society by maintaining vanishing tradition?"

Values: As implied earlier, the literature on "normality" and "mental illness" is suffused with value judgments and critical statements about them. Perhaps we may now briefly outline these values as held, respectively, by psychiatrists, ordinary people, and society.

The psychiatrist is educated, trained, and experienced in psychopathology and the treatment thereof. He sees sickness all around in his patients, colleagues, and friends (rarely himself). He shudders at the possibility that psychotherapy is not the answer to the challenge of illness and lives by one of Masserman's[19] "Ur-fantasies": the power to employ supreme magic. In fact, if he is also a psychoanalyst he retains, despite recurring experiences of failure, the illusion of reconstructing personalities through the omnipotence of his methods. In addition to knowing only patients, by virtue of his geographical location he also sees mostly those engaged in the rat-race of city life. Finally, he is caught in his own middle-class perspective.

The ordinary person has simple and reasonable values. He wants to feel good, work well, love and be loved, play and enjoy life occasionally and have hope for the future. There are wide ranges and many permutations of these values. He settles or is willing to settle for less than he originally hoped for, holding to Freud's adage that life is difficult but it is all we have.

The social and cultural dominant value systems in this country have been studied by Kluckhohn[20] on the basis of her special system of value orientations. Briefly, the middle class American family holds to individuality, future orientation, man being above nature, doing, the inherent evil in man. Spiegel[21] utilized this classification to indicate the source of frequent transference and countertransference difficulties in the divergent value systems of psychiatrist and patient. Such divergencies may also account for the discrepancies between what American families consider to be health or illness and what the psychiatrist says they are.

What we as psychiatrists see to be the goal of American families includes: upward mobility regardless of intellectual, aptitudinal or social fit; doing and becoming which is operationally goal-changing rather than goal-seeking; permissiveness rather than boundary fixing of behavior, work, strict religious belief, and discipline; and child-rearing according to the latest fad based on current theory.

The difficulty is that these cultural values which Spiegel showed not to be entirely held by Irish-Americans or Italian-Americans are also not cherished by upper-lower or lower-middle class and later Protestant-American main-streeters in Kansas, Minnesota, or Illinois or in America as a whole.

Thus what is normality and what is mental illness is confused because of the value discrepancies among psychiatrists, people, and cultures.

Values concerning health and illness are exposed as clearly as in a TAT by those to whom the homoclites have been described. The middle class intellectual and financier consider these subjects sick because "they have no ambition to get ahead." Psychiatrists and psychoanalysts have called them "preadolescent characters" or "latency children" who are destined to break down spontaneously or to disintegrate under stress. Considering the classes of 1958 and 1959, either their parents were children of economic depression or the subjects were World War II infants with absent fathers, hence their personality structure. Yet administrators and teachers at the college confirm the fact that the students are fairly similar year after year (the college is 75 years old), the school has a minimum of breakdowns and employs no student-health psychiatrists; the graduates are sought after and get the best positions in the country after graduation and seldom fail because of illness. They are envied by some observers because they are not racked by ambition and pressures to succeed and move upward. Other colleagues view them from their own positions and anxiously would "hate to be like them." The subjects themselves are unconscious of a need for "becoming" and yet are free from "existential anxiety." Finally, some observers have developed a kind of moral judgment signifying intense anxiety when they imply the question, "Should the homoclite exist at all?"

Many psychoanalysts have difficulty in accepting the parameters of adequate behavior, adaptation, adjustment, etc., as indicating "health," since they are more concerned with internal forces and balances. They ask the strange question: "What are the costs of mental health?" In contrast, general psychiatrists are constantly publicizing the "cost of mental illness."

In all seriousness there is a *cost* as a result of adaptation, but this is difficult to differentiate from the factors related to the *cause*. For example, are the somewhat compulsive character and rigidity, the sharply focused and limited interests, the use of activity to maintain comfort, the absence of creativity, fantasies and introspection, etc., the costs of the subject's stability and "mental health"? Or are these some of the conditions, among others, of clusters or characteristics that lead to "mental health", given the proper environmental conditions?

At the present time we cannot answer such questions which assume linearity of cause and effect until we unravel the time-space sequences by longitudinal studies of many more populations. Viewed, however, from a distance at the time of college-student days we would have to say that internal comfort, adequate adjustment to their environment, goal-directed behavior, and subject-environment fit are associated with stability and a special type of happiness, but also with narrowness and limitations of interests, mobility, creativity, and excitement characteristic of the American postadolescent ideal model. All this from a point of view based on the American cultural model of individual change. From the standpoint of the culture as a whole there is, however, more gain than cost. To have a population of relative stability is a necessary background for the activity of those who possess creativity or who are pioneers.

Our cultural model is mainly derived from the long-past frontier in the development of American society, superseded by pioneers in mental creativity and the frontiers of outer space. We need to remember that it was necessary that the enterprising, restless, dissatisfied frontiersmen were followed by a more homoclitic type satisfied by less accomplishment and more limited goals and mobility in order that a stable civilization might develop behind the leaders.

The homoclite is widely distributed throughout America, yet it is not the only kind of mental health. Silber's[22] competent adolescents, Stein's[13] creative chemists, and Westley's[23] healthy adolescents are examples of different types. Each has its own cluster of inherited, constitutional, and psychological traits; its own family, social and cultural experiences and values; its own best fit for work, socioeconomic and life-style. Even the postanalytic patients have their own social groups in the large cities whose value systems of health emphasize: "Why did I say that?"

The success of prediction regarding health depends on the possible relationship between person and environment. The important question in the current fast-moving and changing social and cultural world is what stresses are, or will be, impinging on the individual. With environments no longer stable even in the previously primitive cultures, the individual is required to make extremely rapid changes. Mental health thus depends less on stability but more on the flexibility of the individual. In other words, internal psychological homeostasis is dependent on the number of environments for which the personality is fit.

The question then that should be raised about populations or samples thereof is not only "how are they doing?" but also "how would they do if the environment shifted or if they moved into a new setting?" This depends on certain aspects of identification, associated with early transactions, which provide a repertoire of roles for the future.[24] The permutations of past experiences, later learning and environmental states and processes lead to an astronomical number of patterns of behavior which can be subjected to rough classification into categories or types.

These capacities for adjustment are learned early in life, rarely later without previous preparation. In a previous paper I pointed out that identifications constitute images of previous transactions that include ego, alter ego and the settings in which the transactions occurred. Thus identifications prepare the subject not only for a variety of implicit roles but also for a variety of settings or environments in which behavior is comfortably possible.

This only throws our important question a step backward for now we must ask what conditions make identification possible or easier. From a study of one specific male group, called homoclites, the empirical data suggest that the proximal causes are a succession, at critical ages, of need satisfactions from first mother and then father. This leads to successful masculine identification and the preparation and capacity for identification with other later masculine ideals. This is probably the basic and essential genetic-dynamic basis for "mental health" but carries with it the limitation of patterned behavior suitable for a few roles and a restricted range of environments—hence, the "homoclite." What prepares the developing boy for multiple roles and a wide range of environments *and* the behavioral and psychodynamic criteria of health, this study cannot answer.

CONCLUSIONS

Despite the current attitude of pessimism concerning the possibilities of research on "mental health" because of the entanglement with value systems, considerable knowledge may be obtained about various kinds of mental health using longitudinal-descriptive, psychodynamic, behavioral, and sociocultural approaches. The implications of this statement are that in the total "field" should be included: hereditary and constitutional data, an accurate description of physical and emotional experiences during maturation and development, a knowledge of resulting psychodynamics insofar as possible, a study of behavior at whatever and whenever maturity is reached (when growth and progress has ceased or slowed), a study of the sociocultural matrix within which development occurred and those matrices in which the subjects function well and the number of these. Rather than considering value judgments as obstacles to research, they become attributes of the culture and suitable for scientific investigation.

Such a field, large as it may be, furnishes the opportunity for the study of permutations of a large number of variables which may be combined into a lesser number of categories or systems in transaction. This should permit the crystallization of types of "mental health" amidst a spectrum of psychopathology and should lead to the finding and formulation of a number of specific hypotheses, some of which are listed below.

1. Ego functions may be described in clusters of traits representing behavioral types which may be correlated with genetic, psychodynamic, and social conditions.

2. The conditions during maturation and development leading to mental health when accurately described without theoretical biases, discloses a rich variety of parameters.

3. Freedom from serious physical illness in critical periods facilitates the development of mental health.

4. Early deprivation of, or excessive, communications are a factor in the type of later health or illness.

5. The constitutionally given quantity of drive energy and/or the influences leading to the capacity for direct discharge in action is involved in a type of mental health.

6. The capacities for the development of mature and so-called healthy behavior depends on a sequence of positive relations (regardless of techniques employed) with mother and then father.

7. Average intelligence with realistic self-appraisal facilitates the use of ego functions for goal directed behavior, albeit minimum goal-changing behavior.

8. A type of mental health may develop in individuals who pass smoothly from one phase of development to another without intervening or visible "crises."

9. Structurally a type of mental health may be associated with a psychological organization which has little access to unconscious processes in the form of fantasy or regression.

10. The capacity of the individual to maintain goal-seeking functions adequately is dependent upon a degree of compulsivity that is not crippling but at the same time maintains a consistent line of behavior.

11. Mental health is not only associated with a balance of internal forces but also with a subjective well-feeling and an objective capacity for adaptation.

12. The prerequisites of such balance are, among others, the experience of satisfactory gratifications in early life without too much frustration, the knowledge of definite limitations or boundaries placed on behavior with reasonable and consistent punishment, and firm sound early religious and ethical training.

13. Mental health is influenced by social and cultural factors, and various types of mental health require for maintenance a necessary environmental fit.

14. One attribute of mental health is a flexibility depending on the number of environments into which the personality type fits comfortably.

15. The number of identifications learned early furnishes a role repertoire suitable for a variety of environments. The capacity for multiple identifications is based on precursors not well defined.

16. Mental health as a definition requires the knowledge of the culturally derived values within subject-patient, observer-investigator, and the culture in which they exist.

17. Subjects comprising a mentally healthy group do not show absolute mental health, which does not exist. It is tempting to view mental health and illness as a continuum using traditional ways of thinking. It is far more sophisticated to analyze the reciprocal and sequential relations among multiple variables to obtain typologies with probabilistic boundaries.

There is no question that our understanding of normal psychodynamics has been facilitated by studies of psychopathology. We, at least, assume that the general and specific aspects of psychoanalytic theory are applicable to the healthy. However, the monotonous reiteration of theory based on the psychoanalysis of one or, at most, a few patients is not conducive to much more progress in our knowledge of health. We need sharply defined hypotheses for scientific observations, descriptions, and experimentation not only to further our knowledge of the abnormal but also of the varieties of *normal*. We cannot be content to discuss the latter as "only a question of values." Systematic psychodynamic studies in addition to other methods applicable to the entire field should be encouraged to define various kinds of mental health. Especially from the point of view of practical application we need to know who is sick and when and how he becomes well.

REFERENCES

1. MURRAY, H. A.: In nomine diaboli. New England Quart. 24:435, 1951.
2. GRINKER, R. R.: A study of mentally healthy young males (homoclites). Arch. Gen. Psychiat. 6:405, 1962.
3. FREUD, S.: Analysis terminable and interminable (1937). *In:* Collected Papers. London, Hogarth Press, 1950.
4. JONES, E.: The concept of a normal mind (1948). *In:* Halmos and Iliffe (eds.): Readings in General Psychology. New York, Philosophical Library, 1959.

5. GLOVER, E.: Medico-psychological aspects of normality. *In:* On the Early Development of Mind. New York, Internat. Universities Press, 1956.
6. BRUNER, J.: The cognitive consequences of early sensory deprivation. *In:* Solomon, P., et al, (eds.): Sensory Deprivation. Cambridge, Mass., Harvard University Press, 1961.
7. MICHAELS, J.: Disorders of Character: Persistent Enuresis, Juvenile Delinquency and Psychopathic Personality. Springfield, Ill., Charles C Thomas, 1955.
8. ERIKSON, E. H.: Growth and crises. *In:* Senn, M. J. (ed.): Symposium on the Healthy Personality. New York, Josiah Macy Jr Foundation, 1950.
9. FREUD, A.: Adolescence. *In:* Weinrub, J. (ed.): Recent Developments in Psychoanalytic Child Therapy. New York, Internat. Universities Press, 1960.
10. JOSSELYN, I.: The ego in adolescence. Am. J. Orthopsychiat. 24:223, 1954.
11. RAPAPORT, D.: The autonomy of the ego. Bull. Menninger Clin. 15:113, 1951.
12. KUBIE, L.: (a) The fundamental nature of the distinction between normality and neurosis. Psychoanal. Quart. 23:167, 1954. (b) Neurotic Distortion of the Creative Process. Lawrence, Kansas, Univ. of Kansas Press, 1958.
13. STEIN, M. I.: et al: Explorations in Creativity: Social and Psychological Factors Affecting the Creativity of Industrial Research Chemists. In preparation.
14. RAPAPORT, D.: The structure of psychoanalytic theory: A systematizing attempt. *In:* Kochs, S., (ed.): Psychology. A Study of a Science, Vol. 3. New York, McGraw-Hill, 1959.
15. ESCALONA, S., AND HEIDER, G. H.: Prediction and Outcome. New York, Basic Books, Inc., 1959.
16. RADO, S.: Psychoanalysis of Behavior: Collected Papers, Vol. I. New York, Grune & Stratton, 1956.
17. BIRNBACH, M.: Neo-Freudian Social Philosophy. Palo Alto, Stanford University Press, 1961.
18. ECKARDT, M.: Review of Birnbach.[17] Arch. Gen. Psychiat. 7:150, 1962.
19. MASSERMAN, J. H.: Faith and delusion in psychotherapy. Am. J. Psychiat. 110:324, 1953.
20. KLUCKHOHN, C., AND MURRAY, H. A.: Personality in Nature, Society and Culture. New York, Knopf, 1948.
21. SPIEGEL, J. P.: Some cultural aspects of transference and countertransference. *In:* Masserman, J. (ed.): Individual and Family Dynamics. New York, Grune & Stratton, 1959.
22. SILBER, E., HAMBURG, D. A., COELKO, G. W., MURPHEY, E. B., ROSENBERG, M., AND PEARLIN, I.: Adaptive behavior in competent adolescents: Coping with the anticipation of college. Arch. Gen. Psychiat. 5:517, 1961.
23. WESTLEY, W. A.: *In:* Galdston, I. (ed.): The Family in Contemporary Society. New York, Internat. Universities Press, 1958.
24. GRINKER, R. R.: On identification. Int. J. Psycho-Anal. 38:Pt. VI, 1957.

AN INVESTIGATION OF PARENTAL RECOGNITION OF CHILDREN'S DREAMS A PRELIMINARY REPORT

By IRVING MARKOWITZ, M.D., JOSEPH C. MARK, PH.D. AND STANLEY SEIDERMAN, M.S.S.S.

THIS STUDY has as its goal the active exploration of dreams, not merely in relation to the child who produced them, but in relation to his parents as well. The analytic literature is replete with clinical evidence that the child often acts out the neurotic needs of his parents; if this is so, and the parents are in truth communicating subliminally their own necessities to the child, they may be more aware of the similarities between their own mental processes and those of their children than they acknowledge. Some experimental verification of the impact of the neurotic needs of the parent on the child's life might therefore be demonstrated by investigating a parent's reaction to his child's dreams.

The procedure adopted was to test out how well a parent could recognize his or her child's dream when a portrayal of this dream was interspersed with similar portrayals of the dreams of 3 other children. The research was conducted in the course of a regular clinic program and had to meet the requirements that it be inexpensive and contribute to rather than hamper the treatment. The child's therapist, when eliciting a dream from a child, reported it in written form to the research coordinator with an interpretation of the dream. An artist then prepared black and white representations of the dream from the written material in an attempt to capture the imagery of the dream. After it had been ascertained that the child had not told his parents the dream, the parents were asked to participate in a "research effort," and were then shown a photostatic reproduction of the dream together with 3 other similar photostats of dreams from other children. Two sets of dreams were used in all, one set for female and one set for male children. The instructions to parents were as follows:

I. Here are some pictures about which I want you to make up a story. Tell me:
   (1) What's going on in the picture?
   (2) What led up to what's going on?
   (3) How will it end?
   Use your imagination and make it as dramatic as possible.

II. Which picture did you like best? Which picture did you like least?

III. Suppose each of these pictures represented a dream and one was a dream that your child had, which one is he/she most likely to have dreamt?

Pictures rather than the verbal accounts of the child were used because: (1.) The picture may more accurately depict the actual dream than the verbal story. (2) The nature of the test is more readily concealed from the parents, since they are unlikely to imagine that we would make the effort of turning their child's dream into a picture. (3) The picture offers greater latitude for self-expression than the mere words would.

Thus far in our study we have been able to evaluate responses to 25 such dream pictures.

One of the first problems in the study arose when it became obvious that parents were over-reacting to their own child's dream picture (which will hereafter be referred to as the target picture), but were not selecting it as their own child's when asked to make the choice. Some parents reacted with avoidance, horror and weeping when confronted with the target picture.*

One situation of many in which mother and father both gave very long stories in response to the target picture but chose a different card, follows:

For 2 years prior to treatment this 10 year old child had practically no communication with his mother except for extremely terse "yeahs" and nods of his head. In the first session, he presented a dream depicted in figure 1. In the actual dream, there were bunk beds as in life and the mother was sweeping a rat out from behind the beds. The brother was afraid of the rat while he

---

*Responsiveness as used in this study means all reactions such as observable tension, overt defensiveness, or lengthy stories. Acknowledgment is a form of responsiveness and is used to refer to a correct choice of the offspring's dream picture.

was not. Despite the fact that this dream was perhaps more poorly portrayed by the artist than any of the others, both mother and father gave long and involved emotional responses to the target picture while remaining completely neutral to the other dream pictures. The therapist's interpretation of this dream was essentially that he felt his mother was not willing to recognize that he was as brave or competent as his brother. Following this interpretation, the child immediately began speaking to his mother and has continued to communicate with her. When asked to choose which of the dreams was their child's, the parents did not acknowledge the target picture despite the lengthy story, and their marked emotional responses. Just as they have been unable to communicate with him in the waking state, so, too, they have been unable to acknowledge his dream production even when they both demonstrated marked reaction to the target picture.

A similar parental reaction to a target picture occurred in the case of a 12 year old girl who came into treatment extremely depressed and withdrawn. Following the first session she immediately began to improve in appearance, brightened up considerably, and was able to relate better to her family and friends. In the second session she told a dream of a monster chasing elves (fig. 2). Her association to the elves was that they might be Santa Claus's elves. This girl's mother had been compelled to marry the father of this out-of-wedlock girl. She was openly hostile to the child, but occasionally felt some distress at not being able to show more motherly feeling towards her. In the test situation, the mother liked her own child's dream the least. When asked to choose which dream was her child's, she looked at the target picture fixedly for 3 minutes and then began to weep. Despite this reaction, she chose instead

Fig. 1.

a more pleasant one. An unexpected dividend of this research procedure was that the mother began to show a different attitude toward her daughter, even making a choice between her daughter and her lover in favor of greater relatedness to the child. In a subsequent session after the daughter's symptoms had disappeared, the mother said that she had been aware that this was her child's dream but had been unwilling to acknowledge it. (For purposes of statistics, this situation is tabulated like similar ones as an unrecognized dream). This interaction of the parent to the target picture points up the possible therapeutic potentials of this procedure.

Since each parent was confronted with 4 picture dreams (one of which was their own child's), the chance of choosing correctly the target picture is 1 out of 4, that is 25 percent of the group could make correct choices by chance alone. When asked to select which dream picture they liked the least, since they had already chosen which they liked best, the chances of a correct selection was 1 of 3. The percentages of the actual choices made to date are shown in table 1.

All these choices were the first ones the parents made. Subsequent retractions, which have all been in the direction of the correct picture, had no effect on the statistics. These are somewhat greater than chance expectation, but we require more cases than we have at present to obtain statistical significance. If the present tends were extrapolated by increasing our N to approximately 40 cases we would then attain statistical significance in some categories.

Fig. 2.

TABLE 1.—*Number of Times a Mother or Father Selected the Target Picture in Three Different Categories*

Categories	Mother N = 24	Father N = 17
1. Chosen as picture liked best	2 (8%)	3 (18%)
2. Chosen as picture liked least	12* (50%)	8 (47%)
3. Chosen as picture that their child might dream.	10 (42%)	4 (24%)

*This score is the closest approach to statistical significance (.15 level of significance).

As listed in table 1, only 5 of 41 individual parents liked the target picture the best. Of these 5, one was a couple who also selected the target picture as their own child's. Another couple liked it best but only the mother acknowledged it as her child's. In this case, the father, a second step-father, did not. The last case was a widower who liked his child's dream best but did not identify it. Since these cases do not fit readily into any statistical pattern and all of them raise questions about the study, they will be discussed briefly:

Fig. 3. This dream picture was that of a 16 year old boy who was seen at the clinic because he had not attended school for a year and was extremely withdrawn and detached. Following 5 therapy session he returned to school. The parents were reluctant to participate in treatment and upon relief of the

Fig. 3.

child's symptoms prevailed upon him to leave the clinic even though he wished to continue. Their reasons for discontinuance were revealed to the school social worker 6 months later when the child again withdrew from school. When questioned by the school social worker about why they had left the clinic, they stated, "Yes, he had improved considerably both in returning to school and socially . . . Yes, the improvement was attributed to his attending the clinic but no son of ours is going to learn to say 'damn it and hell' from that doctor at the clinic." In the test situations they were unanimous in their choices. They liked their child's dream the best and they both chose it correctly. The father was somewhat conscious of his child's loneliness but brusquely brushed it aside. The mother had no awareness of the underlying feeling of the child's dream. They stated uniformly that, of course, any child of theirs would dream this kind of dream because they were a boating family and a child of theirs would naturally dream of the sea and boats. Thus their

Fig. 4.

awareness of the child's problem and their reasons for liking it and being willing to accept it was that the child was willing to stay in the strait jacket that they had imposed upon him both in his waking relationships and when he was asleep. They indicated clearly that just as they had withdrawn from the clinic when he began to exhibit behavior that was in any way unacceptable to them, so too would they withdraw their support if he did not do his dreaming in a format they approved.

Fig. 4. This dream was the only one in the entire series which we considered peer-oriented rather than adult-or parent-oriented. Both parents chose this dream picture as the one liked best. Only the mother, however, chose it as her child's. The natural father had committed suicide when the child was aged 2. The patient had 2 subsequent step-fathers, the second of whom is very devoted to children and keenly concerned about their growth and development. The step-father did not make the correct selection, but picked a less pleasant dream picture as being the child's dream. This is contrary to the general trend of fathers in the group who tended very often to pick more pleasant dreams as representing their children's productions than did the mothers. It is difficult to interpret the mother's choice. We do not know whether this dream was picked by the mother because she liked the thought of her son succeeding in the world separate from her, or because it placed little demand on her for further investment in him and condoned as well her past derelictions in relatedness to him.

FIG. 5.

Fig. 5. The father, a widower, chose the following card as the best liked. The dream picture is that of a disturbed adolescent boy who had spent all his time in sporadic therapeutic sessions alibiing and rationalizing his behavior and placing the onus of blame for his difficulties on a world apart from himself. He had been engaged in mutual brainwashing with his father in which each had almost succeeded in manipulating the other into psychotic-like behavior. Both had become increasingly depressed and divorced from the outside world in the course of their struggle to demean and debase one another. When in the course of therapy the boy did succeed in establishing something of a relationship with his therapist, the father made every attempt to sabotage the situation so as to re-establish control over his youngster. His choices were very discordant. He chose an unpleasant dream as a gay one but not as his son's which it was and then chose a pleasant dream as a sad one and attributed it to his son, which it was not. Thus, in the category of those who liked the dream picture best, there has not been any indication of good relationships between child and parent but there have been instead indications of sicker

FIG. 6

situations than the average in which the prognosis for relatedness between parent and child has been poor.

Figure 6 illustrates the difficulties in interpreting the data in a purely statistical way, but also shows, perhaps more than any other dream picture in the series, how closely parents are tied to their children's concealed communications. The child is a 10 year old boy reluctantly brought to the clinic by the mother for poor school performance and difficulties in peer relationships. The mother acknowledged her extreme competition with the therapist, and indicated in the first session that coming to the clinic represented a great personal defeat.

Fig. 7.

She is an intellectual but dowdy woman who has been highly successful in selling her distorted idealized image of her relationship to her children to some of the best newspapers and magazines in the country. She had had a total of 9 miscarriages in 11 pregnancies, and had a great need to deny any evidence of failure as a mother. The school, however, constantly pointed out her son's unhappiness and his lack of success in the adult world, although she claimed he comprehended it better than most children. The father is an unsuccessful teacher who has been compelled to leave his work because of a psychotic breakdown. The child was desperately trying to maintain the role established for him by his mother and found great difficulty in revealing anything about himself that was discordant with the stereotype established by her. He is a master of passive resistance and is adept at fulfilling the minimal requirements expected of him without producing anything worthwhile. In the test situation the mother showed no affect whatsoever about any of the cards except her son's dream picture, upon which she commented with her only display of feeling, "This is definitely a dream and not a reality." The father stated on seeing his son's dream picture, also with feeling, "I seem to remember this type of nightmare from my own childhood." However, he selected another card as his son's dream (fig. 7) because he felt that his son would be more concerned with the numbers depicted on the card rather than the spiders actually depicted in the dream. The son, he knew, was doing badly in arithmetic. He stated of the dream selected, that his son was "kicking off the numbers," a quality not in either card (fig. 8) but rather in the actual dream narrated to the therapist. The son used almost the exact words to describe his fight against the spiders that the father used to describe the situation in the card he chose. These emotional reactions indicated a definite degree of awareness of the child's problems even though acknowledgment did not actually take place—an awareness frequently masked throughout the study. (Whenever the tester has observed marked emotional responses, it has always been around the child's dream picture, rather than any other). When the child was told the choices made by his parents, he wept more copiously than he ever had. His relationships to his parents have since shown improvement. The most recent dream narrated by this child is as follows: "Everything is all right and every

Fig. 8.

once in a while this roach comes along but I have a fly swatter and I swat it and it goes away and everything is all right." The mother who has improved in therapy along with her son chose this second dream correctly and also liked it the best. The father who has not improved in therapy did not choose the second dream correctly. He did like it the best but chose an even more pleasant one as his own child's, because it indicated great progress which he knew his son had made.

DISCUSSION

We shall define the dream as the emergence of data and affects prepared under the conditions of sleep for the anticipated demands of exigent reality. On this basis, it may be that reality determines directly not only the content of the dream, but its format as well. If the dreamer has been able to be straightforward in the waking state, he should be able to be almost as straightforward in the dream state. If he has been compelled to be devious in the waking state, he should be compelled to be as or more devious in the dream state. The altered nature of the sleeping sensorium as well as the immediate lack of adequate feedback should prevent his formulations from being as exact, concise, or definitive as they might have been in the waking state. His dreaming formulations have to be strategic rather than tactical and are therefore more comprehensive, fluid, and disordered than they would be in the waking state. The individual who has had the greater feeling of acceptance by his possible protagonists and antagonists is likely to be more open in his dream production than the individual whose gambits in life have failed. The child who can be so brazen as to decapitate his parents in his dreams has generally been able to declare his hostility more openly when awake than the child who does not. Few of our children are able to express their hostility so directly. One child who sugar coated her venom to her parents when awake poured hot chocolate on her dying mother in a dream (fig. 8).

Is it that the straightforward child dreamer can more readily communicate his messages to his parents because open and honest communication has been established between them in the waking state? It is our feeling that the basis for responsiveness, regardless of acknowledgment of the parent to the child's dream picture, is the parent's awareness of the role he has had in establishing the child's patterns. It may also depend upon the parent's ability to ferret out the customary devices that the child has futilely employed to escape the parent's designs. If the parent knows that he has been relatively honest in his relationships with his offspring, so that in turn his offspring can

afford to be relatively honest with him, then he will be more responsive to the child's dreams because they are congruent with the kind
of life relationship that has been established between them. If he has
been dishonest in his life relationship with his child, so as to produce
definite kinds of deceit patterns on the part of his child, then he too
will be more responsive to these because they are congruent with the
nature of the game going on between them. It follows from this
hypothesis that if the child moves away sufficiently from the patterns
imposed by the parents' activities and to which they have become accustomed, then the child's dreams may become unrecognizable by the
parents. If, for example, a parent and child both become healthier in
the course of therapy, then from this hypothesis they should still be
able to respond to one another's dreams. If, however, one changes and
the other remains static, then responsiveness to each other's dreams
should become less than if they had grown together. Any escape of
one human being from the design imposed by another would make
them relatively less capable of responsiveness to each other's communications whether awake or asleep. We may find that those parents
and children most cloistered together are most responsive to one another's dreams.

Many directions of research are suggested by the hypotheses that
have just been mentioned. We are contemplating, for example, asking
children to identify their parents' dream pictures. We should like, too,
to be able to determine whether or not parents are as able to respond
to later dreams in therapy as well as they are able to respond to earlier
ones. With patients in therapy we might expect two things to occur:
the dream in mid-therapy would be less oriented to direct conflict
between the parents and child and more geared to the therapeutic conflict; also, at the end of successful therapy the child should be healthier
and more straightforward in his productions with greater feelings of
acceptance and acceptability. If the parents were able to grow apace
with their child even though their child becomes independent of them,
either through therapy or beneficial life experience, they should be as
responsive to one another's later dreams as they were to the earlier. We
would anticipate two peaks of responsiveness, one on the initially sick
basis and another on a healthier plane. If unchanging parents did not
continue to respond to their child's later dreams as they did to the earlier,
this might corroborate the hypothesis that their initial responsiveness
was dependent on the awareness of their own role in the battle for
supremacy between parent and child.

We have been able at this juncture to give very few parents repeated dream pictures in an attempt to demonstrate this point. Some of the technical difficulties have been that, having given a parent 1 dream picture, the experiment is then partially invalidated since the parents may already have surmised that the pictures are in fact, dreams. In the case of one set of parents, we gave them 2 more of their child's dream pictures with 2 additional dream pictures that they had never seen before. The mother in this situation, who had previously chosen correctly the first target picture, chose the other 2 quite unerringly. Her husband who had participated in the therapeutic procedure only sporadically and with great reluctance guessed the first quite accurately, and when asked to pick 2 of 4, he picked only 1 of the later ones. This mother is a woman of great potentiality who had never been able to realize her capabilities because of compulsive deference to the sham maturity of her pompous, alcoholic husband. The youngster in question is a 10 year old girl described by her school teacher as being "like paste," completely unrelated to her peers and despite great intelligence almost 2 years retarded in school. She has, however, been promoted because of her father's standing in the community. In an early dream of the mother's she, an incompetent driver, saw herself having to take control of a moving car with her daughter in the back seat. When she was questioned by the therapist as to where the father was, she wept and revealed all of the feelings and aspirations which she had felt she had to keep submerged in order to survive. The father's refusal to participate in the therapy situation has been rationalized by the great suffering in his life which he relies upon to place him outside the need for involvement with his child, his wife, and the world. Both parents recognized the child's early target picture with ease. The willingness of this mother to perceive accurately her child's activity and to acknowledge all her child's target pictures is very likely related to the great similarity of their common struggle. The mother, much though she may outwardly work to extricate her child from the same difficulties in which she has found herself all her life, has succeeded only in submerging her child's identity further and further.

Other directions for research suggested by some of these hypotheses would be the study of correlations between responsiveness to girl's dreams by mothers or girls' dreams by fathers as opposed to responsiveness to boys' dreams by both parents. We should also like to do a correlation between the degree of illness of the child and the responsiveness of the parents. We propose also, to do objective assessments of the emotional intensity of the responses through direct observation, analysis of the stories, and the use of various physiologic devices. (P.G.R., Respiratory rate, etc.) Another project we have in mind is to correlate the stories told by different categories of parents with the interpretations of the therapists.

It is our feeling that the clinic population does not differ appreciably from the general population, in respect to the factors measured. A control group might be desirable to prove or disprove this point.

SUMMARY OF QUANTITATIVE DATA ON THE FIRST 25 DREAM PICTURES

1. Both bother and father when asked to select the dream picture they liked the least selected their own child's dream to a better than chance degree.

2. Mothers acknowledged the target picture as their own child's in 42 per cent of the cases; whereas father did so in only 24 per cent of the cases.

3. Only 2 mothers of the 24 who liked their own child's dream the most picked it correctly as their own child's. Only one father of 17 did so. This involved only 2 dream pictures. Only 2 other mothers and 1 father picked an incorrect dream as the one they liked best and then chose it as the one their child would dream.

4. Only 3 of the 24 mothers who liked their child's dream least picked it as their own child's. Only 1 father fell into this category. Only 2 other mothers and 1 father picked an incorrect dream as the one they liked least and then chose it as the one their child would dream.

5. Those parents who picked the target picture as the most unpleasant, tended to pick a slightly more pleasant dream as their own child's.

6. Mothers who did select the target picture as their own child's were more willing to select unpleasant pictures to make the correct choice than fathers were.

Our present quantitative data do not justify any sweeping conclusions. The identification of a dream as their own child's seems fraught with danger for most of the parents, perhaps because they fear the dreams may accurately mirror the uglier aspects of their relationship with their children. Mothers seem more willing to identify unpleasant pictures as their child's than do fathers. This may be either because mothers are more perceptive of their children's feelings, or because they are less needful of maintaining an inflated picture of their infallibility as parents. The tendency in this series was for parents to avoid expressing great liking or great dislike for their own child's dream. When they would select their own child's dream as the one they liked least, they tended then to pick a more pleasant dream as the one they thought was their child's.

We believe that parents are more responsive to their own child's dream than the dreams of other children, and that the clinical material offers tentative corroboration of the hypothesis that this responsiveness is due to patterns of congruent development common to both parents and child. Sleep does not permit children to escape the patterns of social reality, at least not in the dreams they narrate to the therapists.

Discussion by James Toolan, M.D.

DR. MARKOWITZ and his collaborators have attempted a most interesting experiment—viz., to see whether parents are more responsive to their own child's dream than the dreams of other children. This is certainly a worthwhile project for, as they state, no similar studies have been reported. Early in their paper they admit that there are too few cases to enable them to analyze their figures as being statistically significant. They conclude "We believe that parents are more responsive to their own child's dream than the dreams of other children."

We could not object to this modest statement and it is one that would have been anticipated. However, they go on to state "We feel that the clinical material offers tentative corroboration of the hypothesis that responsiveness is due to patterns of congruent development common to both parents and child. We feel that the clinical evidence indicates that sleep does not permit children to escape the patterns of social reality, at least not in the dreams they narrate to the therapists.

Although these conclusions are labelled as tentative they represent, nevertheless, sweeping generalizations. Let us examine the data to see whether or not such statements can be supported. Dr. Markowitz stated that it was ascertained that the child had not told the dream or a similar one to the parents. How was this ascertained? Presumably from the child since the parents were not informed of the true nature of the experiment. Even if this were so we must bear in mind that many dreams of children are repetitive as to content and form to a greater degree than adults' dreams. It is possible, therefore, that the parents might have been familiar with these dreams by simple recognition. There are at least two other possible alternative explanations: First, the authors quote Griffiths as stating that most unpleasant dreams of children resemble remembered fears. If this be so might not the parents have been aware of these fears? Second, we know that people use similar defensive operations in their dreams as in waking life. Every analyst soon begins to be quite familiar with the dream patterns of his patients. This would enable parents, therefore, more easily to recognize their own child's dreams. The authors also state that "mothers seem more willing to identify unpleasant pictures as their child's than do fathers and that mothers more frequently recognize their child's dreams than do the fathers. This may be either because mothers are more perceptive of their children's feelings or

because they are less needful of maintaining an inflated picture of their infallibility as parents." Once again, perhaps, this may be because mothers have closer
contact with the child and thus more easily recognize its dreams.

Let us study some further material. Dr. Markowitz offers the following as his
definition of a dream "the emergence of data and affects prepared under the
conditions of sleep for the anticipated demands of exigent reality." He adds
"on this basis, it may be that reality determines directly not only the content of
the dreams, but its format as well." This definition is very close to that offered by
Ullman, but overlooks the unconscious processes of the dream. This is important,
for Dr. Markowitz states that the responsiveness of parent to child's dream is
based on the parent's awareness of the role he has had in establishing the child's
patterns—as well as the parents ability to ferret out the customary devices that
the child has futilely employed to escape the parents' designs. If the parents are
honest and the child is so in turn then they will be more responsive to the
child's dreams as congruent with the kind of life relationship that has been
established between them [and vice versa]. If the child moves away sufficiently
from the patterns inmposed by the parents' activities and to which they have
become accustomed then the child's dream may become unrecognizable by the
parents.

This interpretation is based on a definite philosophy or parent—child relationship—one based apparently on hostility, competition, honesty and dishonesty. It
ignores the child's contribution to the reaction of his parents and to the genesis
of his own neurosis. Furthermore, it overlooks the entire unconscious processes
of both parents and child. If these statements are unproved then further doubt
is cast upon the interpretations offered.

Dr. Markowitz also stated that "the identification of a dream as their own
child's seems fraught with danger for most of the parents, perhaps because they
fear the dreams may accurately mirror the uglier aspects of their relationship with
their children." But mothers acknowledge the target picture as their own child's
in 42 per cent of the cases—twice the expectation of chance, despite denial (as
was the case of 1 parent) on a conscious level due to the reaction to the
researcher, or unconscious fear of facing the extent of their own child's illness.

In another section the authors state "in the category of those who liked the
dream picture best there has not been any indication of good relationships
between child and parent but there have been instead, indications of abnormal
situations in which the prognosis for relationship between parent and child has
been poor."

The data do not support this point. Figure 7 is not necessarily unpleasant and
figure 8 certainly is far from unpleasant. Thus it is not strange the parents liked
those particular dreams.

The authors mention the possible therapeutic potentials of this technique. I
would agree that these may be present for both child and parents although ethical
considerations should be faced. If dreams of parents and children are exposed to
each other are we not violating the principle of confidential relationship? I believe
both parties should be informed as to the nature of the study. I see no reason
not to inform the parents of the true nature of the experiment. It might make it
a more useful study rather than proving a deterrent.

In essence Dr. Markowitz has described a preliminary report on an intriguing subject. As the authors state, much remains to be done: choice of a dream, study at different stages of therapy, sexual differences, therapeutic potentials, and I might add the separation of the parents. The study of dreams of married couples and siblings would also prove of interest. I do not believe, however, that their data allows for the acceptance of more than the statement "We believe that parents are more responsive to their own child's dream than the dreams of other children." The remainder is as yet not proved.

THE DISSOCIATION-ASSOCIATION
CONTINUUM

By HERBERT SPIEGEL, M.D.

THE PHENOMENON of dissociation has been so closely linked with repression that there is a tendency to overlook the two-directional* aspect of this fragmentation process. The fragmentation can occur *from* central awareness to the unconscious, or it can surge from the unconscious *toward* central awareness. The speed, patterning, threshold, intensity and duration of the fragmentation from and toward central awareness are some of the variables that contribute to the complexity of the transition.

Clinically, it has been observed that levels of awareness are in a more or less constant state of flux and even at a given level in the same person, there occur variations in the extent of peripheral awareness as well as the depth of perception.

When Freud expanded the Cartesian dualism into a topographical concept of conscious/unconscious, he postulated that "repression proceeds from the ego, which . . . . does not wish to be a party to an instinct cathexis originating in the id. Through repression the ego accomplishes the exclusion from consciousness of the idea which was the carrier of the unwelcome impulse."

He further stated, "Repression takes place in two distinct situations, namely, when an unwelcome instinctual impulse is aroused by an external perception, and when the impulse arises internally without such provocation."[1]

He then emphasized that the theory of repression became the foundation stone of our understanding of the neuroses.[2] Thus by definition repression refers specifically to opposing undesirable instinctual demands.

---

*Actually a multidirectional nonlinear concept in a 3 dimensional sense would convey my thesis more accurately, but for exposition purposes in this paper the dimensional concept serves adequately.

In recent years, the input/output concept has become an increasingly used paradigm for experimental and clinical work in human behavior. Miller and his group have reported on their studies of input overload with the various adjustive fragmentation processes that can occur before the breakdown of any given system.[7] Hebb and others have opened a whole new field of investigation in studying the many aspects of fragmentation that occur when sensory input is experimentally altered and reduced.[3]

When Magoun described the inhibiting and facilitating roles of the RAS in controlling the spino-motor outflow, a new era opened in neurophysiology.[6] His co-worker Lindsley has proposed that such seemingly diverse phenomena as sensory deprivation, sensory distortion and sensory overload have *one* regulatory process, the reticular formation. And he conceives of it as a regulator and monitor for incoming and outgoing messages, adjusting to its surges as well as to its gradual shifts in levels of excitation, thus functioning as part of the learning process as well as facilitating the elementary perceptual processes.[4] In a sense, this is an open invitation for clinicians to reexamine their hypotheses and "stretch" them when possible in the direction of this opportunity for coordinating observable human behavior with neurophysiological concepts.

In this connection, Whyte has recently stated that the next development in psychoanalytic conceptions will be in terms of biological coordination with the differentiated aspects of the "unity of the mind." He feels that "it is unlikely that the human mind can comprehend its own states of coordination merely by attention to its awareness, or even inferences therefrom, without the aid of guiding principles of organic order gained from the objective study of the organisms." Whereas Freud focused his attention on *conflict* in the psyche, the next development will, he predicts, be in the direction of *order* in the organism illustrated in the human mind. Or, to put it another way, "What is the source and character of organic coordination?"[8]

This thesis then is in the service of reordering our clinical thinking toward a meeting ground with the neurophysiologist.

CLASSIFICATION

From an operational point of view this continuum concept of dissociation-association can be divided into 3 categories, each of which subdivides into input and output, making a total of 6 distinct yet overlapping types (fig. 1), as follows:

(1a) Selective Inattention (Repression)

This includes any fragmentation process that serves to defend against anxiety and fear (or undesirable instinctual demands): e.g., amnesia, neurotic and psychotic dissociations, inspirational experiences.

(1b) Expressive Implementation of the Dissociated

This category is also in the service of fear and anxiety, but its main function is to reinforce and consolidate that which has already been dissociated or repressed e.g., tics, dreams, awakening from sleep, phobias, compulsive triad observable in the posthypnotic suggestion.

(2a) Marginal Awareness

Anxiety is not prominent here. During the automatic scanning that goes on constantly various stimuli are perceived outside of central awareness: e.g., subliminal perception, impact of all afferent exteroceptive and enteroceptive stimuli.

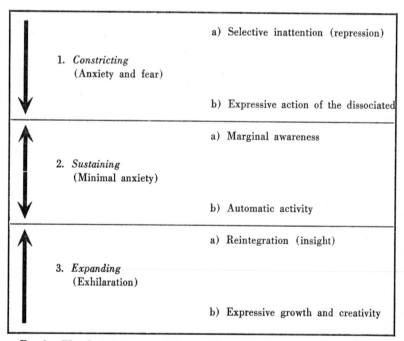

FIG. 1.—*The dissociation-association continuum.*

(2b) Automatic Activity

This is predominantly for facilitating central concentration elsewhere: e.g., inattention or forgetting necessary to establish focal attention, working at routine tasks while concentrating on something else.

(3a) Expressive Uncovering with Reintegration (Insight)

Here the dissociated fragments surge toward awareness and toward reintegration: e.g., dreams, slips of speech, gestures, marginal thoughts, free associations.

(3b) Expressive Growth

Here the dissociated experience is toward *new* concepts and actions: e.g., spontaneity, growth, maturation, creativity.

Categories (1a) and (1b) are in the service of limiting anxiety and fear and are therefore characteristically constrictive. They also tend to be compulsive and rigid.

Categories (2a) and (2b) are in the service of sustaining an already established adaptive level and typically manifest little or no evidence of anxiety.

Categories (3a) and (3b) are in the service of reintegration, growth and development (associated with various degrees of anxiety) leading to a sense of well-being, exhilaration or euphoria. These are characteristically expansive, and are also frequently characterized by tractability, curiosity, and flexibility of response.

This two-directional view permits a more precise operational use of concepts pertaining to levels of consciousness.

OBJECTION TO THE REPRESSION THESIS

If we use the repression concept only, then (1) we imply that dissociation is due to libidinal and/or aggressive conflict exclusively, (2) that what emerges from the unconscious is necessarily chaotic, (3) we then tend to interpret the dissociated phenomena in the sustaining category (2a and 2b) as manifestations of conflict rather than coincidental attention elsewhere, and (4) conceptually, we will have difficulties in allowing for growth and creative expressions as *new* emergent experiences.

While the dualistic repression concept tends to make somewhat static an ever-changing dynamic process, this D-A continuum concept is more dynamic in that it allows for a continuum of action, by acknowledging constant, characteristic changes going on all the time, with maximum awareness as a transitory experience occurring at various times. It also focuses on varying facets of the already existing multileveled unconscious complex.

Actually, the repression phenomena per se are incorporated in this thesis in types (1a), (1b) and (3a).

Value of this Operational Concept

This formulation not only incorporates the phenomenon of repression, but also allows for clinical identification of *other* manifestations of the ever-changing levels and dimensions of consciousness.

Further, this two-directional concept sharpens our sensitivity to the general nature of the mainstream—or the operative belief system—from which or toward which the fragmentation process operates. If the mainstream referred to is the cosmos, then we can safely assume that all individual perception and action is fragmentary or dissociated in relation to the cosmos. But if the mainstream is not the cosmos, but rather a more limited area encompassing man's immediate environment in relation to others, then various theories may be used as media for interpreting his exposure to that fragment of the universe.

If the theory happens to assume the form of psychological man as conceptualized by the libido theory, then percepts and actions can be identified as authentic or inauthentic, associated or dissociated, by the criteria established within that conceptual framework.

If the patient under study chooses to establish his own set of assumptions and beliefs as the main body for reference, then what is identified as authentic and associated will depend on the criteria he establishes for his belief system.

Our task then is to (1) establish and clarify with the patient what is the nature of the "whole" so that fragments can be identified, and (2) to determine the direction of the fragmentation process being observed. Is the direction toward disintegration, or toward integration, or toward growth and creativity.

Uses of this Thesis

To illustrate the usefulness of this continuum thesis, consider this example. Recently, a patient was reviewing a series of events and reflecting upon the nature of his actions. As he protested and attempted to deny the self-destructive implications of his participation, he raised his right index finger to the side of his head. Suddenly, he perceived the pointed finger as a gun to his head. His face flushed with anxiety then embarrassment. He then broke into laughter with a recognition of this unexpected moment of coalescence and insight that expanded his awareness. Following this he described a sense of relief, then exhilaration (type 3a, Reintegration—Insight).

However, if this gesture had occurred as part of a personal ritual to reinforce symbolically his effort to think, and if the gesture had been accompanied with a quality of mild surprise but not much anxiety with an effort at quick accommodation and subsequent puzzlement, this would simply have been an attempt to cope with a marginal perception that was just at the threshold of awareness but not quite perceived (type 2a Marginal Awareness).

If the finger-to-head unit of behavior had been accompanied with anxiety and/or fear with transitory awareness of conflict and quick resolution this would indicate repression and denial (type 1a, Selective Inattention—Repression).

Now, another illustration. For example, a person suddenly awakes from his sleep. If this occurs during a dream experience that threatens the emergence of a repressed thought, then the sudden awakening is in the service of maintaining the status quo of that which is dissociated (type 1b, Expressive Action of the Dissociated). If this happens at a time when the body temperature is lowering because the blanket fell off, then the awakening is simply a corrective maneuver to cover up with the blanket and maintain body temperature, thus enabling the person to go on with his sleep (type 2b, Automatic Activity).

However, if during the sleep when reshuffling of thoughts can occur, a new idea or new perspective crystallizes and leads to a feeling of satisfaction, achievement, or even euphoria, the sudden awakening reflects an emergence of a new or creative idea that supercedes the need for sleep at that time (type 3b, Expressive Growth and Creativity).

Dr. Otto Loewi revealed that the core of his Nobel Prize-winning theory of chemical transmission of the nerve impulse surged into his awareness during his sleep one night in 1920. He awoke, jotted a few notes, then fell asleep again. The next day he was unable to decipher his notes. The following night, at 3:00 a.m., the idea suddenly returned and he awoke with a design for an experiment which included a recovery of an hypothesis that he had formulated and discarded 17 years before. He went directly to his laboratory and performed a simple experiment which became the foundation of his theory. He later reflected that, had he considered this clearly in the daytime, he would undoubtedly have rejected this experiment, and observed that it was fortunate that he "did not think but acted."[5]

If in analyzing the data, the repression thesis alone is used as the referent, the patient would be unnecessarily burdened with expectations of deeper meaning in types 2a and 2b when actually the hand gesture and the sudden awakening are simply accommodating or corrective maneuvers to maintain the established functional state of the moment.

Similarly, if repression and conflict are assumed to be always a factor in dissociated phenomena, then the occasions of expressive growth and creativity are prone to be subject to deep psychopathological exploration when no pathological substrate exists in the first place. It is here that spontaneous and creative actions can be iatrogenically contaminated and natural spontaneous human action can be "psychiatrized" into inaction. In the transference-countertransference phenomenon, the patient can experience this iatrogenic interference as a reinforcement of arbitrary irrational parental control.

SUMMARY

This paper attempts to reformulate a perspective on the fragmentation—coalescence process that releases it from its almost exclusive subordination to the dualistic repression concept of the libido theory.

It allows for its operational usefulness outside of this framework as well, by conceptualizing operational categories of awareness on a continuum extending from (1) constricting to (2) sustaining to (3) expanding categories, each of which is subdivided into input and output aspects: constricting into (1a) selective inattention (repression), and (1b) expressive action of the dissociated; sustaining into (2a) marginal awareness, and (2b) automatic activity; and expanding into (3a) reintegration (insight), and (3b) expressive growth and creativity.

This formulation enables greater flexibility in exploring alternative ways of understanding clinical data; and by this means veers away from the determinism that has enveloped much of our psychodynamic thinking and allows for greater use of the probabalistic, nonlinear conceptualizations of modern day science.

REFERENCES

1. FREUD, S.: The Problem of Anxiety, Chapt. 2. New York, W. W. Norton & Co., Inc., 1936.

2. ———: An Autobiographical Study, Chapt. 3. London, Hogarth Press, Ltd., 1952.
3. HEBB, D. O.: The Organization of Behavior. New York, Wiley & Co., 1949.
4. LINDSLEY, D. B.: Common factors in sensory deprivation, sensory distortion, and sensory overload. *In:* Solomon, et al. (ed.): Sensory Deprivation, Chapt. 12. Cambridge, Mass., Harvard Univ. Press, 1961.
5. LOEWI, O.: An autobiographic sketch. Persp. Biol. & Med. 4:1-25, 1960.
6. MAGOUN, H. W.: The ascending reticular system and wakefulness. *In:* J. F. Delafresnaye, et al. (ed.): Brain Mechanisms and Consciousness. Oxford Press, Blackwell, 1954.
7. MILLER, J. A.: Information input overload and psychopathology. Am. J. Psychiat. 116:695-705, 1960.
8. WHYTE, L. L.: The Unconscious before Freud. New York, Basic Books, Inc., 1960.

ELECTRONIC COMPUTERS IN
PSYCHOANALYTIC RESEARCH

By JOSEPH JAFFE, M.D.

ELECTRONIC computers, which possess superhuman capacity for the processing of information, have already revolutionized general medicine, as in the automated hospital and automated diagnosis. They are a major tool in investigations of neural processes. They have had a profound impact upon biochemistry and physiology, both in the rapid reduction of miles of recorded data, and in the simulation of complex dynamic systems. In the behavioral sciences, we now have models of human interaction ranging in size from small groups to whole societies, playing out their potentialities in a compressed time scale, within the computer. Automated libraries are already with us, in which thousands of publications may be perused in a few seconds in answer to our questions, and there is progress in machine translation of foreign languages. But perhaps the most exciting development is the computer simulation of human cognitive processes. We have finally come to realize that "the digital computer is a device for manipulating symbols of any kind, in any way."[19]

It has often occurred to me, after years of listening to a patient's speech, that my human limitations as an information-handler might in some way contribute to the length of the analytic procedure. I have attempted to remedy this in several ways. First, by a lengthy personal analysis, to free myself from acquired blocks to hearing certain things the patient was saying. Secondly, by hundreds of hours of supervision, in an effort to increase my sensitivity to certain categories of behavior. And thirdly, by continuous study of the developments in theory and technique, in an attempt to increase my general skill. But the nagging question has always remained, "If my brain were

*This research was supported, in part, by Grants M-4548 and M-4571 from the National Institute of Mental Health .

capable of instantly remembering and comparing everything the patient had ever said over the course of the years, and the exact context of each idea, and the emotional flavor of each such occurrence, and how I reacted to each such event, might I be of more use to this person?" In short, do our existing practices of training and education find one of their limitations in the information-processing abilities of the analyst?[18]

A related question is, "In psychoanalytic research, why can we not study the complete process, in detail, word by word for hundreds of hours, instead of speculating on the basis of anecdotal reports or initial and final evaluations? Just a few years ago the tape recorder was hailed as the instrument which would finally permit such objective studies in our discipline. This early enthusiasm has faded. One soon learns that it takes precisely an hour to listen to an hour of magnetic tape, many hours to transcribe it accurately, and many additional hours to subject it to the simplest of quantifying procedures. Thus, research reports of tape-recorded therapy are often as anecdotal as in prerecording days, and relatively few sessions have ever been subjected to detailed exhaustive analysis by quantitative methods. The problem, simply stated, is the overwhelming mass of data that modern recording technology has made available to us. It is our personal area of that more general problem known as "the information explosion."

Suppose we confine ourselves to the typescript alone. Let us multiply the famous "fifty-minute hour" by 3 or 4 times a week over a period of 2 years. We already have a record in the neighborhood of two million words, and this for a single patient! When the investigator is faced with this torrent of information, discouragement sets in, and libraries of tape-recordings accumulate. The remaining undaunted few then begin sampling, to reduce the data to manageable size. One investigator concentrates on the "first five minutes," another on the initial interview, another on only one of the participants. Other solutions are to select only every tenth or twentieth session in a series, or to study every interview but to confine oneself to "brief psychotherapy." Finally, one may neglect the literal process completely and evaluate the patient before and after, treating the therapy session itself as a "black box."[7-9, 14, 17, 21-a, 23, 27]

Can electronic computers, with their incredible capacities for information handling, help us tackle the problem which has generated so many partial solutions? I do not refer to the use of computer programs for doing correlations, factor analysis or other statistical procedures. These are already standard tools of behavioral scientists,[2] but the computers enter the process only at the very end, to do the statistical evaluation. In contrast to this, I wish to call attention to the use of computers for the actual identification and classification of relevant behavior, which it will then proceed to process. Speech is one area in which this is possible since it is already categorized into meaningful units, i.e., words. Given an appropriate transcript, the computer can read, recognize and remember words. Thus, our knowledge of language organization may be written into the machine instructions, and the human content analyst is relieved of the task. This use of computers has been most popularized in its applications to machine translation, and perhaps to a lesser extent in information retrieval projects, such as the automatic writing of literature abstracts.[16] Some of its possible applications to psychoanalytic research are being investigated at The William Alanson White Institute and will be briefly outlined.

Lexical analysis: If, instead of making a typescript of our tape-recorded analytic session, we invest the same amount of time and effort, on an identical keyboard, in punching our transcript on cards or on paper tape, we have a record which can be read by a computer, i.e., a machine-readable text. The further essential requirement is an analyst who can convert his clinical insights into the language of programmed instructions. The computer then does the scanning, counting and tabulation of any number of research "hunches" in a matter of seconds. This was suggested by Dr. David Rioch, and we are in the process of trying it out. Let us begin with a gross illustration, for example, a simple word count, performed completely automatically. The machine lists all the different words in the interview in alphabetical order, and the number of times that each word was repeated. This dictionary gives us a quantitative index of the major themes discussed, which may be automatically compared from one session to another. This is the frequency type of content analysis used in studies of political propaganda and literary style. It is inferred that the frequency of usage is an index of the importance of a concept.[22] You may think, of course, that nonusage is another such index, and I'll come to that later.

Next, our computer program automatically rearranges the accumulated dictionary in descending order from the most frequently to the most rarely occurring words. We usually find in such lists, that the words at the head of a list are just what you might expect, i.e., the articles, prepositions and pronouns that intervene among the more interesting, but less often repeated words. We rapidly look farther down the list of each interview to see if items like "angry," "hurt," "father," "compete," occur as often in one session as in another. But if we instruct the computer to make separate lists for the therapist and patient verbalizations, provocative differences emerge. For example, in Interview III from *The Initial Interview in Psychiatric Practice* by Gill, Newman and Redlich,[7] the 2 participants' counts were produced by the IBM 704. If we confine ourselves to those words which show at least a 5 to 1 ratio in favor of one or the other participant, we get a picture of the parts of the vocabulary that do not overlap to any great extent. The first 14 entries on the 2 lists read as follows:

Therapist	*Patient*
You	I
your	my
mmhmm	a
mm	me
hmm	want
real	mean
these	I'm
sort	seem
who	if
possibility	can't
tell	own
which	there
we	because
yeah	isn't

One might summarize as follows:

Therapist: you, your (references to the patient)
we (reference to the interpersonal relationship)
mmhmm, mm, hmm, yeah (listener's role)
real, possibility (reality, hypothesizing)
who, which, tell, sort (questioning)
these (spatially close specification or categorization)

Patient: I, my, me, I'm, own (self references)
want, can't (frustration)
mean, seem, if (concern with reality)
a (general reference to a class of things, as opposed to "the")
there (spatially distant specification or categorization)

The flavor of the interview comes through in this frankly posthoc and rough classification. A schizophrenic patient is struggling, unsuccessfully, to make sense out of a bewildering set of subjective experiences. She is using logical operations to integrate a vague generalized environment and an egocentric orientation. The results do not make sense. The therapist is the inquirer into the patient's preoccupation and acts to expand her hypothesizing in the direction of his own picture of the world. He also tries to make his reasoning a part of her system. But one may ask, "What would happen to these lists if the patient's delusion were to become more fixed and adaptive?" "What would happen, on the other hand, if she began to accept the therapist's hypotheses and relinquished her own?"

Time will not permit a detailed review of the various investigations that may be developed using such lists. To mention but a few, the early linguistic studies of diagnostic categories[1] may now be pursued efficiently. "Denial language"[10, 13, 28] may be quite evident as when the words, "don't, know" or "in, other, words" appear prominently on the lists, providing hints as to the use of such expressions as security operations. The early interest in the shape of these frequency distributions in schizophrenic language[29] has recently been revived.[21] Some of the word categories describe cognitive dimensions[3] and are clues to the speaker's working hypotheses. For example, the high incidence of self-reference in the schizophrenic speech described might be understood as the patient's use of herself as a reference point in organizing her environment, as seen in developmental studies.[20]

We may further tailor the computer to the unique patient-therapist dyad. Let us suppose that a cumulative dictionary is built up in the computer memory composed of all the words that are spoken in the therapy. In this case the memory would contain the verbal history of the discourse. By comparing every incoming word with the dictionary, the computer could indicate subsequent points at which words were introduced that had not occurred previously in the relationship. Since both patient and therapist have displayed most of their common working vocabulary within several sessions, any influx of new vocabulary might represent a turning point in therapy, or the uncovering of new data. We have already begun investigating such "decision points" or "changes of subject" and found that they tend to precede bursts of "hemming and hawing" (filled pauses) in conversations.[11] This makes sense since such vocal gestures give the impression of "stalling for time," and may allow for restoration of psychological equilibrium following a shift in perspective.

Let us now see how we might ascertain "what a patient might have said but didn't." We may prepare the machine memory with a dictionary, composed of the normative vocabulary pattern of other patients, equivalent in education, intelligence and socioeconomic background. The computer might then tell us what themes were not discussed, by comparing the patient's actual productions with the criterion in the memory. Now it might be going too far to suggest this as an analogue of repression. But may I pose the following question: "To what extent do we suspect repression or dissociation, when the patient fails to say things, in a given context, that other patients say, or that we would say?"

But there is a more subtle way of ascertaining what "was not said." The temporal clustering of concepts is a clue to their semantic clustering. When one word is regularly accompanied by another, we infer that they bear some associative relationship. We become especially interested if words are associated much more frequently than we might expect by chance. But it is equally notable when words are associated less often than might be expected. For example, a patient might be extensively preoccupied with both sex and his sister, but never in the same session. Such disjunctive categories are harder for the human subject to become aware of than are conjunctive categories. The computer has no such problem. Thus, we can explore strong associative bonds as well as specifically inhibited connections. Such contingencies may be traced rapidly, for many separate concepts, and over the course of a whole analysis with the aid of electronic data-processing equipment.

I have listened to numerous unresolvable arguments as to "timing of interpretations." "The therapist makes the connection when the patient is just on the verge of it himself" and similar statements, are frequently heard. The mentioned techniques could be employed to ascertain whether interpretation precedes or follows a change in the pattern of associations. The "timing" of interpretive strategies might thus be brought under experimental control.

Now how much of this has actually been done? At the time of this writing I have on my desk an extensive word frequency analysis of a psychotherapy case, 9 sessions long, performed by an IBM 704 computer. This was possible because Wolberg[30] has had the courage to publish the verbatim account of the complete case. The material is doubly valuable in that it is public, and may be studied systematically from other points of view by different investigators. The formal patterns of word frequency call special attention to numbers 4 and 5 of the 9 session sequence, without our even looking at the thematic "content." For example, there is a progressively falling curve of new vocabulary occurrences over the course of the first 4 sessions, and then an abrupt influx of novel words in Interview 5. This has been explored only from the therapist's standpoint to date.* It was found that in Interview 5 the therapist is involved in verbally repetitive inter-changes to a greater extent than in any other session. Furthermore, a complete analysis of the more than 12,000 words spoken by the therapist throughout the 9 sessions reveal that his word frequency and association patterns in Interview 5 were also atypical of his over-all speaking pattern. It was therefore most intriguing to encounter an independent study of this therapist's operations in a less systematic but more clinical framework.[27] Strupp's study found that Interview 4 scored highest for "interpretive communications" and showed a con-comitant lowest score for "direct guidance." He summarizes by stating that "both depth and initiative (re-educative techniques with the ther-apist assuming the role of authority) rose concomitantly to the middle of treatment, but that the former reached its peak in Interview 4 . . . whereas initiative did so in the following hour, in which depth sharply dropped." Turning to the published comments made by the therapist himself, long before the systematic analyses were undertaken:

> *Interview 4:* "During (this) session the patient explores the dynamics of her problem with beginning insight."
> *Interview 5:* The patient here shows signs of utilizing her insight in the di-rection of change."

Thus, in this as yet incomplete picture, we get a sense of how to measure major transition points in a series of therapy interactions. And the automated analyses seem to reflect clinical judgments.

Vocal Analysis: But, as every analyst knows, our most important cues may not be "what" the patient says but "how" he says it. We attend to the voice channel as much as to word associations and vocabulary. Dr. Stanley Feldstein and Mr. Louis Cassotta of our laboratory, are applying experimental methods of speech analysis and electronic engineering skills to this problem.[4-6, 12] In fact, the vocal analyses bypass the stage of human coding (transcription) required in the lexical studies, and represent our most completely automated stage to date. The ultimate aim is the correlation of all levels of communi-cation, the lexical, the vocal and ultimately the gestural, all by means

---

*A complete analysis of this case has been subsequently presented at the annual meeting of the Association for Research in Nervous and Mental Diseases in December 1962, and will appear in the proceedings.

of computer processing. When the handful of pioneers in this area are successful, we will be able to play our tape-recorded analytic sessions into mechanical devices, unattended by human beings, and come out with a description of communicative style, as well as indices of anxiety and various emotional states which are known to correlate with the judgment of experienced clinicians.

Simulations of Personality: This heading is introduced only to be noted and sacrificed, since this is a research report rather than a review. However, computer programs that embody personality theories are already operative, and constitute important investigative tools. One expects to hear a good deal about such models in the near future.[15]

All these descriptions, rather technical, are research procedures. Toward the end of every such discussion comes the inevitable question of the completely automated psychoanalyst, and this report will not be an exception. I think that this question must seriously be entertained with one major qualification. The therapeutic instrument in psycho-analysis is clearly a human relationship, although the necessary degree and quality of that relationship has never been definitively studied. Thus, the usually facetious question of the robot analyst might be productively rephrased as follows: "Can the computer be used to extend the therapist's neuro-linguistic functioning?" Given powerful engines to supplant his muscles, man leaps for the moon. And the telescope offers the astronomer even greater opportunities and challenges than does his unaided eye. If artificial improvements on human sensory and motor functions enhance human potentialities, may not computers augment the therapist's ability to process symbolic data?

With remarkably little "science-fiction" feeling, I believe we will shortly see the experimental introduction of a computer as a functioning link in the patient-therapist dyad. Receiving physiological, vocal and lexical* data from both participants, the computer will correlate many variables simultaneously, far beyond the symbolic capacity of the most artful psychoanalyst. The results, produced moments after reception of the data, will be "fed back" to the therapist while the transaction is still in progress. Special training will be required to

---

*The roadblock of transcription of words may be circumvented by future development of pattern-recognition devices. But the automatic reading of phonetic transcripts, such as produced by Stenotype records, might permit conversion to machinable text at rapid conversation rates, even as the transaction is in progress.[25]

make use of this additional dimension of information. The results are unpredictable, yet may perhaps be as astounding as was the advent of the x-ray and fluoroscope in chest disease.

The immediate result of this work is a compulsory clarification of our psychiatric language. Machines perform operations which are structurally similar to the clinician's, however, they must be instructed precisely as to the nature of those operations. It has been said that "the computer becomes a valuable 'member' of the research team in that it does not share the experiential background and heritage common to the other members of the staff. In communicating with the computer, there is nothing that can be presumed, assumed or claimed as implicit. Every last term must be explicit or it is not considered. In this sense, the computer represents a developed 'organism' without a past, indeed, an adult 'tabula rasa'."[26] Also implicit in this approach is the frame of reference that views psychopathology as a collection of observations pertaining to normal and disturbed communicative behavior. It implies a focus upon the message exchange rather than upon hypothetical intrapsychic processes, so that generalizations will remain closer to the original empirical observations.[24]

Therefore, it behooves us to become much clearer as to the specific cues which are the bases for our clinical intuitions and "hunches." The immediate yield from thinking in computer terms will be the systematization of the often haphazard state of knowledge in our field.

REFERENCES

1. BALKEN, E. R., AND MASSERMAN, J. H.: The language of phantasy. III. The language of phantasies of patients with conversion hysteria, anxiety state, and obsessive-compulsive neurosis. J. Psychol. 10:75-86, 1940.
2. BORKO, H. (Ed.): Computer Application in the Behavioral Sciences. Englewood Cliffs, N.J., Prentice Hall, 1962.
3. BRUNER, J. S., AND TAJFEL, H.: Cognitive risk and environmental change. J. Abnorm. Soc. Psychol. 62:231-241, 1961.
4. CASSOTTA, L., FELDSTEIN, S., AND JAFFE, J.: A device for automatic extraction and quantification of vocal behavior in interviews. Paper read at East. Psychol. Assoc., Atlantic City, April, 1962.
5. FELDSTEIN, S., AND JAFFE, J.: A note about speech disturbances and vocabulary diversity. J. Communication 12:166-170, 1962.
6. ——, AND ——: Vocabulary diversity of schizophrenics and normals. J. Speech Hearing Res., 5:76-78, 1962.
7. GILL, M., NEWMAN, R., AND REDLICH, F. C.: The Initial Interview in Psychiatric Practice. New York, Int. Univ. Press, Inc., 1954.

8. GOTTSCHALK, L. A. (Ed.): Comparative Psycholinguistic Analysis of Two Psychotherapeutic Interviews. New York, Int. Univer. Press, Inc., 1961.

9. JAFFE, J.: Language of the dyad: a method of interaction analysis in psychiatric interviews. Psychiatry, 21:249-258, 1958.

10. ——: Formal language patterns as defensive operations. *In:* D. A. Barbara (Ed.): Psychological and Psychiatric Aspects of Speech and Hearing. Springfield, Ill., Charles C Thomas, 1960, pp. 138-151.

11. ——, AND FELDSTEIN, S.: Phase relationships of filled pauses and vocabulary change in interviews. Unpublished manuscript, William Alanson White Inst., N. Y., 1962.

12. ——:, ——, AND CASSOTTA, L.: An IBM 7090 program for analyzing vocal parameters of dyadic interaction. Behav. Sc., in press.

13. KAHN, R. L., AND FINK, M.: Changes in language during electroshock therapy. *In:* P. Hoch and J. Zubin (Eds.): Psychopathology of Communication. New York, Grune and Stratton, 1958, pp. 126-139.

14. LENNARD, H. L., AND BERNSTEIN, A.: The Anatomy of Psychotherapy. New York, Columbia Univer. Press, 1960.

15. LOEHLIN, J. C.: Aldous: a computer program that simulates personality. Paper read at Amer. Psychol. Assoc., New York, September, 1961.

16. LUHN, H. P.: A statistical approach to mechanized encoding and searching of literary information. IBM J. Res. Devel., 1957, 1:309-317.

17. MAHL, G. F.: Disturbances and silences in the patient's speech in psychotherapy. J. Abnorm. Soc. Psychol. 53:1-15, 1956.

18. MILLER, G. A.: The magical number seven, plus or minus two: some limits on our capacity for processing information. Psychol. Rev. 63:81-97, 1956.

19. NEWELL, A. (Ed.): Information Processing Language-V manual. Englewood Cliffs, N. J., Prentice-Hall, 1961.

20. OLVER, R. R.: A developmental study of cognitive equivalence. Summary of doctoral dissertation. Dept. Soc. Rel., Radcliffe Coll. 1961.

21. PARKS, J. R.: A committee report on schizophrenic language. Behavioral Sc. 6:79-83, 1961.

21-a PITTENGER, R. E., HOCKETT, C. F., AND DANEHY, J. J.: The First Five Minutes. Ithaca, N. Y., Paul Martineau, 1960.

22. POOL, I. Trends in Content Analysis. Urbana, Ill., Univer. of Ill. Press, 1959.

23. ROBBINS, L. L., AND WALLERSTEIN, R. S.: The research strategy and tactics of the psychotherapy research project of The Menninger Foundation and the problem of controls. *In:* E. A. Rubenstein and M. B. Parloff (Eds.): Research in Psychotherapy. Washington, D.C., Amer. Psychol. Assoc. 1959, pp. 27-43.

24. RUESCH, J., AND BATESON, G.: Communication: The Social Matrix of Psychiatry. New York, Norton, 1951.

25. SALTON, G.: The automatic transcription of machine shorthand. Proceedings of East. Joint Computer Conf., Boston, December, 1959, pp. 148-159.

26. STONE, P. J., BALES, R. F., ZVI NAMENWIRTH, J., AND OGILVIE, D. M.: The general inquirer: a computer system for content analysis and retrieval based on the sentence as a unit of information. Lab. of Soc. Rel., Harvard Univer., 1961.

27. STRUPP, H. H.: A multidimensional analysis of technique in brief psycho-
    therapy. Psychiat. 20:387-397, 1957.
28. WEINSTEIN, E. A., AND KAHN, R. L.: Denial of Illness: Symbolic and Physio-
    logical Aspects. Springfield, Ill., Charles C Thomas, 1955.
29. WHITEHORN, J. C., AND ZIPF, G. K.: Schizophrenic language. Arch. Neurol.
    Psychiat., 49:831, 1933.
30. WOLBERG, L. R.: The Technique of Psychotherapy. New York, Grune and
    Stratton, 1954.

Discussion by Don Jackson, M.D.

I want especially to commend Dr. Jaffe on his use of the occurrence of new words as a mark of changes in the patient-doctor relationship. Naturally, this technique could be extended to any dyadic relationship and not limited just to therapy. However, it is especially appropriate to the analytic situation since, as Dr. Jaffe points out, analysis is a matter of hearing what people do not say as much as it is listening to what they do vocalize. The measure of new words may be important in the positive and the negative sense. I am quite sure that computers will soon listen to single and double bar junctures and other micro-linguistic measurements which will enormously enrich our knowledge of analytic and psychotherapeutic transactions.

Dr. Jaffe has also made an ingenious use of the Redlich interview which further reveals the exceptional uses to which computers can be put. However, this section of the paper reveals one of the problems in the use of computers, namely, that human subjects must program them. These human beings then must interpret the meaning of the outcome of what they have programmed. I, for example, would find a rather different meaning to a set of words picked up by the computer than those selected by Dr. Jaffe. I am not sure this is an important point since differences in viewpoints could be subjected to further computer analysis, etc.

I have a particular interest in this work because of my own interest in communication and because of a worrisome feeling that it is an extremely complicated topic. Consider, for example, some possibilities of ordering communication in carrying on a simple dyadic conversation between myself and an individual who has some importance to me. There are a number of communication operations that I could be engaging in at the same time:

1. I am attempting to influence the nature of our relationship in the immediate present, usualy by asking, offering, informing, exhorting, etc. verbally and nonverbally.

2. I am scanning what I say for needed correction and thus am modifying moment to moment what I say as I hear it. The same modification procedure probably applies to gestures although these seem less available to our awareness.

3. I am observing the other person and modifying what I say in order to increase my influence and/or clarify my messages through the use of humor, stronger tone, more conciliatory approach, etc.

4. I am considering the future effects of my current remarks and as in numbers 2 and 3, this may result in modification.

5. I am anticipating the other person's reply which is not quite equivalent to number 3 in that it involves in addition: (a) Attempting to anticipate change or surprise in order to minimize it, and (b) testing my ability to anticipate change or read minds for purposes of strategy or to demonstrate my closeness to the other individual as in the old saw about two hearts that beat as one.

Obviously, carrying out just this kind of operation is a highly complex and fatiguing process. It seems likely that certain conditions are necessary to keep these various behavioral sequences within reasonably simple proportions. For example, my relationship with the other individual must be of such a nature that the attempt to anicipate and minimize change will need to operate at only a low level. Further, I must operate in a familiar context so that scanning my own messages is minimal and the need to consider future effect is minimized because I have operated within this context many times before.

The thread that runs through the conditions necessary to minimize communication complications is redundancy. I use the term in its technical sense. That is the imparting of information which is extracted because of the patterning or occurrence of a bit of information rather than in the commonsense meaning of unnecessarily repetitions. Thus the more stable my relationship with the other individual, the more familiar the context, the more I need call only upon repetitive behavioral sequences without the need to develop new and untried behavioral patterns or tactics to meet new contingencies.

If these assumptions are valid and not just a representation of certain personal biases, then the computer would be virtually the only hope for validating such premises. This is because redundancy in behavioral patterns involves more than word counting but the combination of a number of variables which must be measured in their relationship to each other, that is, sequentially as well as in the sequences of sequences.

Our own research group is interested in what we call family rules. It is our asumption that when a couple marry, they establish covert rules which represent a blending of their own premise systems into some kind of modus vivendi. Right now, we can only guess at these rules by scanning transcribed and taped material of marital interaction for repetitive patterns. In one of our so-called normal families, the couple appears to have a rule that neither will behave in a manner that will put himself ahead of the other spouse and thus they maintain status balance. It is possible to notice on transcripts of their interviews that if one individual makes a statement about himself, he immediately seeks confirmation from the other spouse. If he does not do this, the other spouse will insert himself into the conversation by modifying it slightly and the first spouse always accepts the modification made by the second. This is a couple incidentally who have not quarreled in 20 years of marriage. The last time they quarreled, they were on a bicycle trip and rode off in opposite directions angrily. Each thought the better of his move, turned around, and they met exactly in the center of town.

The kind of rules that we can label under our present system are more obvious and crude compared to the variations possible if we could have a machine programmed to pick up all redundancies and group them into sequences and these into sequences of sequences. In the family described, we can see with present efforts that there are two apparently sequential patterns which may be noticed by the word "I" followed by "we," or "you" or "I" followed by the acknowledgment of "we' 'or "us" by the other spouse. However, when the content is not appropriate for this sort of crude scoring, we are lost. I feel a machine would not be.

Any good discussant, according to the rules of the game, must not allow himself to be merely a yes man or he will never contribute to the deification of confusion which makes the long journey to these conventions so worthwhile. Therefore, I must raise 2 points tbout Dr. Jaffe's paper:

1. Whereas I feel that computers are infinitely better equipped than the human subject to pick up abstract relationship patterns over a number of interviews, I doubt that this information can be made therapeutic without the interposition of a human personality. I feel that doing therapy and having a theory of therapy are very different things as has been demonstrated by Fiedler, Strupp, and others.

2. Dr. Jaffe's paper has not touched upon the basic question of whether human communication is ultimately reasonable in a computer sense. When we can program computers to deal with metacommunication, that is, messages about messages, I will lessen my doubts. I look forward to the day in fact when the computer can act sensibly in a chess game when faced by human opponent who acts as if he wishes to win, secretly wishes to lose, and moves in a fashion which is calculated to keep the issue of either winning or losing from ever coming into question.

Part III. Techniques of Therapy

THE ROLE OF THE PSYCHOANALYST

by MAY E. ROMM

IN VIEW of the uncanny uniqueness of each individual, therapy has to be modified and applied to each patient within the framework of the dynamics of psychoanalysis. In a paper written in 1913 on "Further Recommendations in the Technique of Psychoanalysis," Freud[1] stated "The exceptional diversity in the mental constellations concerned, the plasticity of all mental processes, and the great number of the determining factors involved prevent the formulation of a stereotyped technique and also bring it about that a course of action, ordinarily legitimate, may be at times ineffective, while one which is usually erroneous may occasionally lead to the desired end. These circumstances do not prevent us from establishing a procedure for the physician which will be found most generally efficient."

Fenichel in his book "Problems of Psychoanalytic Technique," (p. 1)[2] stated that "The infinite multiplicity of situations arising in analysis does not permit the formulation of general rules about how the analyst should act in every situation because each situation is essentially unique."

Since the days when Freud held that the analyst was to assume the role of the "Tabula rasa" much has been added to the understanding of emotional functioning both in the so-called healthy individual and in the one seeking help for emotional illness. In turn, a great deal has also been added to how the analyst should react to the patient, and what, how and when he should interpret the patient's verbal and nonverbal production and behavior, and what his aim is in establishing a relationship with his patient.

173

It is essential to keep in mind that the psychoanalytic climate within the relationship of the therapist and the patient is by and large an artificial one. In no other situation in life can a person disclose not only all that is conscious to him, but what comes up from the unconscious, and be free from repercussions from the environment. Since the analyst encourages the patient to free associate in the therapeutic hour and stresses the importance of not censoring any thoughts that come to the patient's mind, it is also his duty to enlighten the patient that free association should be limited to the analytic session. Occasionally when this is not pointed out, the patient may carry over the permissiveness of the analytic situation into his daily life with detriment to himself and others.

We frequently hear about goals in psychoanalysis. It seems to me that the only goals which the therapist has a right to have for the patient are that the latter should free himself from his infantile and childish relationships, that he develop sufficient ego strength to meet unalterable situations with a minimum of conflict and that he should be ready and willing to accept without guilt propitious and pleasurable situations which could prove productive to him and to others. He has to develop independent critiques of his own concepts and viewpoints and to evaluate his relationship with other people in a realistic manner. The analyst must be on guard lest the patient utilize him as a model in toto through identification. There is no question that no matter how impersonal the analyst may be, the patient may adopt him as his ego ideal and take him over as his conscience in the beginning of therapy; but as the treatment continues, the analyst through interpretations and confrontations must help him to develop independent critical thinking and an identity of his own. Through the proper and timely interpretations by the analyst of the transference, both positive and negative, the patient should be able to recognize that how he felt toward his parents as a child and how he has transferred on the analyst his dependent needs of childhood and his early feelings toward the important figures in his environment are at present anachronistic. It is the role and duty of the analyst to confront the patient with the factual material that as a child he was realistically dependent on the adults in his environment, primarily the parents or parent surrogates and later on teachers and other mentors, but that now, in his adult life, he has to substitute for dependent, and/or unjustifiable rebellious feelings and actions, realistic concepts, functioning and behavior. Passive aggressive maneuvers of childhood have to be transformed into productive interpersonal relationships.

Glover in 1928 stated[3] that the classification of the analytic method might be related to the maintenance of complete detachment on the analyst's part. He questioned whether the analyst does preserve complete detachment. He later added that there were isolated occasions when the analyst abandons his attitude of neutrality. Webster defines neutrality as not taking part in either side of a quarrel, giving no active aid to any belligerent, being indifferent to one thing or the other. English and English in their dictionary on Psychoanalytical Terms (1958) define neutral as being in a zone closely surrounding the zero.

Can the analyst at all times be of sufficient help to his patient? Are there occasions and situations when his own emotional make up, his life history and his values may create obstacles in the treatment of his analysands? Is his role always objective and benevolently nonjudgmental? We have to accept the fact that the analyst is a human being with reactions to his own childhood, his background and his present status. It is therefore mandatory for him to evaluate his own concepts and feelings toward each specific patient. When he becomes aware that the values of the patient such as they may be, create either "unlust" or irritation within himself, he must either through self-understanding resolve these feelings or he has to transfer the patient to a therapist whose personality does not react in this form. I wish to demonstrate this with a clinical example.

About 12 years ago, I treated a patient who was referred to me by her internist because she had innumerable psychosomatic symptoms and severe anxiety. She was literally crippled somatically and psychically. She had gastrointestinal symptoms of an intense variety and her anxiety prevented her from leaving her home. It was with great tension and effort that she was able to come to my office for treatment first accompanied and later by herself. She feared to drive her own car and was inordinately tense even when driven by others. Within a short period of time after therapy started, I came to the realization that this woman was intellectually inhibited, and belonged to a social stratum in which competition among women for material possessions was intensely high. This particular patient seemed to me to be the arch offender in that department. In addition, not only did she weep and wail because some of her friends were in a higher fashion bracket and wore more expensive mink stoles and gave more elaborate parties but she would use the phrase "In other words" and would then repeat what she had already said. A therapeutic hour with her became very trying for me and I am loathe to admit that during 1 hour, in order to repress my distaste for her, I distracted myself by counting the number of times she said, "In other words" and repeated the same thing. It added up to 14.

Because the transference was positive and probably because she knew of people who were helped by me and, no doubt, because of some interpretations that I made to her which she was able to accept, she became relatively free from her somatic symptoms and I not only encouraged her to discontinue treatment but egged her on to do so.

Three years later after her only daughter married, the patient reacted with the return of her old symptoms in full bloom. Her internist insisted that I take her back for treatment. I frankly told him that I felt uncomfortable in treating this patient and recommended in her interest as well as mine that she should seek therapy with someone else. I offered to find her a competent therapist. However, she insisted on coming in for one session during which she informed me that she would not go to any other analyst and wanted to be treated by me. I told her that I would perhaps reconsider taking her back in treatment after 2 weeks had elapsed. During that time I evaluated through self-analysis why I was so allergic to this particular woman. Interestingly enough I discovered that I identified her with an important person in my own past and this identification intensified my dislike and depreciation of her. I took her back in therapy and determined to treat her with the dignity and interest to which each patient is entitled. I began to seek the meaning of her phrase "In other words." It became clear that it was a defense against her feelings of her inferiority about her lack of comprehension and her fear of expressing herself improperly and hostilely. I was agreeably surprised to discover that underneath her layer of defenses which largely expressed itself by her striving for material things, there was a relatively intelligent and warm human being who was highly traumatized by her father who wanted a son, and by her mother who expected her to be in constant attendance. As long as the patient could take refuge in being sick and immobile she could refuse her mother's inordinate demands for attention without guilt. When her masculine protest was analyzed, she was able to sublimate it by entering into social activities which had philanthropic goals. She began to feel that she, too, could be productive and with that her rivalry with her husband decreased. She began to take an interest in her daughter on a maternal basis and relinquished her role of the little girl who reached out to everyone around her including her daughter, for protection. When she became a grand-mother, she was able to be of value to her daughter and got pleasure and satisfaction in frequently taking care of her grandchild.

When the therapy was terminated after 2 years of intensive work on both her part and my own, I felt that the change for the better in her character, personality and in her functioning fully justified the mutual investment in the second phase of her treatment. I also felt justifiably guilty that when I treated her previously, I withheld from her my usual attitude toward patients which is one of interest, compassion and respect.

The patient entering analysis is conflicted between his wish to remain ill, be taken care of, be dependent, be protected and loved and his desire and pull toward becoming independent, productive and having the capacity to love as well as to receive love. In the process of helping him to uncover the dynamics of his illness, bringing as much as possible of the unconscious and preconscious into consciousness, the analyst cannot be neutral. He obviously joins forces with the healthy part of the patient's ego and becomes his partner in the battle to defeat the neurosis which is keeping the patient unhappy and symptom-ridden. The technique is slanted to permit the patient to become cognizant of his dependent needs and/or desire for suffering, be it somatic or psychic. The application of the acquired insight is then at the service of the patient. The analyst through further interpretations and benevolent confrontations hopes and expects that the patient will utilize the acquired insight productively. A physician, irrespective of his specialty, cannot actually cure a patient. The organicist, by removing the diseased organ or by altering the biochemistry through various available methods, aims to produce a physiological versus a pathological climate in which the tissues can heal themselves. The same holds for psychoanalysis wherein the analyst, through the fostering of the transference and analyzing it with proper timing, creates a propitious psychic climate. By being benevolent and nonjudgmental he thus offers the patient an opportunity through free association, interpretations by himself and with the help of the analyst plus the evaluation of the unconscious through dream work, to understand his resistances, his anxieties and his fears. The patient in due time comes to the realization that his present reactions are based on early frustrations, misunder-standings and conflicts and that in his present state these feelings are anachronistic and do not fit in adult functioning.

Does transference and the patient's faithful compliance by keeping his regular appointments and lying on the couch and speaking at random constitute good psychoanalytic therapy? Perhaps there are unique patients who can through this method gain sufficiently to give up their neuroses. In my experience, I have found that it is essential for the analyst to work actively, hand in hand, with the patient. Taking for granted that the patient through his own efforts can make part of his unconscious conscious and may gain sufficient knowledge of himself to repattern his attitudes and thus give up his neurotic trends is, in my opinion, problematical. A human being is not born with an all knowing unconscious. He represses selectively what he has experienced and learned. What he never knew or acquired, he has no possibility to repress into his unconscious. Hence psychoanalytic treatment is inherently a learning process during which the patient adds to his knowledge concepts and ideas to which he has never been exposed. This does by no means exclude his own knowledge, experiences and feelings which he has suppressed, regressed and distorted. The analyst must also be on the alert to recognize the resistances of the patient which may express themselves through special selectivities. On occasion he may fall into the trap of helping the patient to bring out hostility and interpret it to him over and over again when actually the patient is using this material to protect himself from his fear of tenderness. The following example illustrates this.

A man in his late thirties came to me for treatment after he had had psychoanalytic therapy for over 6 years during which he was seen 5 times weekly. His presenting problem was that he felt hopeless and unworthy and he was fearful of his suicidal thoughts. He freely admitted that he agreed with his former therapist that he was an extremely hostile person incapable of loving anyone. He frankly said that he did not trust anyone and that he was constantly on guard lest his superiors, his peers and his employees take advantage of him. His favorite expression was "I cornered him like a rat." He suffered from innumerable somatic symptoms including gastrointestinal spasms and frequent severe migraine headaches.

Within the first 2 hours, he disclosed his intense hatred toward his mother whom he described as ignorant, avaricious and paranoid and his derision toward his gentle, weak and submissive father. He was perfectly willing to continue treatment with me on a 5 times a week basis and he was most willing to describe in minute detail his hostile, aggressive and depreciating attitude toward every person in his environment and, in fact, to people in general. I offered him 3 hours weekly. After obtaining his history, I speculated that his hostility could well be a screen for deeper feelings. After telling me that I "cornered him like a rat," he poignantly admitted that when he reacted in a hostile manner to those about him, he was on firm ground. He knew, he expected and he was prepared for retaliatory hostility. According to him the idea of reaching out to anyone with tenderness carried with it the unknown, the possibility of being rejected and of getting as he expressed it, "egg on his face." Further work with him disclosed his inordinate need for love, his intense sibling rivalry and his fear that no matter how successful he could or would be as a person, as a business man and as a philanthropist, he could never really please anyone (mother) or himself.

Confronting him with pertinent material which clearly showed how he himself created a world of hostility about him and pointing out to him repeatedly how he feared to take a normal calculated risk by reaching out with tenderness to others in addition to evaluating with him his qualities and his ego strength in many directions, resolved his paranoid reaction to life and permitted him to see himself as a worthwhile person who was entitled to rewards for being productive. His fears that he was an ugly hostile individual were dissipated when he began to realize and appreciate that he could get warmth from people when he reached out toward them in a friendly tender fashion. His reaction formation to his former isolation and hostility took an exaggerated form so that for a relatively short period he planned to dedicate himself in toto to the welfare of humanity through a Schweitzerian attitude. Continued active work with him permitted the pendulum to swing within the mean.

This patient was not only willing but anxious to focus his interest and that of the analyst on his hostility. He registered anxiety and irritation when I confronted him with his manipulating intent to keep the analysis fractional in order to avoid delving into the dynamics of his intense anger. When I mirrored to him that he was conducive, through his own hostile manipulations, in creating a threatening environment where he constantly fenced with his opponents, he admitted his intense opposition to investing tenderness in people for fear of being rejected. It required a great deal of activity on my part to balk the patient's constant attempts to veer the analysis into what he labeled as his hostile sphere. Left to his own devices, this man in his erroneous concept of free association, would unquestionably have remained fixated on dwelling on his own hostility as well as attempting to prove to himself and to me how misused he was by every person that came on his horizon. Only when this mechanism of defense was resolved by my repeated confrontations and interpretations, given in a nonjudgmental climate to which he had either not been previously exposed or could not appreciate it, was he finally able to accept his own role in his creating an astigmatic concept of the world around him. This led to his acceptance of himself as a person who possessed tenderness as well as hostile feelings and who could afford to chance a calculated risk in reaching out to others on a tender basis.

Invariably in the process of an analysis some negative transference is bound to occur. The desirable technique is to permit the patient to bring out the hostility and aggression, whether conscious or not, and to help him understand the meaning of it with the hope that he will be able to apply his insight and resolve it within physiological limits. On occasion the amount and intensity of the transferred hostility may overwhelm the patient's ego to the point where he either interrupts therapy or blocks the progress of it. The analyst has to be at all times aware of the role he plays in the transference and through confrontations and interpretations attempt to modify the patient's reaction to the extent where he can continue the therapy without blocking or interrupting it. A case in point is as follows:

A young man in his twenties came for therapy because of intense anxiety and what can be called a "fate neurosis." Progress in his therapy was slow and extremely painful for him. His hostility toward his father was inordinate although partially justifiable. After he had been in therapy for almost a year during which period he asked me on several occasions to have a conference with his father, I felt that it was indicated to see the latter. During the interview with his father, it became apparent that he considered his only son an extension of himself and wanted both to be proud of him and to mold him into his own image. He reacted with considerable tolerance when I pointed out to him that the aim of therapy was to make his son an independent mature person. The following day the patient came in a fury. Before he asked me what transpired between his father and myself, he vehemently stated that he was certain that his father influenced me against him. He expressed his conviction that I "sold him down the river." He was so overwhelmed by his hostile feelings that he picked up an ashtray and threw it across the room, no doubt symbolically destroying me as he wanted to destroy his father.

It was impossible for me to interrupt his ranting and raving against me while he was lying on the couch. I insisted that he sit up and face me. Only then was I able to relate to him my conversation with his father. I think that his very facing me had a calming effect on him. He burst into tears and in a pitiful tone admitted that he saw his father in every person with whom he had any sort of a relationship. Before he left he was, at least, consciously aware that on many occasions he had interrupted friendships because of his belief that all human beings would treat him as his father did. Because my voice was soft, calm and reassuring, he apparently had a corrective emotional experience since his father has never been able to talk to him without yelling at the top of his voice. Whether my seeing his father was timely or not is open to question. The result was that the patient finally realized that he identified me in toto with his father. He also became aware of his pattern of projecting on all people the fear he had of his father and the hostility he felt toward him.

Continued interpretations and confrontations on my part of his lack of security and his inordinate mistrust of everyone finally dissipated greatly his negative transference toward me. There occurred a turning point in the therapy on a positive basis. While in the course of the continuation of the analysis negative transference occurred from time to time, it was on a modified basis without flooding his ego so that he could handle it with eventual insight which he was able to apply. His insight increased to the point where he was able to bring in the following dream and to analyze it with little help from me. He dreamt that he was lying on a narrow hospital cot. A woman was sitting in a chair by his side. She repeatedly kept leaning over him and turning on an electric light at the head of his bed and he consistently reached up and turned the light off. The dream faded as the woman turned the light on. Since at the occurrence of the dream he had been in treatment for over 3 years, he himself realized that he was blocking the progress of his treatment as he blocked the advantages in his interpersonal relationships and in his work. In a manner characteristic of such an individual, he accused me of never having pointed out to him that he had a tendency to ignore what was offered to him. This particular area was worked on with him innumerable times. Until the patient was ready to accept what was offered to him, he literally reacted with a sort of psychic blindness and deafness, and yet his preconscious and unconscious stored away these pertinent interpretations and confrontations until they could be utilized by him when his ego became strong enough to handle them. In the positive transference he finally resolved his resistances and was able to acquire insight and to utilize it.

On occasion the erotic transference becomes so intense that it interferes with the therapy through the patient's conviction that he is desperately in love with the therapist. He may demand a relationship beyond the therapeutic situation. This happens more frequently when the patient has a therapist of the opposite sex although there are times when the homosexual transference may overwhelm him. I have treated several women who were transferred to me by male therapists because they became erotically involved with the analysts so that the therapy had to be discontinued. To demonstrate: a married woman was in therapy for over a year with a very experienced male analyst. She began to demand a real love relationship with him including sex. Repeated interpretations of the transference made no impression on her. She spent the hours in therapy weeping constantly and inordinately in her intense frustration. She pleaded with him to gratify her erotic demands and threatened suicide if he rejected her advances. She came to me under duress. For several months she continued to weep and wail and to convey to me that her feelings toward her former therapist were not based on transference but were due to genuine love. I could not make any headway with her until she began bringing in homosexual dreams involving a friend of hers and later myself. She then confessed that she had had a sexual relationship with the husband of her friend and later a homosexual relationship with this friend. It became clear that her inordinate erotic transference to her former therapist was a defense mechanism against her homosexuality. My interpretation of this phase in her sexuality which she at first denied vehemently resolved her erotic feelings for her former therapist. Her homosexual trends stemmed from the seductiveness of her mother when she was in the oedipal phase so that she was never able to experience any deep feelings for her father. She expressed surprise that I could accept her as a decent person despite her acting out and the therapy continued and was brought to a satisfactory conclusion.

My opinion is that the transference should be analyzed from the very time that it makes its appearance; on a superficial basis at first, and then on a deeper level. Failure to do so may create the concept in the patient's mind that the analyst is welcoming the erotic transference and is willing to participate in it.

Whether an analyst accepts a patient for therapy or whether he refers him for treatment to someone else, it is indicated to attempt to evaluate which therapist is best suited to this specific person. Some women who apply for treatment, because of their symptomatology and background, may have more difficulty in relating if the therapist is of the same sex. On the other hand, some women relate with less tension to a woman therapist. By and large, in my experience, men have less difficulty in disclosing their problems and their symptoms to a woman since consciously and unconsciously these particular men cannot handle rivalry with members of their own sex and they may have intense fear of their homosexual components when dealing with male therapists.

The age of the therapist may also, at times, be used as a resistance by the patient. If the therapist is young the patient may question his ability. If he is old, the patient can utilize that as a resistance. As an example of the latter: a patient in a state of negative transference gleefully told me that he doubted his choice of me as a therapist. He confronted me with his concept that if after the analysis was terminated he might have a problem in the future, I would be dead of old age at that time. This man had an inordinate fear of old age and of death and he also had intense death wishes toward his mother from whose death he stood to benefit financially. He was an only son whose mother had intense guilt toward him because of her numerous marriages. During his formative years, she was either sporadically clinging to him and telling him how important he was to her or else she was gallivanting with a lover or a new husband. I doubt whether this man could have been so frank with a male analyst.

There are times when in a situation of crisis in a patient's life a woman therapist, particularly of mature years, can step in and utilize a protective attitude toward such patient which in a younger person or a member of the opposite sex might represent to the patient seduction. To exemplify: one of my patients in a state of depression whose parents were in Europe and whose husband was hospitalized, came in for her therapeutic hour in a state of despair. She admitted feeling hopeless and suicidal. She had deprived herself of food for the last week and had lost a great deal of weight. The question of hospitalization had to be considered seriously. She gave the general impression of a lost child reaching out for help. When she told me that she felt aimless in how she would spend the day—she saw me in the morning—I asked her whether she would like to have dinner with me at my home, taking pot luck. After faintly protesting that she did not wish to interfere with my life, she consented to accept my invitation. During dinner she ate in an almost ravenous fashion and interestingly had 3 glasses of milk during the meal. When she said that she would like to go to a movie, I offered to go with her. She did the driving to the theatre, purchased the tickets and also bought 2 large pieces of chocolate, one of which she gave to me. Since I left the choice of the movie to her, she picked one in which there was a great deal of violence. Again, while watching the picture, she ate her chocolate bar ravenously. She drove me home and left, literally a different person. This was the end of her depression. Following this she reacted to the realistic vicissitudes in her life productively without anorexia and without weeping and wailing as she did before her dinner date with me. It is interesting to note that this patient constantly stressed that while her mother frequently offered to help her, whenever there was a crisis, her mother was in another part of the country. Apparently my standing by her in her hour of need was a corrective emotional experience for her which neutralized her pattern of turning the aggression against her mother on herself. This protective attitude toward a patient which had desirable results in this case because of my sex and my age, might have been out of order and possibly detrimental for her had the therapist been a man.

A sophisticated patient will occasionally ask, "Am I being analyzed or am I just getting psychotherapy?" Invariably this goading of the analyst occurs when the patient is either angry at the therapist or an interpretation or confrontation touched on material to which he was resistant. The following exemplifies the above: a 53 year old male patient who had had therapy for many years with several analysts was determined to control not only the persons in his immediate environment but also his analysis and his analyst. When I interpreted to him that his sibling rivalry and his need to have special attention from everyone about him, as he wanted mother to treat him, caused him to be inordinately demanding, hostile and controlling, he retorted that I was unfair to him and that he still needed to "dredge up" early memories which in effect he expected to give him the magic key which would resolve his tensions and his problems. To a direct question he admitted that he has been "dredging" for the last 10 years without too much change in his reaction to life and he also admitted that his question was deliberately provocative.

This patient as well as others of his ilk frequently indulge in what

I label as "emotional bookkeeping." They not only fear being controlled by others, but they cannot tolerate the idea that fate may dole out to them vicissitudes in which they had no voice. Having been inculcated, as we all are, with the concepts that life is difficult, that one is bound to have pain in the process of living, they, so to speak, arrange their own way of handling the situation. They determine to play life on a ratio basis: they suffer, create difficulties for themselves, avoid pleasure with a vengeance and hope that if they suffer ad lib for a certain period of time, fate or God or the gods will then credit them with the allotted necessary suffering and then at a certain period of life they will be rewarded exclusively with pleasure. Since this form of bookkeeping is under the control of the super ego which is consistently rigid in these people, it cannot be appeased. These patients continue their expiation interminably unless they are repeatedly and actively confronted with their sado-masochistic behavior and the guilt, fear and hostility involved in such omnipotent and irrational concepts and behavior. This has to be analyzed to its source. Invariably it has to do with early feelings of rejection by parents or parental surrogates, sibling rivalry and infantile insatiability with omnipotent thinking of personally controlling the emotional universe. It is as if each one of these patient were to say "I am willing to pay a price but then the world must single me out, love me and gratify all my needs and wishes—I am special." The reaction formation to such unrealistic desires for personal control consists of hostility, guilt, depression, psychosomatic symptoms and at times, acting out. The latter can take the form of alcoholic or drug addictions, antisocial or a social behavior and character disorders.

These people, in their need to control, fight tenaciously and avidly against any progress in life as well as in analysis. To be benefited through environmental situations of which one is analysis, is interpreted by them as dependence which is inordinately threatening to them. They reject the utilization of their endowments, natural or acquired, ignore opportunities and wallow in their self-imposed miseries. It takes active and patient participation on the part of the analyst finally to help such patients.

There are situations during the analytic process in which it takes almost heroic efforts on the part of the psychoanalyst to detach a patient from a symbiotic fixation. I wish to demonstrate briefly the following case: a woman patient became fixated in her associations on an early period of her childhood during which she felt rejected by her father. She wept copiously as she described in great detail how between the ages of 3 and 5 she literally anguished when she "pitifully" reached out to her father and he showed no interest in her. Since her dreams indicated that she identified me with her father and since I suspected that her concentration on her oedipal conflict to the exclusion of everything else in her life was a defensive maneuver, I attempted through interpretations and confrontations to convey to her that her problems in her interpersonal relationships which were acute at that time did not stem exclusively from the circumscribed oedipal situation. Her reaction was dramatic. She became enraged and her fury gathered momentum as she railed at me. She accused me of being like her father and of not permitting her to tell me how she really felt. She said that I disliked her and that I deliberately demeaned her to the point where she thought that she would have to leave treatment in order to free me of her presence which she knew was obnoxious to me. When her anger had spent itself, I was able to confront her with her apparent resistance to facing certain painful situations in her life at present. I pointed out to her that as long as she could agonize over the injustice done to her by her father in her early childhood, she experienced pain without guilt. Her intense fear of assuming her responsibilities for her present situations was repressed because of the guilt and self depreciation connected with it and she hid her real feelings behind her oedipal lament. It took time, patience and active participation on my part to detach this woman from her comfortable oedipal island wherein she felt guiltless and justified in blaming all her difficulties on her father.

She far I have focused on the various phases of intense transference, both hostile and erotic which needed the active participation of the analyst and the underlying desire of the patient to continue treatment. However, on occasion the analyst discovers that a patient who may enter treatment with what appears to be a sincere wish to be helped will not or cannot develop a transference relationship with the doctor. Treatment then becomes a futile exercise and has to be terminated. Frequently under such conditions the patient refuses to continue with another therapist or if he does, he repeats the same process. To exemplify the aforementioned: an intelligent, creative and successful man entered treatment in order to rid himself of somatic symptoms and a germ phobia. His somatic symptoms decreased rapidly and his germ phobia got under control. However, his lack of consideration for others continued and there was no improvement in his interpersonal relationships.

He treated me as if I were one of his numerous employees. He would have one of his secretaries phone me several times that he was delayed and would be late. He would then either not appear at all or come in 10 minutes before the time allotted to him was up. During the few appointments that he kept by coming on time, he expected and demanded advice or praise or else he would chit chat about the happenings in the lives of others. When confronted with these resistances against facing himself, he would retort that he was willing to pay me for my time whether he kept his appointments or skipped them. He also added that he was under the impression that what came to his mind was free association and therefore I had no right to criticize him. While I was trying to decide how best to handle the situation with him, he himself precipitated my decision to discontinue his treatment with me. During a subsequent session to which he was 20 minutes late, he disclosed how he intended to juggle several untenable situations. I pointed out to him that he was thinking as if he were omnipotent and that no one could have his cake and eat it. He expressed his opinion emphatically that irrespective of what other people could or could not do, he was convinced that he could have his cake and eat it too. He refused to evaluate the deplorable situation in which he intended to plunge even though he agreed with me that he was imitating his deceased father who entered a similar situation with disastrous results. He defiantly and belligerently told me that neither I nor anyone else could tell him how and what he should do. He added that he knew the dangers of the situation under discussion but that he, in contradistinction to his father's unfortunate plight, would overcome the insurmountable obstacles. My interpretations that he had a need to identify with his father and to triumph over him and at the same time through the identification to rescue his father, fell on deaf ears. I felt that his resistance was due, in part, to a fear of delving deeper as well as a need to deny his feelings of inferiority by acting out in situations where angels feared to tread. I suggested that he interrupt treatment with me and offered to help him choose another psychoanalyst. He willingly agreed to stop treatment but refused to accept my recommendation that he continue with someone else. This occurred 15 years ago. I am sorry to report that after this brilliant and talented man ate his cake, he had none left.

One of my reasons for reporting this case is that there is a tendency on the part of psychoanalysts to report case histories describing progress and/or some complications but usually the follow up is either avoided or not mentioned. In his report Marmor[4] stated that "The psychotherapist in practice needs to be constantly on guard against the defensive tendency of the ego to take refuge in arrogance. It is natural for the ego to minimize its failure and cherish its successes." I feel and think that the analyst should realize that he may evaluate a patient as food material for analysis and then after a certain period of treatment discover that the patient either cannot benefit from therapy or that it may be contraindicated in the interest of the patient to continue treatment. There are also situations where it is in the interest of the patient to transfer him to another therapist.

The cardinal factors among others which may block or obviate progress in therapy can be classified as follows:

1. Lack of sufficient intensity in the transference.
2. Inordinate erotic transference wherein the patient's demands for direct gratification cannot be resolved.
3. Inordinate negative transference wherein the patient's formidable hostility and fury frighten and overwhelm him to the point that progress in treatment is stymied and blocked.
4. Regressive passive dependence with intense gratification from the recaptured infantile symbiosis. This transference gratification more than compensates the patient for his suffering entailed in his neurosis. He actually prefers his illness to separation from the analyst. Unless the analyst takes an active part in helping him resolve this symbiotic dependence the analysis may become interminable.

Despite the tediousness of psychoanalytic treatment and the prolonged time and expense involved, there is as yet no better or shorter way of adequately helping people to free themselves from the torments entailed in emotional malfunctioning. Neither the soma nor the psyche is exempt from pain. Not only is the patient paying an inordinate price for his unconscious indulgence in a neurosis, but each person in his milieu is obviously affected through dealing with him.

In the above I have tried to exemplify certain untoward reactions on the part of patients in the process of psychoanalysis and I evaluated some of the possibilities of ways and means in which the analyst may meet these interfering situations. I am fully aware that many patients work satisfactorily in treatment so that the therapist can permit them to cue him when and where an interpretation is indicated and when it is desirable to permit the patient to face the need of working through his resistances and transference feelings by means of his own efforts. My general opinion and, in fact, my conviction leads me to believe that active participation on the part of the analyst, although occasionally overlooked, is frequently indicated.

REFERENCES

1. FREUD: Further recommendations in the technique of psychoanalysis. 1913.
2. FENICHEL: Problems of Psychoanalytic Technique. p. 1.
3. GLOVER: Lectures on technique in psychoanalysis, vol. 9, 1928.
4. MARMOR: The feeling of superiority: an occupational hazard in the practice of psychotherapy. Am.J. Psychiat. 110:No.5, 1953.

Discussion by Leon Salzman, M.D.

DR. ROMM has the rare capacity for exploring psychoanalytic theory and techniques with clear, pointed vignettes from case material which highlight her point of view. This invariably makes her presentations interesting as well as illuminating. Her charm and warmth are revealed not only in her presence, but in the material she presents.

Since, cliches and oracular pronouncements are long in dying, particularly when they contain a spark of truth, we must continue to offer evidence and argument in the activity-passivity controversy. Dr. Romm's material is quite convincing in this regard. She demonstrates how an honest self-appraisal and a recognition of her own distaste for the patient resolves a situation which, in the long run, serves his best interests. We could draw an alternative scene in the tradition of the Hollywood idealization and oversimplification of the psychoanalyst as a combination of the compassionate Jesus and the omniscient Freud, who has only love for everyone, and thus benignly confronts the patient, whom he covertly dislikes. To complete this picture, we would need to show how this arrangement has a long and friendly history of, say, 10 or 20 years duration. But we now recognize this to be a caricature of the role of the psychoanalyst. We now know that the psychoanalyst is a human being who reacts to his patients with both positive and negative feelings, sometimes in a manner which might seriously interfere with the conduct of the analysis. Recognition of this may necessitate transferring the patient, or exploring whether it springs from one's own neurotic trends, or are a proper and adequate response to the behavior of the patient.

Such countertransference reactions can be a most potent influence in the therapeutic work since, if they are in response to the patient's behavior, they can reveal, in camera, the effect which the patient's techniques and patterns of behavior have on others. The therapist's response, whether it be hostility, lust, disinterest, boredom, or excessive maternal or paternal feelings, requires activity of some sort, rather than the passive and sublime illusion that the wisdom of the unconscious will make everything come out just right. These notions have nothing to do with psychoanalysis as a science or an art, but with psychoanalysis as a mystique, based on ignorance and fear of the therapist's potentialities, and thus relegating all power to the unknown, magical forces presided over by the "libidinal god of happiness."

The question of activity versus passivity is best explored in the sado-masochistic problems which occupy the bulk of the psychoanalyst's practice. Dr. Romm refers to the "emotional bookkeeping of the masochist." I think of it as the magical belief that by suffering, one can claim and demand higher rewards. Dr. Romm indicates the extreme efforts which are often needed to pry an individual loose from these symbiotic attachments, and she describes a fairly typical situation of a patient who railed and fumed at her for not acknowledging the patient's needs. The patient accused Dr. Romm of not believing her, and of demeaning her. It was necessary to confront the patient actively with her resistance, and to free her, as Dr. Romm put it, from "her comfortable Oedipal island." I fully agree with the formulation of the necessity for active, assertive behavior in overcoming the inevitable therapeutic impasse in the therapy of the masochistic and compulsive character disorders. I feel the therapist should directly intervene and make overt the true nature of the patient's distortions. The classical detachment of the analyst only arouses intense anxiety and stimulates further masochistic defenses which remain covert and unavailable to analysis. Under these circumstances, the patient is entirely cooperative, obsequious, and pleasant, but therapy remains at a standstill. This is the typical relationship which a masochist sets up in dealing with the world. The direct, active intervention attempts to appraise the realistic situation while correcting falsifications of the past and the present. It also takes into account the masochist's need for contact and interaction. Such activity must be an expression of what the therapist really feels, and it must avoid the cautious and refined statements we are often forced to make in order to avoid hurting the patient's feelings. One must always remember, in this connection, that the definition of a sadist is one who is kind to a masochist. Skill, tact, and above all, a human capacity for warmth and tenderness is required to perform this difficult, but necessary maneuver.

Dr. Romm places some emphasis on the role of the psychoanalyst as a teacher. Franz Alexander and his co-workers have recognized the role of learning in the development of the neuroses when they developed the concept of the "corrective emotional experience." Conditioning, both of the Pavlovian and the operant type (Skinner) also illuminated the dynamics of the process of change. What is the practical effect of these conceptions on the therapeutic process?

First, our view of the neuroses has been altered by the awareness that neurotic development does not occur at a single moment in history as the result of a trauma, or a repression, or even a libidinal fixation or regression. Rather, it is a developmental process which takes place over a period of time and is designed to deal with, or adapt to a situation or event in the life of an individual. The dynamic consequence is a pattern of behavior which, in the process of repetition, follows the laws and principles of learning. It ultimately becomes fixed because of its adaptive usefulness, or its capacity to reduce anxiety, or to resolve painful conflicts. The neo-Freudian theorists (Horney, Sullivan, Rado, Alexander, Grinker, Masserman, Millett, Silverberg, Thompson, Weigert, and others) have documented and developed this aspect of the neurotic structure. If this is the case, then it is clear that the illumination of the problem, either through a moment of truth, or a detailed examination of the structure of the neuroses, or the dynamics of the interpersonal situation, is not sufficient to resolve or reorganize the personality structure. This type of insight was considered intellectual, and it has long been known that this alone could not end the neurotic process. The dilemma was thought to be resolved when the notion of emotional insight was introduced, and the understanding was accompanied by an emotional reexperiencing and reliving of the original traumatic situation. While theoretically this was profound and neat, it still left the problem unsolved, for even with both intellectual and emotional insight the patient remained trapped in his neurosis and still seemed unable to alter his behavior or change his way of life.

In recent years, the goal of treatment has been formulated in terms of producing change rather than insight, and this introduces the issue of learning. Insight and understanding become the prerequisite for the necessary steps in learning and relearning more adequate patterns of behavior. At this juncture, learning theory, the significance of trial and error, rewards and punishments, learning through identification, and the need to lower the anxiety gradient, etc., must be taken into account. The ultimate resolution of the neurotic process becomes a matter not only of following through, but one of prolonged and compassionate assistance in learning to live, re-experience, and to perceive and conceive the world in a newer orientation. This cannot be better exemplified than by referring to the phobic states or the masochistic character disorders.

It has been a privilege and a pleasure to discuss Dr. Romm's paper, and to offer my support and substantiation of her views. Dr. Romm is a good teacher as well as a good scientist. It is this combination which makes the best psychoanalyst.

OVEREVALUATION OF ANXIETY
IN THE TREATMENT PROCESS

By MARIANNE H. ECKARDT, M.D.

OUR AGE is often called the age of anxiety. There is a fascination with and a centering on anxiety that can be compared to Freud's pre-occupation and focussing on sex. Freud reacted to the Victorian and, in fact, Hebrew-Christian tradition of thinking about sex as evil. We may be reacting to the discovery that our society and culture are not as naturally stable as we had supposed, that progress is by no means inevitable, that we cannot assume that the eternal forces will look out for us, that war and pestilence are not evidence of an understandable divine wrath, temporary in nature but always for the future good of mankind.

Freud, reacting to the existing Victorian morality, visualized a world centered around libidinal energy, which he phrased and perceived in overly literal images of sexual drives. We, too, are children of our age and a manifestation of this fact may be our particular fascination with and approach to the phenomenon of anxiety. I do not imply with this statement that we are no longer influenced by the Judean-Christian code of morality. All too often, the word neurosis has simply replaced the word sin and exerts just as much pressure in the name of good mental health as sin did in the name of salvation. But this is not the focus of my essay.

Freud's emphasis depicted man with his libidinal drives caught in an unavoidable and insoluble conflict with family and society; a conflict which he had to cope with to the best of his ability. One never thinks of Freud's man as weak or helpless. He is the battle ground of strong vital urges and energies with a conscience and with the integrating, performing self that has to deliver the goods.

The portrait drawn of man in more recent times is quite different. The accent has been on man's sense of helplessness and weakness in an overwhelmingly unfriendly world. Several major trends have co-operated in painting this picture. Psychoanalytic investigations have broadened out to include personality difficulties and gradually have become all inclusive of man as we meet him. Normality has become nonexistent and the word has been perverted to mean an ideal norm, mostly rather ill defined as to what it is, although very much defined as to what it is not. Ego defenses, defense mechanisms, neurotic trends have become the characteristics of man. They seemed to have taken over, and the key to these defenses is anxiety.

Fromm-Reichmann[1] describes this trend well in a paper called "Psychoanalytic and General Dynamic Conceptions of Theory and of Therapy. Differences and Similarities," which appeared in 1954 in the Journal of the American Psychoanalytic Association. Speaking of the classical and the more dynamic group of psychoanalysts she say: "At present, however, both groups put therapeutic emphasis primarily on the investigation of anxiety aroused by unearthing repressed material and of the anxiety operating in the relationship with the therapist who helps patients to resolve repressive processes. Psychotherapeutic interest is focussed only secondarily on the content of that which has been repressed. In other words, both groups have shifted the center of their therapeutic interest from the investigation of the content of the operation of the id, to the investigation of the dynamics of the operation of the ego." Fromm-Reichmann touches briefly on Sullivan's and Whitehorn's too narrow conception of anxiety as relating chiefly to the anticipated disapproval of others. She then continues: "I have asked myself, therefore, time and again for an additional or a more satisfactory explanation of the most significant emotional content of people's anxieties, which cause the self-disapproval and the fear of punishment and disapproval by others, held responsible for the rise of anxiety in the current analytic and dynamic concepts. In going over the literature on anxiety in children and adults, from M. Klein, Sharpe and Spitz, to Ferenczi and Rank, Freud, Rado and Sullivan, Fromm, Horney and S. Silverberg, it seems that the feeling of powerlessness, of helplessness in the presence of inner dangers, which the individual cannot control, constitutes in the last analysis the common background of all further elaborations on the theory of anxiety." She then develops a hypothesis which, she hopes, might be acceptable to both psychoanalysts and other dynamic psychiatrists. I will not quote it here as it adds little to my discussion.

As mentioned, the image of Western man reflected in more recent psychoanalytic writings, stresses powerlessness, helplessness, anxiety, and a society not conducive to the development of mature individuals. On the whole, the image, as described, is a deplorable one: man is alienated from himself, he is insecure, neurotic, and Fromm castigates Western man as dead and a robot. The picture of our society fares no better. A recent, excellent book by Birnbach[2] called "Neo-Freudian Social Philosophy" appraises the implications of psychoanalytic theory for contemporary social and political problems as revealed in the writings of Neo-Freudians. Summarizing the chapter "The Individual in Western Society," he states: "Neurosis, or to speak more broadly, mental illness, was shown to be the upshot of insecurity and anxiety (Sullivan); insecurity and anxiety were shown to be generated most frequently—almost infallibly—by competition (Horney); competition was shown to be the necessary consequence of the quest for individual self-validation in an egalitarian society of conflicting values (Alexander); and our egalitarian, competitive society was shown to be the product of a long-term evolution of social institutions (Kardiner). Neo-Freudian social philosophy therefore seems to point to the melancholy conclusion that an extensive incidence of mental illness is inherent in modern Western Society, to say nothing of an unavoidable trend toward social breakdown.

"There is little satisfaction in nominating one's fellow citizens for candidacy for a psychopathic ward. Neither is much pleasure to be had from foretelling the impending doom of one's social order. The Neo-Freudians, on the whole, are averse to enjoying the cruel delight of playing Cassandra. The safest generalization that can reasonably be drawn from this chapter, and from the work of the Neo-Freudians as a school of social critics, is that the conditions of life in American society are notoriously conducive to the contraction of mental illness."

Birnbach takes these gloomy appraisals with a grain of salt and I am glad he does. I do agree with him that this trend towards bewailing our society and the depicting of enmeshing neuroticisms in all members of this society exists, and I feel that a self-appraisal is in order. We do not approve of mothers who denigrate their children by a constant negative appraisal of all their action; we do not approve of their lack of trust in their children's basic ability and power to cope with life. Yet we so easily do the same in our manner of speech and writing.

This denigrating appraisal would concern me relatively little if it were purely a matter of public verbalizations and did not reflect itself in the performance of therapy. But I am afraid it does affect therapy.

Psychoanalytic therapies have become longer and longer without evidence of increased effectiveness. These long therapies show a preoccupation by patient and analyst with what causes the patient to be anxious; a preoccupation with needs that were not met in childhood and are not being met now; and show a peculiar passive nonattention to the patient's capacity to engage in his immediate environment more creatively and to make life more satisfying by his creative effort. I have known a series of individuals in such therapies where I felt that the patient's vitality, ability, and common sense was vastly underrated by the analysts, while the anxiety and the so-called repetition compulsion was much overrated.

Our estimate of the patient influences the patient. Marmor[3] made this point well, although in a slightly different context, as follows: "The fact is that in so complex a transaction as the psychoanalytic therapeutic process, the impact of patient and therapist upon each other, and particularly of the latter upon the former, is an unusually profound one. What the analyst shows interest in, the kinds of questions he asks, the kind of data he chooses to react to or ignore, and the interpretations he makes, all have a subtle but significant suggestive impact upon the patient to bring forth certain kinds of data in preference to others."

We all depend to a high degree on the mirror of ourselves reflected by the world we touch. The patient cannot help being deeply affected by what he sees of himself mirrored in the analytic hour and by the image of himself reflected by the comments of the analyst. A one-sided emphasis on the defensive structure often produces a negative image consisting of undue demands, dependence, self-inflation, self-contempt and manipulative maneuvers. A one-sided emphasis on anxiety and trauma produces an image of smallness, helplessness, impotence and a feeling of incapacitation.

If I thought in terms of id, ego, and superego, which I do not, I would ask whether we have not thrown out the id, left the ego-defenses, and then replaced the id with anxiety. Sullivan, in fact, does this in some of his formulations that make anxiety the key of the self-system. He sees anxiety as derived from reflected appraisals of others, or directly caused by the anxiety of the mother, but with no relation to inner impulses.

By the word id I refer to our wishes, our yearnings, our inner wisdom, and to the volitional and intended aspect of our personality. Sullivan describes the superdependence on other people's appraisals.

This we see in our office every day. But it is symptomatology, by which I mean consequences arising out of a certain mode of being.

A dream image told by a patient will illustrate this best. The patient reported: "I was wading in water and had a barometer which fell into the water. I picked it up and realized that it was not working as before. It seemed to register the temperature of my hands, rather than the atmospheric pressure outside, and fluctuated widely." What a helpful image. My patient dealt with life outside by using a barometer that registered atmospheric pressures which he then used as guides for his own behavior. The dream occurred after his first hour with me and registered his apprehension that his inner temperature fluctuations might be revealed. The fluctuation suggests waves of intensity of feeling.

The patient had many an anxious moment in his daily existence for the simple reason that anyone who lives on the principle of that sort of a barometer does. On the other hand, the patient never impressed me as an anxious, helpless person. Nor was I impressed with the presence of feelings of inadequacy, which another therapist of his had emphasized a great deal. The patient knew he was very able and had a rather low opinion of most of his colleagues. His mode of adjustment was in the nature of a defense, designed to keep his own reactions from entering into the interplay. But it also had the characteristics of a policy. He had had a very chaotic childhood that could have come from John Steinbeck's pen. It was a senseless, tearing, crude and cruel kind of a world. The patient had coped with this world better than any of his siblings by a rather deliberate compartmentalization of private and public. He catered to the public world on its terms, not because he feared or respected it, but to keep it from intruding. I am using words like deliberate, policy and intent. These words can obviously get me into trouble, because a conscious formulation of attitudes is often lacking. But they reflect the view that there is a system to our madness in living, often obscured by a facade; a system which is sick only from our mental health perspective, but which otherwise reflects an appraisal and a philosophic statement of the world as experienced by the child. Many patients will recall formulating certain attitudes at a young age and dream images will tell about a patient's main bearing of life.

The main problem of my patient arose less out of the compartmentalization and his attitude to society, then out of the increasing neglect of the private sphere of his existence. This was very evident during his weekends which were like empty spaces filled with waste and trivia even though the patient had two major resources to draw on: an exquisite enjoyment of nature and considerable artistic talent.

The points I wish to make with this example are the following:

1. While I have to grasp the patient's mode of relating to the world or to himself which are usually called defenses or operations of the ego, exemplified by the barometer, there is no question in my mind that my main task lies in allowing the patient to register his feelings from within which in a very liberally extended sense means concern for the substance of his id.

2. There is a danger in focussing on the defensive system as the patient uses the very focussing on other people as a means of not focussing on himself. Patients are delighted to describe their dependency on other people and will do so forever unless we shift the focus.

3. What we are apt to call neurotic defenses are patterns of behavior evolved by the person out of his experiences with his world. These are by no means only responses to anxiety but involve, rather, complex appraisals, judgments, philosophical statements and policies. These are invariably logically founded in his own experiences and make an immense amount of sense. But it is also true that the patients we see have been caught in dead end streets and in their own imagery. The general course of therapy with the patient I described, is to first aid him to reregister his private life, no matter how intense the fluctuation, and then to encourage him to re-experiment and to dare to integrate some aspects of his personal life with his more public existence. This involves new experiences. It is a process of learning, experimenting, forming new judgments and new philosophies.

The experience of anxiety can be most anything. It can be a temper tantrum to have one's way, or a threat, or a genuine apprehension because one is getting into something one cannot handle, or a facade covering competence, etc. But I would like to comment on the two anxieties most often used in our formulations and discussed by Freud in his "Problems of Anxiety."

While Freud gives castration anxiety a prominent place in his speculations, he emphasizes that the apparent anxiety encountered in patients is mostly an anxiety that belong to the ego. It is a signalling device intended to increase the ego's control over the rambunctious id. I think of this signalling device as a red light, saying stop, equipped with a television screen that quickly rehearses in dramatic form all the dire happenings that would result if one did not heed the signal. While these dramatic warning have a memory source, I do not believe that they give us any information as to whether the person would be afraid or would have reason to be afraid if he followed his inclination and disregarded the warning. This kind of anxiety has a purpose and that is to discourage whatever the person was up to.

These anxieties are dramatic productions with the patient being producer, actor, and audience. Patients with a vivid imagery are very good at this. They start with little discomfort but by the time the show is over, the audience has become fully seduced by the imagery presented. The intensity of these anxieties often bears more relationship to the dramatic ability of the patient, than to a fear of whatever would happen if . . .

I have seen these anxieties appear in full force one day, and seen the patient proceed the next day with whatever he insisted he could not possibly proceed with, and do a superb job with total ease and not a flicker of apprehension. The change was often accompanied by some sort of a decision to do rather than not to do. In other situations the fears involved are of a much greater complexity.

These anxieties are treacherous therapeutic problems. They tend to shift focus from an inclination or impulse, mostly of a reaching out nature, to the potential dire happenings and thus discourage the initial inclination. The moment we ask why, or the patient asks, "Why am I so anxious?", and we investigate the past sources of anxieties, we fall hook line and sinker for what might be called a neurotic device.

> A husband on his way home had a fleeting, affectionate thought of seeing his wife greet him warmly and seeing himself kissing her with affection. A minute later his thoughts drifted to an insult she threw at him a week ago, and before he knew it he had re-enacted that scene and was in a state of fury and anxiety. He entered the house tense and ready to pounce. If we take the insult association literally we will direct the association in a certain way, probably elaborating on features of the wife that remind him unpleasantly of his mother. But if we take the insult association with a grain of salt and point out that he started out with a rather affectionate thought, we might get a completely different kind of material. It would probably stress his difficulties in reaching out affectionately. While this difficulty has its developmental source its discussion, nevertheless, focusses the problem on where it should be, namely, on his difficulties in allowing his warm impulses to show and not on the wife's or mother's insults. I have no way of knowing what are the most frequent mistakes in analysis. But my guess is that one of the most frequent ones is to miss the boat by asking the question why at the wrong time and in the wrong direction.

Most formulations relate the anxiety of the ego in the service of defense to the primary anxiety of castration. The imagery of castration has definitely engaged us into a picture of the young, helpless child as being traumatized by the punitive behavior of the adult world. I will use the word castration in a nonliteral way meaning "to make impotent, small or ineffectual." Just as I feel we have taken anxiety too literally, so do I feel that we have thought of trauma too much in terms of the nasty world and the poor, little child. The word trauma belongs to Freud's vision of the Victorian world that was dead set against any form of libido and did make people feel guilty for their sexual impulses. Since then we have extended the meaning of trauma to include any behavior of significant adults that tended to be responsible for a neurotic pattern in the child. The word trauma suggests a hurt. I do not believe that an intense hurt is always involved although, of course, it may be. The child reacts to the way things are around him and digests it all into a pattern of his own. It is perfectly true that he makes the experiences that many of his thoughts and ways do not seem to have a place in the world around him and he takes measures accordingly. Whatever the situation, the course of his future development depends less on the experiences made with his environment than how he digests these experiences into ways of his own. In this sense the process of castration is more a process of self-castration than anything done to him by the outside. It is a self-curbing of his vitality or potency because he feels that his vitality is not wanted or misunderstood or disapproved of and, particularly, because he is afraid to be disappointed if he permitted his intense longings, hopes, and enthusiasms to come alive. Better not hope or desire than to have one's hopes crushed.

Again, let me illustrate with a few images from dreams. A patient drives his car with the brake on. A patient sees a huge penis behind the closed bathroom door. A patient holds a San Sebastian statue in his hand and suddenly discovers that a long penis stands out at the base; he immediately covers it with his hand so that no one should see it. A patient in a dream with many sexual overtones felt the roots of a tree heaving and sees the tree swaying with might. All of these images suggest the apprehension of the intensity of their vitality coming to the fore. A college girl said to me, "People resent it, if I am strong and smart." She tended to present herself as the confused help-needing girl.

Let me add to these dream images a sonnet by St. Vincent Millay,[5] which was quoted to me by a patient who managed the world well enough with his little finger and yet never gave his whole hand. It is entitled "Sonnet to Gath."

"Country of hunch backs!—where the strong, straight spine,
jeered at by crooked children, makes his way
through by-streets at the kindest hour of day,
till he deplore his stature, and incline
to measure manhood with a gibbous line;
till out of loneliness, being flawed with clay,
he stoop into his neighbor's house and say,
'your roof is low for me—the fault is mine.'
Dust in an urn long since, dispersed and dead
is great Apollo; and the happier he;

since who amongst you all would lift a head
at a God's radiance on the mean door-tree,
saving to run and hide your dates and bread,
And cluck your children in about your knee?"

Our view about this process of castration is important, as it will be reflected in our therapeutic approach to the patient. An emphasis on the anxieties of traumatic experiences stresses the search for feelings of anxiety, for memories of traumatic happenings, for feelings of helplessness and, somehow, favors resentments. A stress on the aspect of self-curbing and on submerged intensity and potency in living with due appreciation of its developmental source, will highlight potential strength and introduce the challenge of emerging.

The preoccupation with anxiety and with defensive operations contains the danger of underestimating the individual, of focussing on the wall of fortifications and camouflages rather than on what is hidden within. By giving these defenses an order of primary importance as if they were the individual himself, we run the danger of strengthening the neurosis rather than dissolving it. By focussing on anxiety as an expression of the individual's sense of helplessness and powerlessness we underestimate the person's creative intent and purpose as an architect in building the unique structure of his life.

If this be indeed the age of anxiety, the irony may be that we help to make it so.

REFERENCES

1. FROMM-REICHMANN, F.: Psychoanalytic and general dynamic conceptions of theory and of therapy. J. Am. Psychoanalyt. A. 2:716, 1954.
2. BIRNBACH, M.: Neo-Freudian Social Philosophy. Stanford, Stanford University Press, 1961, p. 128.
3. MARMOR, J.: Psychoanalytic therapy as an educational process. To be published.
4. ST. VINCENT MILLAY, E.: Collected Poems. New York, Harper Brothers, 1956, p. 626.

Discussion by Judd Marmor, M.D.

DR. ECKARDT directs our attention to a common psychoanalytic tendency to focus unduly on the patient's anxieties and weaknesses, and relatively to disregard his strengths and creative values. This is an important and valid point. It is sometimes assumed that people repress only their fears, hostilities and inadequacies, when in actuality patients often are equally unaware of their assets. To confront them with their strengths, therefore, is just as important an aspect of the analytic objective of making what is unconscious conscious, as is the uncovering of repressed ego-dystonic material. It is not uncommon to see patients who cling tenaciously to a depreciated self-image as a defense against the interpersonal responsibilities, intimacies, and expectations in which an acceptance of their actual capacities would otherwise involve them. To be little and helpless is to invoke the protection of others; to be strong and capable is to run the risk of arousing envy, hostility and rejection.

Eckardt also points out, however, that behavior is not only defensive. It is also positively and spontaneously *adaptive* even in the absence of frustrations or threats to the organism. It has long been a criticism of classical psychoanalytic theory that it conceives of personality development as taking place primarily around instinctual frustrations and ego defenses. Hartmann's concept of a conflict-free sphere of ego-instincts is an effort to correct this deficiency and still remain within the classical theoretical framework. Rado's adaptational theory, of course, is a more thoroughgoing effort to break away from the defense-centered orientation of classical libido theory. The principle of homeostasis, important though it is, cannot be the total basis of a theory of behavior. We must be equally aware of the principle of spontaneous growth, which in human subjects includes forces which play a part in creative drives, play, and nondefensive adaptive behavior. But Eckardt points out that we can see only what we are prepared to see. Psychologists have long ago demonstrated that perception is not a mechanical register of "objective reality," but is a highly subjective process determined by our own expectancies and frames of reference. Horney, Alexander and others have pointed out that some patients are capable of showing remarkable powers of spontaneous recuperation after only a brief amount of psychotherapeutic support or insight. This is an area of study which has been relatively neglected by psychoanalysts, who have generally tended to operate on the assumption that genuine emotional maturation can occur only with long-term analytic working-through. We need to know more about the kinds of patients who have this capacity for self-help and about what kind of techniques are most likely to call forth such responses in them.

Dr. Eckardt makes another important point that the assumption that clinical anxiety is always a reaction to a consciously or unconsciously perceived threat is not always valid—that patients may sometimes use anxiety as a way of manipulating others, a kind of "sham-anxiety" whose basic purpose is mastery rather than defense. However, I am sorry that Dr. Eckardt chose to equate the creative potentials in man with mysterious inner forces akin to the Freudian id. I know that she has been careful to caution us that the equation is more literary than literal, but I'm still afraid that the verbal analogy confuses rather than clarifies! Freud's concept of the id was, if anything, the antithesis of the positive forces with which Dr. Eckardt is concerned. It was a "seething cauldron of animal passions," amoral, self-seeking, concerned totally with the pursuit of pleasure and the avoidance of pain—much more akin to Hobbes' concept of "brutish" man than to what Dr. Eckardt is describing. Dr. Eckardt's conception, in fact, sounds more like Rousseau's man, with his presumed "basic feelings" of strength and "inner wisdom." Indeed, I am a little troubled by Dr. Eckardt's use of the term "inner wisdom" as though it is something innate in all of us. I am not sure that man has any wisdom that is not born out of experience—the same basic biological drives which under one set of life experiences can lead man to new heights of creativity and self-fulfillment, can in a different life setting result in fantastic capacities for destruction and annihilation. I must confess that my own bias is for a view of man which sees him neither as innately evil, selfish or destructive, nor innately good, wise or creative. Man comes into this world with an extraordinary central nervous system which has the capacity of adapting itself in countless ways to the demands of his environment, and whether we call those ways good or evil, wise or stupid, depends on many complex factors, including our value systems.

There can be no quarrel with Dr. Eckardt's statement that we must allow the patient to register his feelings from within, but I cannot see that this means concern for the substance of his id even "in a very liberally extended sense." The id is not observable by psychological means—only the ego is. No less a Freudian than Anna Freud pointed this out as long ago as 1936. A patient's inner feelings represent ego responses also, responses which have highly complex roots, social and experiential, no less than biological.

I have some question also about Dr. Eckardt's positing the self-curbing or self-censoring aspects of "castration-anxiety" as though this were antithetical to some originally experienced threat rather than the historical consequence of such a threat. In terms of psychotherapeutic technique, Dr. Eckardt is quite correct in emphasizing the purpose for which the patient is using such anxiety in his current life, but I find it difficult to conceive of such a pattern of self-censorship existing without the individual having subjectively experienced or perceived at least a threat of punishment or a threat of the withdrawal of love, even though, of course, an actual punishment need not have taken place.

In closing, I would like to underline one of the central philosophical implications of Dr. Eckardt's thesis. It is true that there is much in modern society that is destructive of man's capacity for individuation and love. Yet despite all the evidence that exists for man's existential anxiety, his loss of identity, his "escape from freedom," and his seeming inability to control his capacity for destruction, to see only this image of modern man is to see but one aspect of the coin. Side by side with these gloomy observations we can also find a ceaseless striving for self-realization and freedom, a constant pushing forward of the frontiers of his knowledge, and a creative capacity that has put him on the threshold of vistas more exciting and wonderful than have ever before been thought possible. In our sociopsychological approach to modern man no less than in our clinical work with our patients, we must not let ourselves lose sight of the positives, for if we do we are in danger of losing that core of rational faith and hope without which neither we nor our patients can achieve our objectives of a fuller life and a better world.

THE SIGNIFICANCE OF SOMATIC SYMPTOMS IN PATIENTS DURING ANALYSIS

By JACK L. RUBINS, M.D.

THE ANALYTIC situation represents the confluence of many dimensions of personality growth and change, and the analytic process brings into play emotional and characterological factors to such an extent that it is to be expected that some psychosomatic symptoms will appear. In fact it could be legitimately asked whether a treatment is truly psychoanalysis without the occurrence of such symptoms. In my own experience every analysis of adequate depth and length has been accompanied by some somatic symptom formation.

According to a holistic view, personality (or the totality of feelings, attitudes, drives, behavior traits, etc.) is seen as constantly changing throughout life. These changes are the product of forces in process, acting along two dimensions: the developmental or longitudinal, and the here-and-now experiential, cross-sectional or horizontal. The former occurs under the impetus of inherent constructive potentialities for growth and self-realization from childhood through adulthood, is colored by individual temperamental qualities, is subject to the modifying effect of external influences (perceptual, cultural, parental) and internal influences (instincts, physical conditions, body-image, etc.), and is given direction by more healthy or more neurotic development. The latter dimension consists of the interplay between the various inner events occurring at any particular moment which are experienced, expressed or reacted to characteristically. According to this multidimensional modification of Horney's theory of neurotic development,[9] the child who is exposed to distorted parental influences will develop characteristic attitudes in his attempt to relate to them so as to provide him with the greatest feeling of security and safety and minimize his "loneliness in a potentially hostile world." He may attempt to move closer to them and to please them, emphasizing love;

or move away from them, emphasizing his self-sufficiency; or move against them, showing his aggressiveness. But since such attitudes are needed to avoid anxiety, they may become compulsive; being fundamentally contradictory while acting simultaneously, they create conflict and further anxiety. The child, and subsequently the adult, is then obliged to seek secondary means of allaying this anxiety and resolving the conflict. It is this further evolution which constitutes neurotic development.

The individual may then adopt a predominant self-effacing personality orientation to life (morbidly dependent or self-eliminating), or an expansive one (perfectionistic or arrogant or narcissistic), or a resigned one (detached or rebellious). Although one of these attitudes may predominate at any one time, the others are repressed from awareness but remain dynamically active. Each orientation will be accompanied by corresponding needs, standards, inner dictates, values and claims upon others and on the self, whether overt or repressed. What gives these various elements their peremptory, driving effect is that, in keeping with the context of his particular neurotic orientation, the person creates an unconscious, irrational, pride-invested idealized concept or image of himself. Since this is a solution for the conflict engendered by the existence of these incompatible attitudes, he is thus driven to actualize this image, so rising above the anxiety and conflict, by ascribing to himself the irrational attributes of this image. Any awareness of flaw, weakness or failure to achieve this ideal in performance will result in feelings of hurt pride, self-contempt or humiliation, directed against his actual self.

The over-all result of this distorted emotional development, be it neurotic or psychotic, is a loss or numbing of his inner emotional experiences, his identity and body-image, his wants, desires, talents, i.e., an alienation from self. During the psychoanalytic process these different neurotic compulsive attitudes and conflicts which are largely unconscious, emerge into awareness and so may be actively experienced. Such dynamic movements were related to the variations in the clinical picture of somatization in my patients.

These variations were found to be considerable from patient to patient, but a few gross generalities could be noted. (1) Where the somatic symptoms have been present for some time previously and have been an important cause for seeking treatment, patients are often free from the symptom during a first short period of analysis. This may be due to a strengthening of a neurotic attitude, e.g., dependency on the analyst, which temporarily alleviates the conflict. (2) The somatic symptoms occurred in cycles of varying length and intensity, which may begin early in the analysis or late. (3) The system affected varied not only from patient to patient, but usually in the same patient. One patient with a long asthmatic history showed mild asthmatic attacks for some time, then shifted to a cyclic involvement of other systems. Another patient with an equally long history of asthma showed an early cessation of attacks, then a late recurrence. The system which could be affected was most varied: respiratory (asthma, colds, cough), skin (pruritis ani, acrocyanosis, sweating), gastrointestinal (heartburn, gastritis, diarrhea, constipation), motor (stuttering, trembling), ocular (itching, poor vision, lacrimation), genitourinary (pollakiuria, premature ejaculation, pseudopregnancy), or muscular (headache, back pain, chest pain, fainting spells). (4) At times they seemed related to the presence of anxiety in direct proportion; at other times not so related, i.e., decreased even though the anxiety was high, increased when the anxiety was lessening. (5) They did not constitute a problem *per se*, nor did they often interfere with the patients' coming to the sessions. Indeed, this discrepancy, the apparent intensity of the symptoms contrasted with the minimal functional disability, furnished an important index of their functional nature—as contrasted with purely organic symptoms which also occurred from time to time. (6) They decreased uniformly toward the latter part of the analysis.

Body-Image Distortion

These patients seemed to have a characteristic distortion of their unconscious psychological body-image. A number of writers have considered details of the development of the body-image in the infant, and more recently emphasis has been placed on the necessity of adequate and healthy external stimuli for this development—such as mothering contacts and the constant inflow of sensory percepts. We know that the infant begins to develop a self-concept, a sense of "I", probably by the first year, derived from the first awareness of his surface contactual stimuli, his perceptual emotional relationships, and his inner experiences related to satisfaction of needs. An important part of this self-concept is the body-image (body-schema, body-ego) which seems to have two aspects: a physical (postural model) and an emotional, both of which influence each other. The former includes the appearance of the body and its inner and outer configurations: its boundaries, dimensions, depth, inside-outside, up-down, and organs. The importance of the relationship between body-image boundary, for instance, and the patterns of both physiological responses and socializing experiences, has recently been re-emphasized by Fisher and Cleveland[5] who tried to validate their conclusions with various psychological test series. Although this physical aspect may be partly conscious, it is largely an unconscious image which may not agree with the actual body form.

The emotional aspect consists both of the primary feeling tone associated with the various body parts and functions, derived from their importance in fulfilling early needs, as well as the emotional value secondarily ascribed through parental or cultural influences. Not much has appeared in the literature on the relationship of this body-image to the total self-concept nor on its importance in the production of somatic symptoms. Hoffer,[8] Greenacre,[7] Linn,[15] and Keiser[11] have focussed on the inclusion of particular body parts, such as the mouth, the hand-arm, the skin and the genitals, into the body-ego. They have postulated that these organs may remain or later become detached from the body-image, explaining the later appearance of somatic symptoms in them. They relate this process solely to psychosexual factors, so that the body-image becomes libidinized and fragmentary rather than a unitary whole.

Using a somewhat more holistic approach, Schilder[21] has described numerous factors which enter into the formation of this body-image, including developmental, libidinous and social ones. Bender[2] extensively studied distortions of the body-image in children, as evidenced in their behavior, their reactions to postural tests and their drawings of themselves. She found that some distortion of this image was a basic condition for many psychopathological states, including childhood schizophrenia.

Zuger described early personality development in three overlapping stages which he linked to the body-image concept.[25] The earliest is the stage of "self discovery," followed by a stage of "self possession" which continues through adolescence, and finally, a stage of "self-direction." In this schema he stresses the importance not only of external emotional stimuli, but of the formation of the physical self-image through discovery and awareness of the body; and of then having to assimilate or incorporate this body-image into the self-concept. He suggests that certain early psychosomatic conditions may result from undue or distorted parental emphasis upon the part involved, e.g., the bladder and enuresis, so that it is excluded or otherwise distorted in the body-image. This viewpoint has the advantage of going beyond the purely libidinal theories in that it treats the growing person as a whole, and stresses the importance of the acceptance of the physical self as basic to self identity.

A more inclusive explanation of some psychosomatic conditions can be found in part by considering not only the early developmental distortions of the body-image, but more specifically those which occur with neurotic development. This concept postulates that the body-image continues to change constantly with physical and emotional growth through life. It is influenced by internal conditions which can be related to the body, such as instinctual urges, illnesses, physical defects; and also by external stimuli, percepts, as well as by symbolizable concepts, such as parental or cultural attitudes toward sickness. In particular, distortions in the developing body-image may occur as a result of abnormal emotional (neurotic) development, each affecting the other as interchanging cause and effect. These changes are derived from its being implicated in the unconscious idealized concept of the self. Since emotional qualities are associated with physical aspects of organs, neurotically needed aspects of the physical-emotional self are exaggerated or enlarged, and unwanted aspects are decreased or eliminated. For instance, neurotic pride in one's intellectual capacity may be accompanied by enlargement of the image of one's head or cerebral capacity; pride in sexual prowess by enlargement of the image of the genitals. Excessive self-esteem related to size or strength might be accompanied by the image of being taller or huskier than one really is. Conflict about identity might result in a fuzzy definition of appearance. Contempt for the sexual role might go with an image of smallness of the genitals, or of the breasts or other sexual contours.

The alienation from the self, noted above as characteristic of all neurotic development, particularly implicates the body-image in these somatizing patients.[18] Furthermore, they are estranged not only from their actual physical attributes but also from their emotional reactions. Yet since they often are subject to the compulsive inner dictates ("shoulds") of having proper emotional-physical reactions like other people, they have to find a means of expression which will at once be inner-abstract-emotional and outer-concrete-physical. This relationship was noted by Kepecs[13] and by Kubie,[14] who made the distinction on the basis of the actual location of organ systems. It would seem, however, that the real position of organs is of less importance than the psychological location and value made by the patient within his unconscious (and often irrational) body-image. The real position of an organ system is significant only insofar as it will correspond to the psychological function needed by the somatic symptom, i.e., use of the skin for communication, expression, etc. Somatic reactions are more superficial simply in the sense of being more evident, more tangible, more available for conscious attention than direct emotional experience; therefore can best serve this dual function. They would thus be a way of both experiencing emotionally unpleasant qualities, and keeping them at a distance at the same time—the greatest possible distance while still being felt as belonging to the person. They are a means of saying "I have" and "I have not" emotions and body simultaneously.

This greater superficiality and accessability to awareness of somatic symptoms also permits a greater degree of pretense (duplicity) to the individual. For example, a person might be more able through physical symptoms to show others (and himself as well) that he has control over them when he might be feeling helpless. Or to give an appearance of suffering, sorrow or other emotion, when there may really be an underlying absence of affect. With such manifest evidence, the person can convincingly feel honest, real, justified or righteous, thus avoiding deeper awareness of the basic duplicity.

Personality Traits

These patients seemed to show certain dynamic tendencies which predisposed to the appearance of somatic symptoms. I do not feel that these constitute a "personality profile" or character typology, such as many authors have described, in that they are not fixed, static or descriptive attitudes or behavior traits. They are rather driving or energizing forces—which might be seen as needs, drives, demands, restrictions, shoulds—which have a peremptory effect and direction but which may not be concretized into behavior.

The first of these was a pride-invested glorification of absolute health, in some cases emotional health, in others mainly physical health. It constituted an outstanding aspect of the idealized self-concept, and included a feeling of omnipotence in being able to overcome any illness or handicap. It resulted in corresponding claims on life, namely, that the individual be invulnerable and immune to physical ailments. In some cases where the pathological self-esteem was fixed mainly on emotional health, the physical symptom was accepted, even preferred, as less threatening. While such feelings may be partly conscious and behavioral, their intensity, compulsiveness, irrationality and ramifications are entwined with many other personality traits. In one patient they were related to perfectionistic strivings, in another to the power to control feelings absolutely; in another to the feeling of being able to dupe others.

Secondly, as a derivative of this idealization of "strength," sickness becomes highly charged emotionally, again both on a conscious and unconscious level. It becomes synonymous with weakness, fault, imperfection, and as such is accompanied by feelings of self-rejection (self-contempt, humiliation, self-hatred). More precisely, sickness may have different emotional significances depending on the dynamic configuration of the personality at the time and on what is occurring in the analytic process: it may be experienced as a lack of self-sufficiency, as dependency or submission, as masculinity or femininity, as loss of control, as being less smart or less intellectual, as a means of dominating others. With some patients even genuine health may be conceived of as sickness since it means acceptance of normal everyday aches and pains.

A third quality was a characteristic form of intellectualizing (used as an auxiliary defensive solution to relieve conflict and anxiety). It was not the absolute intellectual detachment seen, for example, in some schizoid individuals, where the existence of the emotional-body is denied psychologically or put out of consciousness. In such cases, where there is extensive living in imagination or intellectualizing, somatization reactions seem to be less frequent; feelings are more completely transformed into thoughts. In these patients where there is a partial, conflictual emphasis on intellectual functioning, the body functions are partially admitted to awareness but are felt to intrude. The intellect is often experienced as a means of controlling both the self and the presence of illness. In addition, many such persons have inner dictates involving both their intellectual ability and their emotionality; in their idealized self-image they are both intellectual and feelingful to an absolute degree.

Specificity

The interactions between definable psychic and somatic events have been well reviewed in a recent article by Kaplan[10] and need not concern us further here except that the degree of relatedness has been seen to vary from a precise specificity (a definite affect or personality type producing a definite somatic symptom) to complete nonspecificity (any affect producing different somatic reactions). Some authors espousing nonspecificity have attributed any consistency of pattern in the same person, or differences between individuals, to vague temperamental predispositions, to total life experiences, or to development of a so-called psychosomatic character.[3]

In my patients, even though changes in the somatic symptoms seemed to coincide with more or less definable emotional changes during the analytic process, it was questionable whether this indicated any fixed specificity. This correspondence seemed to be a temporary functional relationship rather than any constant symbolic equivalent. Varying emotional factors came up at different times in relation to the same somatic symptom, or conversely, a similar dynamic factor might seem to coincide at different times with different somatic symptoms or changes in a somatic symptom. For instance, in one patient, respiratory symptoms (colds) were exacerbated when she was experiencing needs for attention and/or affection; or with needs to dominate, or to distance herself; or as she became aware that she herself was frustrating these needs; or as she was taking a stand against her rigid compulsive "shoulds" (projected on to her parents whom she was then experiencing as authorities); or with her feelings of self-hate and self-contempt. In another patient, asthma appeared at one point as a conflictual crying out for help; at another as an ambivalent laughing; or then again as a conflict over "letting go" to breathe freely, to express emotions. Eye itching could possibly be related to emotionally "seeing," becoming aware of something in one's self; nausea to self-disgust; dysmenorrhea to conflict over self-acceptance as a woman or to the feeling of "freely-flowing" in conflict with rigid restrictions; pseudo-pregnancy to feelings of expansiveness, to awareness of creativeness, or to the experience of inner aliveness in the face of emotional deadness; and various sphincteric openings or closings (diarrhea or constipation, for instance) to emotional letting-go or holding-back. Nevertheless, even with the apparent concurrence of such psychic and physical events, it is difficult to affirm how valid the connection really is, whether there is any one-to-one psychosomatic specificity. Certainly from the therapeutic viewpoint we attempt to define the underlying theme or movement in the context of the analytic process at that moment, and perhaps to bring it into awareness as part of analytic technique. At times, anxiety may be diminished by doing so.

However, I feel that even such symptomatic change does not prove the assumption of a specific causal connection. In the first place, the anxiety-relieving effect may be due to other mechanisms. It may be due to the relating of some particular body-part awareness to total inner activity; or of rhythmic somatic changes to psychic changes or other body rhythms, all of which result in enlarging and familiarizing the experience of self. In the second place, every trait, attitude or dynamic movement is in relation to other reinforcing or opposing tendencies, to the conflict which may be produced and to the anxiety resulting from it. This was emphasized by Schilder[22] in his concept of inner functional "spheres" or groups of interrelated unconscious affects. It is doubtful that any particular trait can be isolated from the constellation of total inner experience in which it is embedded and connected more exclusively to the somatic symptom than some other concurrent trait, even though from a descriptive level we may do so. For instance, a person may be bringing up unconscious anger at the same time that he experiences a headache or pruritus ani, and may benefit from an interpretation to this effect. We cannot assume that it is only the rage relating to the headache; it may equally well be expansiveness coming into conflict with self-effacing needs; or the threat of loss of control in conflict with the need to control; or the expression of any emotion at all in conflict with the need to benumb feelings.

Anxiety and Conflict

The somatic symptom at times seemed to be related to the presence of anxiety (limited specificity) but this was not a simple or direct quantitative relationship. There were intense somatic symptoms with a minimum or absence of anxiety, or no symptoms with considerable anxiety. This observation agrees with those of Reid[17] that the degree of somatic involvement does not correspond necessarily with either the intensity of anxiety or the conflict. That is, although body participation may be a physiological component of any affective state, and has been related to emotional conflict,[16, 23] the presence of anxiety or conflict *per se* does not lead to a predominating somatic expression.

The qualitative nature of their anxiety appeared to be of special importance in these somatizing patients, regardless of the particular characterological conflicts which may have engendered it. There seemed to be a distortion of their total experience of anxiety. This was not the simple blocking or damming-up of its adequate discharge, as has been proposed by some analysts.[24] It seemed rather that this distortion involved two faculties. First, it was a blurring of experiential awareness of the anxiety as an *immanent* or arising inner emotion, as a "pure fact"[12] or immediate experience. Such an awareness is both perceptual and conceptual although not necessarily intellectual; it does not refer to either conscious or unconscious as these terms are conventionally used. In short, it is an inability to identify the anxiety.

Secondly, it was a decrease of the capacity to assimilate or become involved with the anxiety as an *emergent* affect, however, distortedly it might have been first immanently experienced. In this sense, the somatic symptom represents both a limited and limiting expression of the anxiety. Both of these tendencies are a result of the neurotic process; the former is part of the general alienation from self characteristic of neurosis in general, the latter is a fear of experiencing anxiety associated with disintegration of defensive solutions. Accordingly, as the person becomes less estranged from all his inner feelings, more able to identify them and more able to involve himself with them (including his anxiety), the somatic symptoms may also be expected to diminish—although at the same time the intensity of the anxiety may be decreasing through resolution of his neurotic conflicts. This occurred in all the cases studied. Since the somatization decreases as the anxiety can be more freely entered into, it is in this sense only that we can speak of "tolerating" anxiety, or in the phenomenological sense, as the person becomes his anxiety.

Somatization as Constructive and Restitutive

Implicit in the concept of acceptance of anxiety is the notion that the presence of anxiety may be a normal phenomenon, consistent with the healthy state. It is more difficult to conceive of psychosomatic symptoms as other than pathological, indicative of neurotic process. I am not referring here to somatic manifestations which are the physiological components of intense emotions occurring as part of "fight or flight" reactions; these cannot be truly considered as pathological. These may be related to simple or rational affects, with or without anxiety, and are constructive in that they lead to effective and appropriate action. However, even the somatic symptoms in these patients may be seen as constructive in certain ways. Thus, they may be a means of the individual's indicating to himself inner experience—albeit in a distorted way of which he otherwise might not be able to be aware.

Not only may somatic symptoms disappear or change with significant emotional movements in a neurotic direction during the analysis, but they may first appear during changes in a constructive direction. For instance, the neurotically detached or intellectualizing person may first somatize when he is shifting constructively toward a greater emotionality, a closer contact with himself. Likewise, somatic symptoms may arise late in analysis when the person's constructive forces may be becoming predominant and threaten the total neurotic structure. During this period of analysis, designated by Horney as the period of Central Conflict,[9] the quality of the anxiety and intrapsychic conflict often changes, to become more intense but also more variable and shifting. At this time, somatic symptoms may likewise first appear or may change in system or intensity.

In addition to indicating either a constructive or neurotic psychic movement, somatic symptoms may represent a third type of function which I would call *restitutive*. This is neither solely neurotic nor solely healthy; it is both. Or it might be considered as the constructive use of a neurotic function. That is, the somatic symptom might be seen as neurotic or destructive at one level but healthy or constructive at some other physiological or psychic level. It constitutes basically a way of maintaining or affirming the integrity of the organism. This form of function has been attributed to other emotional traits, for instance by Eckardt in relation to detachment,[4] by Goldstein for pathological physical functions,[6] and by Bartemeier[1] to the alternation of somatic illness with psychotic episodes, where the somatization is seen as protective.

This restitutive function had three characteristics as evidenced in the somatic symptomatology. First, it seemed to be a self-regulating process in which the focalizing on to the body influenced the rest of the body, other parts and the total state of tension. Second, and as a result of the first, it was an equilibrium-seeking or homeostatic tendency. It tended to bring the patient not only to a uniform state of tension throughout, but to that level of tension or anxiety which could be best tolerated and accepted. This tendency could be sensed sometimes in connection with a particular somatic symptom as a testing either of a neurotic resistance or a constructive strength. The somatic symptom thus constituted a degree of "pain" which could be adequately handled at the moment, which in turn affected the degree of anxiety or other "painful" experience coming into tolerable awareness. They permitted a plateau, a pause for the consolidation of previous intrapsychic movement, a temporary experiencing of a newer psychic organization.

Third, these two properties are not inconsistent with the direction inherent in constructive growth toward increasing tolerance for anxiety. Equilibrium-seeking at any level of anxiety, conflict or tension, is neither static or regressive. It does not imply a lessening, although this may temporarily occur. In this characteristic, somatization differs from what is ordinarily considered as psychological mechanism of defense or solution to conflict. Defenses are directed at avoiding psychologically painful experience. On the contrary, while somatization may permit a temporary lessening of anxiety or conflict, it results in a moving toward a higher level of tolerance at the same time. Paradoxically, periods of freedom from previous somatic symptoms may often indicate movement in the direction of neurosis, i.e., more successful resistances or solutions in operation. This is notably what may occur immediately after entering analysis, when somatic symptoms may temporarily disappear due to strengthening of neurotic self-effacing or dependent trends. But occurring after longer periods of consistent low-level anxiety or somatization, the disappearance of such symptoms may indicate that the patient is now ready to proceed further into the conflict-producing area.

Restitutive function as expressed in somatization, is thus a basic pattern of psychological expression which differs from neurotic patterns in that it is not necessarily adopted for security-safety needs and is not compulsive, although it may become intricated with particular neurotic trends and take on a compulsive quality.

The Somatization Process

Even though we may be aware of the various factors within the personality which dynamically relate to somatization, such as the compulsive attitudes toward sickness and health, the intellect-emotion conflict, the distortions of the body-image as it is involved in the neurotic idealization and rejection of the self, it is still necessary to consider how these factors translate themselves into a somatic symptom. These are motivational or functional factors; they may explain the "why" or the "what" but do not explain the "how." Somatization may represent neurotic, constructive or restitutive movement in the psyche, but such movement must become somatic in its expression. This intrapsychic translation constitutes the *process* of somatization.

This process must be considered within the concept of *modes of reflexive self-presentation of inner experience* which I have presented elsewhere in detail.[19] In brief, I submit that all stimuli arising within the self—feelings, perceptions of organ activities, instinctual impulses, etc.—regardless of their nature or source, whether arising primarily within the self or secondarily in reaction to external factors, are available to awareness and are self directed. The total pattern-process in which such inner experiences present themselves to the individual's awareness would be designated as the "mode of experience." This self-presentation is neither conscious or unconscious in the usual meaning of these terms. It is more a total self-reporting which may be either, an inner awareness which may or may not be conscious or intellectual. It is neither ego function nor id activity, but more inclusive than either. And it is not the subject "I" experiencing something occurring in the body as object, such as the "having" a stomach or hand or headache or anxiety. It is rather a total assimilation or involvement in the body or emotional experience, which is an active process and therefore has been termed reflexive. That is, the self has constant awareness of this process at the same time that it is directing it. What is ordinarily experienced as attitudes, subject-object polarity (I-me experiencing of self), concepts and images, thought or ideation, are simply modes of self-presentation.

These different modes can be brought about because of the inherent symbolizing faculty of the human being—taken in its broadest sense as the representation of one experiential event by another. To account for these different forms of expression, various psychological mechanisms may be used to insure the greatest representative value to the symbolizing process: in other words, to enable the self to acquire the greatest possible awareness of the primary inner experience. Among these mechanisms might be mentioned objectification (translation of inner experience into object-concepts or images), temporalization (experiencing as past, present or future), and externalization (seeing inner events as external occurrences). Externalization, is particularly important insofar as somatic symptoms are concerned, since inner space is as significant as external space. The body as it is conceived to the individual (body-image and body-concept) becomes the framework for inner experiences to be externalized upon.

Conceptual distortions of this framework may give rise to psychosomatic symptoms. Since the body-image is relatively more stable than psychic changes, and since the symbolizing process operates at many levels of self-experience, somatic symptoms will thus vary less than psychic-emotional events. And the same somatic symptoms may thus express varying intrapsychic stimuli, from the more simple to the more complex. Similarly, several self-presentatory modes of experience may be used at the same time for a particular emotional stimulus, for instance where gut pain may be felt simultaneously with a mental image as a result of some emerging inner experience. It might be said that the reflexive circuits are of different directness and degrees of distortion. By the same token, the patient who has a shift in somatic symptoms from headache to respiratory to intestinal, is representing a shift in the configuration of constellations of psychic factors. The same shift could be expressed in other ways, for instance as changes in one or a series of dreams, or by the selection of memories or actual events involving change or movement.

The various body symptoms are thus not only the direct overflow of one or more affects or affectively-associated ideas but also the self-presentation of the inner organization (configuration) of this momentary psychic-affective state. The patient who has contradictory compulsive dynamic attitudes may experience anxiety; his somatic symptoms express not only the anxiety, but more specifically represent his way of becoming aware of this anxiety in a particular inner context. Somatic symptoms are thus symbolic, but not simply object symbols. They are rather symbolizings of intrapsychic movements or peremptory emotional forces (needs, affects, drives, inhibitions, demands, etc.) in dynamic relationships with each other.

REFERENCES

1. BARTEMEIER, L.: The structure and function of the predominating symptom in some borderline cases. Am. J. Psych. 116:825, 1960.
2. BENDER, L., AND KEDER, W.: The body-image of schizophrenic children following electroshock treatment. Am. J. Orthopsych. 22:335, 1952.
3. BLAZER, A.: The psychosomatic character. New York State J. Med. —:1587, 1950.
4. ECKARDT, M.: The detached person. Am. J. Psychoanalyt. 20:139, 1960.
5. FISHER, S., AND CLEVELAND, S.: The Body-Image and Personality. Princeton, Van Nostrand, 1958.
6. GOLDSTEIN, K.: The Organism. New York, Am. Book Co., 1939.
7. GREENACRE, P.: Early physical determinants in the development of the sense of identity. J. Am. Psychoanalyt. A. 6:612, 1958.
8. HOFFER, W.: The development of the body ego. In: Psychoanalytic Study of the Child, New York, Internat. Univ. Press, 1950.
9. HORNEY, K.: Neurosis and Human Growth. New York, W. W. Norton, 1952.
10. KAPLAN, H. L.: A psychosomatic concept. Am. J. Psychoth. 11:16, 1957.
11. KEISER, S.: Disturbances in abstract thinking and body-image formation. J. Am. Psychoanalyt. A. 6:628, 1958.
12. KELMAN, H.: The symbolizing process. Am. J. Psychoanalyt. 16:145, 1956.
13. KEPECS, J. G.: Some patterns of somatic displacement. Psychosom. Med. 15: 425, 1953.

14. KUBIE, L. S.: Central representation of the symbolic process in psychosomatic disorders. Psychosom. Med. 15:1, 1953.
15. LINN, L.: Some developmental aspects of the body-image. Internat. J. Psychoanalyt. 36:36, 1955.
16. MARTIN, A.: The body's participation in dilemma and anxiety phenomena. Am. J. Psychoanalyt. 5:28, 1945.
17. REID, J. R.: The concept of unconscious anxiety. Am. J. Psychoanalyt. 16: 42, 1956.
18. RUBINS, J. L.: Psychodynamics and psychosomatic symptoms. Am. J. Psychoanalyt. 19:165, 1959.
19. ———: Notes on the organization of the self. Am. J. Psychoanalyt. 18:171, 1958.
20. ———: The self-concept, identity and alienation from self. Am. J. Psychoanalyt. 21:132, 1961.
21. SCHILDER, P.: The Image and Appearance of the Human Body. New York, Internat. Univ. Press, 1950.
22. ———: Medical Psychology. New York, Internat. Univ. Press, 1953.
23. WEISS, F.: Neurotic conflict and physical symptoms. Am. J. Psychoanalyt. 6:15, 1946.
24. ZETZEL, E. R.: Anxiety and the capacity to bear it. Internat. J. Psychoanalyt. 13:1, 1950.
25. ZUGER, B.: Growth of the individual's concept of self. Am. J. Dis. Child. 83: 719, 1952.

Discussion by Simon H. Nagler, M.D.

DR. RUBINS' paper, despite its deceptively modest clinical title, is an ambitious undertaking. For, while presenting valuable clinical observations and generalizations, it most cogently addresses itself to casting light on a highly important theoretical question, namely, the nature of somatization. This is one horn of the mind-body dilemma which has plagued Western intellectual history from the earliest Greeks, posing the mystery of how the mind exerts its effects on the body: in a word, the riddle of somatization in all its forms and configurations. Descartes, who most clearly formulated the modern form of this fateful duality, solved the riddle by locating the soul in the pineal gland and assigning to it the role of mediating between the psyche and the soma. In recent years, modern research has returned to the vicinity of the pineal gland, assigning the mediating role to the so-called visceral brain, the functions of which Herrick, Papez, and MacLean have done so much to elucidate.

To facilitate discussion, let us briefly summarize the body of the paper. After a critique of the term "psychosomatic" as basically inadequate from a dynamic point of view, Dr. Rubins presents a valuable set of clinical aphorisms on the variation of somatic manifestations as they were observed by him in a rich clinical experience. He then proceeds to the kernel of his argument by delineating the dynamic factors which he considers as predisposing to the generation of somatic symptoms. The formulations that follow are distinctly in the line of the Horney theory of personality formation and neurosis. The psychosomatic individual, so to speak, has a pride-invested glorification of absolute health in all its aspects. He has a need for intellectual brilliance and the fullest sort of emotionality, which can only coexist because of compartmentalization, which permits at least the partial achievement of these contradictory demands, through the process of somatization. Furthermore, such individuals, presumably because of the earliest childhood experiences, have acquired a distortion of their unconscious body-image, which subsequent neurotic alienation from the self only aggravates. Somatization is a way of both "feeling" and "not feeling" emotional states, and by thus permitting greater self-deception facilitates the maintenance of the fraudulent self-image. And, finally, such psychosomatically-prone individuals characteristically distort their experiencing of anxiety in that there is both a perceptual and conceptual blurring of the existential state of anxiety. There is a type of inability to identify one's anxiety and a diminished capacity to deal with emerging anxiety, so that the somatic symptom serves as both a limiting and a limited expression of the painful affect. The therapeutic conclusion that follows is obviously that the more the patient becomes capable of both identifying and experiencing his anxiety in its totality, the less somatic disturbance he should display.

All of the predisposing factors to somatization enumerated indicate only the "why" but not the "how" of the process. Dr. Rubins' contribution toward a solution of this problem is his formulation concerning what he terms the "modes of reflexive self-presentation of inner experience," upon which he elaborated in a previous publication. According to this concept, all stimuli from within, whether primary or secondarily derived, are available to self-awareness in pattern—processes designated as "modes of self-presentation."

This brings us to the highly complex symbolizing process, over which throughout the history of ideas literally oceans of ink, if not blood, have poured. It is because of this innate human capacity for symbolization, for representing anything by anything else, that the different modes postulated by Dr. Rubins can be achieved. Among the various avenues of the symbolizing function, such as objectification, temporalization, etc., that of externalization is of special importance to somatization, for intrapsychic experience is projected upon the body as conceptualized by the individual in his body-image or body concept. Distortions in this framework of reference, so to speak, result in somatic disturbances. The somatic symptoms are not simply symbols, but rather symbolizings of dynamically related emotional forces, the ways in which the individual becomes aware of anxiety in particular contexts.

These formulations appear to have an inner consistency but require further validation—just as all contemporary schools of psychopathology accept the nuclear significance of the concept of anxiety, but disagree as to the nature of the conflicts that generate it, so too all concerned with the question of psychosomatic illness agree that emotional tensions arising in varied personalities under diverse circumstances are casually operative. There is disagreement as to the variables and how they are translated into somatic dysfunction.

Ten years ago, Kubie published a paper which touches closely on the mechanism of somatization as propounded by Dr. Rubins, although obviously written from a different orientation. Kubie, like others, finds that it is the symbolic process that renders possible the transmutation of the psychological experience into the somatic disorder or symptom. And in keeping with the significant neurophysiological findings concerning the visceral brain, which I briefly mentioned in my opening paragraph, it is through the pathways and mechanisms of this complex system that the symbolic process operates in psychosomatic disorders. The development of the uniquely human function of speech and language—in fact, of the entire organismic function of employing symbols—is intimately involved with the formation of the body image or concept, which is the evaluative mental representation of one's body both as to structure and function and especially as to how it appears to others. The visceral brain is at the juncture of external and internal perceptual processes and is thus the point of integration of the multipolar symbolic function. By way of the visceral brain, the visceral components of memory enter into psychological functions, and contrariwise, the psychological perturbations are reflected in visceral activity or dysfunction. Of course, organs and their processes are not equally or similarly available to the symbolic function, and thus they must be differently involved psychologically. Certainly, normal growth is never exclusively somatic or psychological, but always psychosomatic and holistic. Kubie offered an elaborate classification of the body and its organs based on the degree of their accessibility to awareness, and the relative values of the the roles played in the function by the somato-muscular and somato-sensory systems and the autonomic nervous system. In the first category, the somato-muscular-sensory system is primary, while the autonomic nervous system is of little importance. This category includes those organs which implement one's relationship to the world (exteroceptive sense organs, voluntary muscle, organs of speech, etc.), the instruments of the ego, so-to-speak. Disturbances of these functions are generally classified as conversion-hysteria and are excluded from the psychosomatic disorders in this country, but not by continental writers. These organs are clearly in consciousness, belong to the body "I," mediate our relation to the non-"I" and may represent the non-"I" on an unconscious level. The second category includes the organs of the internal economy which are not available to direct awareness, and whose disturbances are considered "organ neuroses." In these, the autonomic nervous system is practically the sole agent, and the organs have a very vague symbolic representation, if any. The third category includes the organs of the primary instinctual functions of intake and output of air, food, water, wastes, etc. These organs and their symbolic representations are chiefly concerned with the functions, control, gratification and frustration of the various apertures of the body. These functions are invariably initiated on the somato-muscular level only to terminate by purely autonomic behavior, as for example, swallowing, urination, ejaculation, etc. And, finally, in this interesting survey, there is the category in which the sole member is the body-image as a diffuse representation of the entire soma. In this function the higher conceptual and symbolic processes predominate and there is little activity of the effectors. ("The Central Representation of the Symbolic Process in Psychosomatic Disorder" : L. Kubie, Psychosomatic Medicine, 1952).

It must be clearly understood that while the foregoing considerations are illuminating concerning the roles of the symbolizing function, the divisions of the nervous system, emotional tensions and the body image in the generation of psychosomatic symptoms and syndromes, they are largely descriptive. And, parenthetically, it is necessary to recall that Alexander does not ascribe any symbolic significance to vegetative neuroses, although he considers that each psychosomatic disorder has its specific conflict. Emotional tensions are usually expressed in the symbolism of language and sensory imagery, but they may also find expression through the language of the body in varied disorders of function. Conversion hysteria, organ neurosis, and somatization are still largely descriptive terms.

Dr. Rubins in his generalizations on psychosomatic symptom variation noted that the system affected varied in the same patient. This characteristic of psychosomatic disturbances has been familiar to clinical medicine for a long time, and has come to be a hallmark of this class of disorders. A very well known example, of course, is the occurrence of asthma with the disappearance of infantile eczema. This is an illustration of what has been termed syndrome shift, chiefly by continental writers, who also call attention to syndrome suppression, namely, the disappearance of a psychosomatic syndrome under conditions of emotional tension as, for example, the clearing of ulcers during the bombing of a city during the last war. While relatively few studies of the phenomena of syndrome shift and syndrome suppression have been made, several were reported in this country by Kepecs under the title of "Some Patterns of Somatic Displacement," and by Seitz on the hypnotic substitution of other symptoms for the original conversion reactions. It is of significance to the thesis set forth by Dr. Rubins that only the symbolically equivalent reactions could be substituted hypnotically by Seitz. Even the spontaneous formation of symptoms following posthypnotic suggestions would occur only along symbolically equivalent lines. Furthermore, Kepecs observed that symptom shifts which occurred under the pressure of psychic events were not along random pathways, but along highly personal paths only to be understood in terms of the individual's experiences. I, too, have observed as migraine "cured" only to be replaced by duodenal ulcer, and postpartum depression yielding to a florid hyperthyroidism with extreme exophthalmos, and alternating depressions and asthmatic attacks, one of which yielded to ACTH along with a psychosis.

THE SIGNIFICANCE OF THE EMOTIONAL EXPERIENCING OF DREAMS IN PSYCHOANALYTIC THERAPY

FREDERICK A. WEISS, M.D.

PSYCHOANALYTIC therapy has become more difficult. The gap between the therapeutic needs of the patient and the development of psychoanalysis has widened. More patients show an increasing degree of inner dissociation and emotional withdrawal. Freud's age of hysteria was followed by the age of psychosomatics, and this has been followed today by the age of alienation. The main characteristic of patients has become their estrangement from their own feelings and experiences.[1]

Psychoanalysis, born as a child of the period of enlightenment, overestimated the therapeutic value of knowledge in itself; and the recently reemerging ambition to become an "exact science" often lets psychoanalysis become what Ferenczi called "a kind of descriptive analysis, actually a contradiction in itself . . . The dynamic factor of experience was neglected."[2] After termination of analysis a training candidate and very often a patient could go to the next clinical conference and give an excellent description of himself in the terminology of his analytic school. Basically, however, they did not change.

Psychoanalytic therapy, if effective, fosters basic emotional change through emotional experience and emotional insight. In the warm climate of the mutually trusting doctor-patient relationship in which he feels fully accepted as he is, the patient can gradually abandon his defenses. Steadily growing self-awareness and self-confrontation become possible and lead the patient to a genuine and realistic acceptance of his self with its human limitations but with awareness of the potentiality and responsibility for further growth.

In this therapeutic process the dream can become a decisive, mobilizing force due to essential qualities inherent in the process of dreaming itself.

DREAMING—A CREATIVE EMOTIONAL EXPERIENCE

Dreaming is the expression of a basic organismic need. Dream deprivation leads to a compensatory increase in the number and length of dreams and, if it continues further, to a severe impairment of health.[3]

Dreaming is by no means a merely *reactive* phenomenon, reactive to a "vis a tergo" such as instinctual pressure or reactive to inner or outer stimuli, to a traumatic past, a disturbing present, or a wish for the future. Any or all of these elements may enter the dreaming. In doing so, however, they lose their isolated nature and become transformed into symbolic aspects of a new integrated whole: the dream.

Dreaming is an *active*, creative, integrating process.[4-6] It is steered by the total needs, feelings, strivings, emotional conflicts and attempts at solution which the dreamer is experiencing at the time of the dream.

The dreamer may attempt to solve the conflict more neurotically, for example, by magic wish fulfillment, approximating Freud's original view of the function of the dream, or more healthily by confronting the conflict in a creative spirit of self-assertion and courage.

Dreaming expresses the interplay between two main emotional forces in man: (1) Strivings which move man forward in the direction of healthy growth, greater freedom for self-expression and self-realization; and (2) anxiety-charged, compulsive needs for safety which interfere with growth and self-expression and which, if the anxiety is excessive, lead to a regression in the direction of self-effacement and self-elimination.

Like man himself, his dreams are neither only neurotic nor only healthy. The dream is not merely "a neurotic symptom"[7] or "a psychosis with all the absurdities, delusions, and illusions of a psychosis."[8] Neither, however, is the dream always part of a "curative process of the soul" as Poul Bjerre postulated in his constructive, but too teleological view.[9] Yet we may agree with Bjerre that there are "creative, life-affirmative forces at work in us, and that dreams are one of their most important expressions"—a view which has also been expressed by Karen Horney and Franz Alexander.

Originating in the patient as a most personal and individual experience, the dream carries with it a convincing power greater than any statement coming from the outside, including comments by the therapist.

LESSENING OF SELF-ALIENATION

Dreaming occurs in a state of lessened self-alienation.[4] The superstructure of repressions, rationalizations, and self-deceptive illusions, built up for protection and defense during the waking state is shrinking. There is less need to keep masks on, to over-adapt to others and to conform with the stereotyped norms of the surrounding culture.

Dreaming is a "primary" process. This does not make the dream a psychotic phenomenon. Similar aspects of "primary process" characterize the creative process. The affects in (and after) dreams are the most significant and the most reliable aspect of the dream. Even Freud, while devoting the major part of his "Interpretation of Dreams" to the complicated mechanism of the "dream-work" which has to be undone by the equally complicated many steps of dream interpretation, says: "The dream presses its claim to be accepted as part of our real psychic experiences, by virtue of its affective rather than its ideational content."[10]

In dreaming the patient is closer to his true feelings, be they more neurotic or more healthy. The dreamer is freed from temporal and spatial constrictions. More truly free associations emerge. Unessentials recede. The essential moves into the center. "Shoulds," imposed by society and by the patient himself are weaker. Spontaneous "wants" become stronger. Dreaming brings the patient closer to experiencing himself as he is and as what he can become.

WIDENED SCOPE OF SELF-AWARENESS

In dreaming the scope of inner perception and of self-awareness is widened. As the pupil widens in the dark, the dream enlarges the inner horizon, the scope of self-awareness which during the day is restricted by compulsive focussing on emergencies, on action, on defense.

Bergson thus commented on the enlarged perceptive power of the dream:

"Our senses continue to function . . . they embrace a host of subjective impressions which pass unnoticed in the waking stage—when we live in a world of perceptions common to all men—and which reappear in sleep when we live only for ourselves. Our faculty for sensory perception, far from shrinking in every respect when we are asleep, broadens its field of operations."[11]

Bergson refers to the inclusion in the dream of auditory, tactile and particularly of internal body sensations which explains the occasional illness-predicting capacity of the dream. He also observed that dreams often relate "to objects that we have perceived almost without awareness." This highly significant observation was later experimentally confirmed by Poetzl and recently, by Charles Fisher,[12] who in their studies of subliminal perception showed that the dream often symbolizes that which in the waking state had not been perceived.

The enlarged perceptive power of the dream, in a unique way, includes the perception of the self. The dream has access to aspects of the self which the patient rejected or repressed: neurotic aspects which he denied or idealized; or healthy aspects: for example, the courage to be and realize himself, his capacity for affection and love which he was afraid to experience and express; or spiritual aspects which he disregarded or deprecated; or physical and emotional needs, the experiencing of which was blocked by pride, attempts to control, and self-doubt or taboos. Thus the dream becomes a door to the "larger self."

Dreams confront the predominantly dependent patient with the rage and aggression within him, of which he has remained unaware. The predominantly aggressive patient may experience his strong dependency needs which pride prevented him from feeling. In severely alienated or resigned patients, who appear shallow or emotionally dead, dreams often show a surprising aliveness, emotional depth, violent conflict and passionate feelings of whose presence neither patient nor therapist had been aware.

Owning the Dream

The dream can exert its full therapeutic impact only if it is emotionally fully experienced and "owned" by the patient. Such experience often reaches the intensity of an "Aha" experience: this is *my* dream; yes, these are *my* feelings, this is *me*. Only such "owning" gives the dream sufficient power to lead to basic emotional change. This dynamic impact, however, is very often prevented by the patient or by the therapist, and frequently by both.

The Patient

The fact that the patient brings a dream to his analytic hour, in itself does in no way evidence his genuine interest or emotional involvement in it. On the contrary, he may do it without any emotional experience or—not too rarely, even to *prevent* it.

Particularly in the beginning of therapy the patient often looks at the dream as "only a dream" for which he is no way responsible, a product of the unreal world of phantasy which he separates completely from the "real" world of his actual life. While Oedipus still doubted his responsibility for his dreams, Nietzsche and Freud held a very different opinion. Nietzsche wrote in "Morgenroete" ("Dawn") : "You want to own everything, but not your dream. What weakness, what lack of courage. Nothing is more your own than your dreams. Nothing is more your own creation." And Freud states:

"Obviously one must hold oneself responsible for the evil impulses of one's dreams. In what other way can one deal with them? Unless the content of the dream is inspired by alien spirits, it is a part of my own being . . . I shall perhaps learn that what I am repudiating not only 'is' in me but sometimes "acts" from out of me as well."[13]

The patient may bring his dream in a disinterested spirit of fulfilling his duty. Or he may bring it as a "gift" to the therapist: "Today I have a dream for you, Doctor." This does not only reflect the transference aspect of his "offering," but the formulation "for you, Doctor" clearly reveals the unconscious wish: "But please *keep me out.*" Here the dream affords to the patient, in the words of Glover, "respite from the recital of other and more obviously affective material."[14]

Other ways to avoid emotional experiencing are used by the detached patient who reports his dream as if it were a story or a movie plot dealing with somebody else, and by the competitive patient who tries and often succeeds in using dreams to involve his therapist in an intriguing game of puzzle solving in which he, the patient, of course, presents more ingenious solutions although they may actually only cover up or distort the truth contained in the dream.

WRITING DOWN OF DREAMS

The writing down of dreams may interfere with their being experienced emotionally. Freud considered it "superfluous." Other analysts definitely reject it. For example, Lipschutz states: "The written dream is always a transference dream produced specifically for the analyst, to deceive, confuse, blockade or please him."[15]

There is no doubt that spontaneously reported dreams are closer to experience and therefore more valid and more valuable; but if the interval between sessions is too long one may use the written dream. In such a case, however, it enriches the experiencing of the dream if the patient, in addition, is asked to report the dream. Often slight, but sigfiincant differences between the two versions fertilize the analysis.

THE THERAPIST

The dynamic, affective impact of the dream, however, is very often lost due to the therapist. He may take the dream out of context as an interesting object in itself. He may give one-sided emphasis to its aesthetic or dramatic aspect, to the decoding of symbolism and the search for the latent meaning of the dream. Most papers dealing with dreams which were published in the recent years fall into one of those categories. I am a great admirer of the creative artist in us who produces dreams; but from the viewpoint of effective therapy the *looking at* the dream (although often with awe and fascination which the patient is only too ready to share) maintains, even increases, the experiential distance between dreamer and dream. The therapist has to be on his guard against being seduced by the patient into a mere aesthetical or symbolistic approach, or being led into the trap of a parlor game of dream interpretation. Often he has not even to be seduced. He may welcome such activity to relieve his own unconscious or conscious anxiety about lack of progress in therapy.

More deleterious and almost universal, a result of present psychoanalytic training is the fact that the therapist approaches the dream with preconceived notions, formed and definitely colored by the very specific concepts and "complexes" of his psychoanalytic school. Such restrictive approaches, together with a dogmatic symbolism which reduces the experiential richness of the dream to stereotypes, interfere with the spirit of creative exploration that is required for the activating of the patient's spontaneous experience. It makes the therapist a 'killer of the dream."

There exists a close relationship between dreams and myths which Abraham called "dreams of nations." Mythical and universal symbols may be used by the dream if they pertinently convey the dreamer's feelings. Nevertheless, dreaming is a highly individual experience. Binswanger sees the dreaming mode of being in the world characterized by our being totally involved in our "Eigenwelt" (our own world), the mode of relating to ourselves.[16]

Many psychoanalysts still see dream symbols as having predominantly libidinous and fixed meanings. But symbols are neither restricted to libidinous meanings nor are they fixed.

Dream symbols have a holistic character. It is the whole realm of human experience which is being symbolized: the dreamer's feelings about himself, about others, about his "being in the world."

Dream symbols are not stereotyped. The human symbol, according to Cassirer, is "not characterized by its uniformity but by its versatility. It is not rigid or inflexible but mobile."[17] The same symbol, for example, a horse, a bird, father, may acquire new and changed meanings in the course of therapy. Indeed, the change of a symbol or of a symbol pattern in dreams often indicates (or sets in motion) significant emotional changes in the patient.

Symbols Condense Emotional Conflicts

Symbolization in dreams is not a reductive, disguising process which occurs in a state of lessened apperception. It is a creative process. Symbols are dynamic crystallizations of the dreamer's feelings and conflicts, in the original sense of "symbol." "Symbol," derived from "symballein" means: that which is thrown together, formed by being fused. What the dream image fuses is: two conflicting affects or strivings.* Not the reduction of the symbol to stereotypes, but the opening up and the full experiencing of the emotional conflict which is condensed in the symbol promotes the experiential owning of the dream. The experiencing has to take place in the context of the whole dream as well as the dreamer's life. The symbol of the "wife-mother" in which the dreamer gives the wife features of his mother, lets him experience his conflict between his striving for a mature marital relationship and his dependency needs. A slick, "masculine" flashy racing car which had the shape of a baby carriage crystalized the conflict of a girl concerning the infantile qualities of her pseudomasculine boy friend.

The same holds true for sexual symbols.[19] A knife or sword is not simply a disguised penis, but it may symbolize a penis if the dreamer's experience fuses sex and aggression. In his dream a man gives his penis to his wife, feels first good and relieved by it, but then sees it wither and fears that it will no longer be useful when he wants to put it back again on himself. The dream symbolizes the conflict between his compulsive passivity and his wish for masculine identity.

The Past Intensifies the Emotional Experience of the Present

The symbol fuses unconscious and conscious experience, past and present. The past appears in dreams as a dynamic symbol of the present.[20] It is called forth by the emotional constellation of the present. It

---

*A similar view was expressed by Schilder who stated: "Symbols express two conflicting tendencies. They appear on the crossroads of two drives."[18]

deepens and intensifies the dreamer's experience.

At times of increasing anxiety past symbols of dependency and help-lessness may enter the dream. At times of lessening alienation and stronger self-feelings, constructive symbols of the past may enter. Chronologically they may lead back to childhood of adolescence, but dynamically they are by no means regressive. They indicate construc-tive moves in which the patient reconnects himself with a time when his heart was still alive, his feelings were more genuine, a time when he was able to take a stand for himself, when he had a greater sense of personal identity.

Concepts Recede Behind Emotional Experience

The emphasis on the emotional experiencing of the dream lets the differences between orthodox and holistic interpretations recede. De-cisive is: which interpretation will promote best emotional insight in *this* patient at *this* stage of his analysis. Thus the dream in which a patient's father took away a letterbox key from him could be seen as symbolizing castration. The patient, however, experienced mainly the arbitrary use of power and control by his father and connected it constructively with his own lack of self-assertion. In a later stage of his analysis, the castration interpretation may prove more meaningful to him. Erikson also makes the choice of possible interpretations depend-ent on the specific therapeutic need which prevails at the time of the dream.[21]

Anxiety dreams are by no means always a negative phenomenon in therapy, connected with fears of physical or sexual aggression. Often they occur because the last analytical hour questioned successfully a neurotic solution or penetrated effectively some aspect of the defense. Such anxiety often is threshold anxiety. There is fear about giving up the status quo which, despite its restrictions and illusions (or rather because of them), provided some safety. How possible will life be with-out the crutches of the neurosis? Often the anxiety dream reflects the "dizziness of freedom," (Kierkegaard) and has a positive significance regarding the prognosis in therapy.

Not only the presence, but the absence of feelings in dreams is im-portant, especially when this absence appears paradoxical as, for ex-ample: absence of fear in danger situations (due to belief in magic or omnipotence?), absence of sadness when sad events occur (due to hostility, need for control of feelings or self-anaesthesia?), or absence of rage in humiliating situations (due to basic self-rejection or self-effacement?).

CHANGE OF EMOTIONAL EXPERIENCES IN DREAMS DURING THERAPY

The character of the emotional experiencing of dreams changes in the course of effective therapy. Early dreams let the patient experience the self-defeating aspect of his attitudes and his magic expectations regarding the therapist. What I have called "split-image" dreams, occur later, in which the patient experiences conflict between the restricted neurotic self, which may be idealized, and the emerging larger self. Finally, dreams of integration supervene which reflect stronger personal and sexual identity, self-acceptance and self-realization.[22] Limits of space[23] permit the inclusion of only one dream which was accompanied by deep emotional experiencing. A woman under the pressure of a perfectionistic idealized image had become filled with violent self-contempt. She rejected herself to the degree of making several suicidal attempts. She resented being a woman and rejected body and sex. At the mere mention of these words during the analysis she displayed strong reactions of disgust. Now she dreams:

> "I was beside a crib in which lay a little girl who was just waking up. I had a very strange feeling. I loved her very much and it did not frighten me. I picked her up, held her and loved her. I asked her whether she had wet her bed and she said she had not. But I felt it would not make any difference to me whether she had or had not. I took her into the bathroom, and there she started to urinate and she filled a big pot just to the brim, which was remarkable. I kissed her all over, from the forehead down to the lower body and finally, on the sex organs. A year ago I would have wanted to kill her because she was a girl. I would have felt horrified and disgusted. But she had a lot of personality. Passive but quite outgoing. I had a new feeling of happiness."

The feeling of happiness which the patient has in this dream reflects that basic emotional change which Bjerre calls "transformation of feeling." The love which she feels for the girl, even if she has been "bad," shows a lessening of the extreme demands she made on herself. That the girl "fills the pot just to the brim" still shows remnants of her perfectionism. But her kissing of the child's body "down to the sex organs although she was a girl" and her statement that "she had a lot of personality" made this dream a pacemaker on her road to genuine self-acceptance and a stronger sense of personal and sexual identity.

THE DREAM—A DOOR TO THE LARGER SELF

As it is important for the patient not merely to *talk* about the dream, but to feel the dream until he is back in it, the therapist too has to feel himself (not think himself) back into the dream with the patient. He may "dream along," as Gardner Murphy expressed it. But he must also help the patient to integrate the dream into his life and to use it as a door to his "larger self." The morbid dependency which the dreamer experiences is *his* even though in his daytime awareness he called it "love." The sadism which he experiences in the dream is *his* although while awake he saw it as "strength." The need for closeness which he experiences in the dream is *his* although he glorified himself proudly as self-sufficient and needing no one. But also the courage or affection or love which he experiences in his dream is *his* although in his actual life they may still be blocked by anxiety or pride.

"While dreams entertain us, Santayana writes, the balance of our character is shifting beneath, we are growing while we sleep."

Summary

Psychoanalytic therapy promotes basic emotional change through emotional experience and emotional insight. In this process the dream can become a powerful mobilizing force due to essential qualities inherent in dreaming:

1. Dreaming is a creative emotional experience which originates in the patient himself.

2. Dreaming occurs in a state of lessened self-alienation. The dreamer is closer to his true self.

3. The dream has a widened scope of self-awareness. The dream, however, can exert its full therapeutic impact only if it is emotionally experienced and "owned" by the patient. Such "owning" often is prevented unconsciously or consciously by the patient. The therapist may become a "killer of the dream" by a mere detached or aesthetic approach or by using a narrow reductive concept of symbolism.

Both patient and therapist have to feel themselves back into the dream. In effective therapy the psychoanalyst helps the patient to experience the dream fully and to use it as a door to his "larger self."

REFERENCES

1. WEISS, F. A.: Self-alienation: dynamics and therapy. Am. J. Psychoan. 21: 207, 1961.
2. FERENCZI, S.: The Development of Psychoanalysis. Nervous & Ment. Dis. pp. 51-52, 1925.
3. DEMENT, W.: The effect of dream deprivation. Science 131:1705, 1960.
4. HORNEY, K.: Neurosis and Human Growth, Chapt. 6. New York, W. W. Norton, 1950.
5. ALEXANDER, F.: Fundamentals of Psychoanalysis. New York, W. W. Norton, 1948, p. 289.

6. FRENCH, T. M.: The integrative process in dreams. *In:* The Integration of Behavior, Vol. II. Chicago, Univ. of Chicago Press, 1954.

7. FREUD, S.: A General Introduction to Psychoanalysis, Garden City Publishing Co., 1943, p. 397.

8. ——: An Outline of Psychoanalysis. New York, W. W. Norton & Co., 1949, p. 61.

9. BJERRE, P.: Das Träumen als Heilungsweg der Seele, (Dreaming—a Curative Process of the Soul) Zurich, Rascher 1936.

10. FREUD, S.: The Interpretation of Dreams in: The Basic Writings of Sigmund Freud. New York, The Modern Library, 1938, p. 434.

11. BERGSON, H.: The World of Dreams. New York, The Wisdom Library, 1958, p. 32, 55.

12. FISHER, C.: Subliminal and supraliminal influences on dreams. Am. J. Psychiat. 116:1009, 1960.

13. FREUD, S.: Moral Responsibility for the Content of Dreams in Collected Papers, Vol. V. London, Hogarth Press, 1950, p. 156.

14. GLOVER, E.: The Technique of Psychoanalysis. New York, International University Press, 1955, p. 88.

15. LIPSCHUTZ, L.: The written dream. J. Am. Psychoanalyt. A. 7:477, 1954.

16. BINSWANGER, L.: Traum und Existenz (Dream and Existence) in Ausgewaehlte Vortraege, Vol. 1. Bern, Francke, 1947, p. 92.

17. CASSIRER, E.: An Essay on Man. New York, Doubleday Anchor Books, 1953, p. 57.

18. WEISS, F. A.: Sex as a holistic symbol in therapy. Am. J. Psychoanal. 18: 7, 1958.

19. SCHILDER, P.: Psychotherapy. New York, W. W. Norton, 1951, p. 121.

20. WEISS, F. A.: What is effective in the therapeutic process. Am. J. Psychoanal. 17:18, 1957.

21. ERIKSON, E. H.: Identity and the Life Cycle. New York, International Univ. Press, 1959, p. 136.

22. WEISS, F. A.: Constructive forces in dreams. Am. J. Psychoanalyt. 9:30, 1949; Am. J. Psychoanal. 13:17, 1953.

23. ——: Dreaming—a creative process. To be published in Am. J. Psychoanal., 1964.

Discussion by Walter Bonime, M.D.

FEELING in dreams is potentially one of the most productive areas to explore in analysis. Affect is, nevertheless, clinically and academically one of the most neglected elements of the dream. Dr. Weiss does a service in focussing upon emotion; but the value of his paper lies in the emphasis upon the patient's full subjective acceptance of his dream as a reflection of his personality, for this acceptance fosters the recapture and exploration of the dream emotion and its integration into the engendering waking contexts.

The importance of pursuing the feeling in dreams always lies in this access it offers the patient to the emotions in his waking life—emotions which in every patient are to some degree unperceived, misperceived, denied, synthesized, exaggerated or sometimes obscured in ambivalent mixtures. It is one of the diseases of our culture to hide emotion—to play it cool. It is another disease of our culture to play it warm—to learn 'how to make friends and influence people.' There is constant and mostly unaware tactical dissimulation or simulation of emotion in the pervasive competitive interpersonal maneuvering of everyday life. There are endless discrepancies between the individual's concept of his feelings and the reality of his feelings. A mother heaps resentments upon her offspring in the form of restrictive oversolicitude. The rejected boy-friend kills his sweetheart in a vindictive act that supposedly is a gesture of supreme love, captioned "I can't live without you." The depressive wallows in a supposed sense of guilt over the injuries he has done to those closest to him, while in unrecognized rage he continues to blight their daily existence with grim unconsolability. The stake each patient has in his particular pathological ways of living makes for him the detection and identification of feeling and their communication in analysis difficult, threatening and undesired tasks. The frequent clear presence of emotion in dreams, however, allows at least an initial detection and identification. Once captured through the dream, it becomes possible to acknowledge the authentic existence of a feeling and then to begin the associative tracing of such discovered feeling into the interpersonal contexts of waking experience. It is through this kind of pursuit of the emotions that the most significant and valuable corrections are made in the distorted concepts the patient has of his personality, his values and his related behavior. It is essentially, I believe, the subjective initiation of this indispensable process to which Dr. Weiss refers as "owning one's dreams." Interference with this indispensable pursuit of the affective data of dreams is, essentially, what he refers to as "killing the dream."

The degree of commitment with which an individual approaches a dream as a significant manifestation of his personality ("owns it," to use Dr. Weiss's term) depend upon how much value he comes to find in working with dreams. Much of this value derives from a clinical approach implicit in Dr. Weiss's discussion, but not adequately emphasized. I refer to therapeutic collaboration. An emphasis upon the fundamental role of collaboration in the therapeutic use of dreams leads me to disagree with certain of Dr. Weiss's attitudes. For example, I am utterly opposed to his disregarding or underplaying first or early dreams. (He spells out this attitude more forcefully in the unpublished paper to which he refers.*) Almost nothing offers greater opportunity than a dream, whether it be a new or obsolete one, to get the patient therapeutically involved at the very start of therapy. Through work with an early dream the patient may quickly be introduced into a number of important aspects of the therapeutic process—the search for significance in seemingly meaningless manifestations; the nature of associative activity; the awareness that the analyst is not omniscient, and that he usually only hypothesizes or suggests directions for exploration. This immediate joining of forces in the pursuit of dream data moreover itself sets the tone of collaboration as an essential element of the total therapeutic experience. In that spirit the patient does not regard his memories from sleep as "only a dream," nor does he say, "I have a dream for you, Doctor." Furthermore, in a serious collaborative framework the writing down of dreams is not a resistance nor an intellectual disowning of dreams but rather a testimony to their value. I encourage patients to keep pad and pencil by the

---

*The Dream—A Mobilizing Force in Therapy.

bed. Patients who forfeit the value of dreams do not lose through the mere act of writing, but rather through all the means of avoiding therapeutic involvement, applied diffusely to both dream and other data.

As a final comment, I wish to relate the roles both of the emotional experiencing of dreams and of therapeutic collaboration, to the case at the end of the paper. Dr. Weiss rightly accents the wonderful transformation in this misogynistic woman's feeling about herself. The curative process, however, particularly because of most patients' emotional alienation, requires in their dealing with dreams not only a full acknowledgement, an emotional experiencing of the dream material—*the curative process requires also a genuine emotional experiencing of the reciprocal interpersonal exchange through which the meaning of dreams becomes illuminated.* Dr. Weiss's patient, symbolized as the little girl in her dream, was "just waking up" to a new personality. In the telling, moreover, her emotional interpolations indicated a full acceptance of the dream. Something had happened during analysis which made it possible for this woman not only to have the new feeling about herself in the dream, but also to have the all-important waking experience of confidently communicating this feeling to her analyst. It is this interpersonal aspect of working with dreams, perhaps even more than the emotional experiencing of dreams, which promotes healthy change in the patient.

REPORT ON DREAMS IN A LIFETIME STRUGGLE WITH CONSCIENCE

By JOHN A. P. MILLET, M.D.

THE patient from whose dossier these dreams were selected was a man in his early sixties, who had been destined by strange circumstances for a career in the priesthood, but who at the eleventh hour of his attendance in the Seminary, had found himself unable to face the task of perpetuating credal dogmas which he found to be at best survivals and at worst the relics of primitive and magical beliefs and rituals.

His complaints included the following:

Terrific tension in the head, constantly present, in the frontal region. Duration 2½ years.

Constant pain in back of the head for 37 years, recently increasing in intensity.

Several past failures in life, with one "nervous breakdown."

Constant fear and self-pity.

Confusion and inability to concentrate.

Significant figures in his life history were his mother and her brother. His father had been disabled by an accident when the patient was a small boy and had died a few years later. He was for the patient of little significance except in a negative sense. At the time of this disabling accident the patient's uncle had stepped in to take charge of the boy's physical, intellectual and social welfare. He was a rigid churchman whose material wealth had assured him a high position in the society of lay believers. He was thus able to assuage his own self-doubts through consciousness of his own allegiance to the dogma and ritual of his church. It only remained for him, since he had no son of his own, to insure his spiritual survival through delivering his nephew to the ranks of the clergy.

With this absorbing ambition in mind he sought every opportunity to admonish his nephew in the ways of righteousness and piety, to insure his conformity, to inculcate a sense of absolute loyalty to the forms and dogmas of the church service, and to prepare the way for him to secure a streamlined education directed toward admission to the priesthood. The patient's mother thereby also fell under a debt of gratitude for his interest and efforts on behalf of her young son, and, being herself devout, felt that the career which was so thoroughly outlined and planned was indeed a blessing from on high. In later years, after her brother's death, when the patient had exposed to her what he felt to be the cause of his unhappiness, she had expressed her amazement in these words: "You should have been a doctor as you wanted to be: I thought you wanted to enter the church!"

The patient was not able to face graduation from the Seminary and assumption of the priestly role. However, he accepted a position as teacher of English in a church school where he achieved recognition as a teacher, a skilled craftsman, and as an athletic coach. With some of his old college classmates he enjoyed the society of a group of Bohemian intellectuals and eventually was married. Soon afterwards he was invited to assume the position of assistant principal of the school—a prelude to eventual leadership. He became anxious and eventually refused the promotion. This indecisiveness, reflecting his sexual immaturity, so angered his wife that she asked him for a divorce.

In his initial therapy, he became acutely depressed and was hospitalized for a brief period. As he convalesced he concluded that he had failed in his obligations to the church authorities who had made possible the opportunity for him to teach. He sought the advice of a classmate from seminary days, recently elevated to an administrative position in the church in charge of youth activities, and exposed to him the continued story of his obsessive doubting. His friend, however, who knew of his past success as a teacher and leader of youth, persuaded him that he should disregard such old conflicts and devote his energies and talents to meet the challenge of service. This friendly reassurance could not be gainsaid. He re-entered the service of the church as a lay assistant, carrying with him the same old doubts and self-critical attitudes which had pursued him throughout his early years.

The death of his mother some 30 months before his coming into treatment, although long expected, was followed by an increase in symptoms as recorded above, and seemed to provide the straw that broke the camel's back. The diagnosis was obsessional neurosis, chronic, severe, complicated by an acute depression with marked involutional features. The total number of sessions was 66 over a total period of 5 years.

The material quoted is drawn from written communications brought by the patient to the therapeutic sessions. The first dream was reported on the occasion of his fourth visit:

"I remember a dream that I had which I told to my first therapist. An unidentified woman, maybe woman as such, whose body from waist to feet was dressed with a very heavy and thick garment, as though made of concrete. The doctor's remark was 'It does not show very much imagination,' and it was dismissed."

The patient said: "Somehow, I feel that I have not gotten to the root of my trouble. The tension in head and neck areas have lessened somewhat because you have shown me how to meet with fear, and the hate that I engendered against my uncle has been eased.

"As I think of it now, I feel as though I had surrounded the woman with a concrete curtain because she was forbidden."

On his next visit: "The uncle I have talked so much about had in my own mind taken over my father's place. He was as I see it now a bully. . . . Mother respected him so much or was indebted to him for what he had done, when father had the accident, for the family, so that I felt she wouldn't understand my confusion."

He then related a recent dream: "I appear as a sorry looking priest, in a black topcoat, alone, walking at night, without purpose, with a clerical collar. Then something changed. I was suddenly seized by crooks, and tough thinking men, who said, 'We don't care if you are a priest,' and they rolled me and tripped me, and mugged me, and I noticed after they left me for dead, I got up, and I was still alive, without the clerical collar, but pretty badly beaten, and alone; no longer afraid, but very tired and just about able to walk. And the last sort of comment that my mind made was 'But you are still alive!', a hopeful comment."

He added: "The theological strait jacket prevents me from using my imagination—it is like a dead weight. I have tried and tried to accept it but when I feel hypocritical, and when I don't I feel hypocritical, and so I escape by working in the garden or do some woodwork."

"One of the things, tendencies, in my motives is the fact that I do things in order to prove to myself that I can do them.

"This has been a pattern in my life. To prove that I can do it, but the proving has always caused tension, never fun."

One week later he reported a dream of the previous night: "Somehow, I had got back to the Seminary, and had robbed a suit of clothes, very stealthily, and all the students and professors were on the lookout for me, but apparently I escaped, holding the suit on my left arm, and was wandering around, and I met a woman who said she needed someone to take care of her furnace, and when she asked if I were a handy man, and I said no, she apparently thought I was a beggar, and she gave me pennies and said, 'So sorry to trouble you,' but I didn't want the pennies but still took them."

"When I awoke I tried to recall more of the details but couldn't. I do not know any priests in the church who would understand, with whom I could feel at ease, and the reason for it is that just as I have fought orthodoxy, and became obsessed with it, perhaps also I too have been obsessed with the freedom of the individual, his independence, so that the conflict is obsession with literal orthodoxy and literal independence.

"As I write the tension is not as bad as it was yesterday, and I wonder whether because I am not as tired, or whether it is because I am trying to compromise or resolve the conflict. I do hope it is the latter. I feel the basis of my trouble is the fact that I lied to my uncle, and the fear that I have been harboring is the fear that the lie will be detected by those in authority That is why I fear all people."

During his seventh interview he commented: "What I wonder is: 'Who is lying? The super-ego, or the real self?' Is the real self escaping from the super-ego? Because I know, am quite sure that I am fundamentally not a liar, not a cheat, but one who within human limits is really decent, kind, good, religious without theology, but so anxious and afraid that I may say or do the wrong thing. In other words, I have become outside a perfect, deliberate literalist, a stick-in-the-mud, a pain in the neck. I hate myself, but an inner hope has been a comfort. I feel that somehow I am punishing myself because of the fact that I lied and deceived my uncle and my super-ego. They are doing their best to make me suffer."

A few sessions later he expressed a sense of gratitude and a revival of hope: "At the interview I was pretty deeply disturbed as a result of the tension of the previous days. At any rate, I began to feel that all was not lost, and a sense of gratitude and hope mildly touched me." He spoke of having enjoyed a day in the country and a fishing expedition. He then related a dream:

"I found myself strangely sitting at a table, a restaurant, alone, and before I had even ordered anything two rough looking men grabbed me and before I knew it, they had taken my wallet and I was not hurt and they left me. It had something to do with a suit of clothes that they told me I had to buy. I don't recall whether I got the suit of clothes but I felt that unimportant, but they did get my wallet. Then there was a break in the dream and I found myself with an old friend, a minister, telling him about the suit of clothes that were well tailored, etc. And he wanted such a suit. Again I found myself in the hands of these two rough looking men, arguing with them and fighting with them, that the suit of clothes I ordered was not what they were giving me. The old friend disappeared out of the picture and I found myself objecting to the various suits these two men were showing me, and they were struggling with me, holding my arms back of me, and I shouted and ran, looking for a policeman, and seeing someone dressed in a uniform, with a corporal's or sergeant's cap, with a chevron of gold, I asked him for help and I recognized him as a phony. And then the dream seemed abruptly ended and I awoke."

He went on to give his associations to the dream: "The two men who held me and stole my wallet were Fear and Hate, when I first was breaking down. They took my wallet, my treasure, 'My Faith,' which experience I covered over with a suit, which I did not seem to get, a suit of the priestly garments.

"What seems important is the fact that I recognized the creature whom I called for help dressed as a cop as a phony; the chevrons on his cap were gold, which I very clearly saw. In other words, though at the time I entered the church service the second time I had induced a conversion, it was not real as I tried to believe, but I really did so to prove that I was good, and also to make a living, and to save myself. The gold stripes on the cap seem to be a symbol of money.

"One of the things in the dream I penetrated was the need of earning a living, which I know is real, good, and wholesome."

The next session[14] was remarkable in that it developed the most satisfying resolution of his conflict that he had been able to conceive.

"I wonder if a technique that I have sort of arrived at through much bungling, to help me with the problems and conflicts that I have been struggling with, sounds to you sincere and sound.

"The technique that I have been thinking of, its validity if you wish, is this. The super-ego tyrant is breeder of fear, doubt and hate. These are my fake gods. These I have so completely sold to myself so that fighting them, rebelling against them, makes me more fatigued, more worn out, more tense, and cause more suffering than if I just said 'OK' which I cannot do. How else to get rid of them because I feel in my own case I need a religious point of view, a spiritual point of view (because of my background, etc.) then to admit they are gods made by my own hands, and substitute gently but firmly a God into this super-ego subconscious realm, a God who loves, who is kind, who is merciful, who does not expect [humanity] to be perfect, but to be human and affectionate and kind with the gifts and talents that I have, not to try to be a Christ, but rather a humble follower of his spirit."

After an interval of 6 weeks therapy was resumed. (Seventeenth session) He brought in a dream: "Last night, a dream. Somehow I was to be an actor in a play. I can't quite make out the content in detail, but the main point was that I had lost the script, and was looking furiously for it, and the headgear I was supposed to wear got tangled up with my feet, quite confused, and I found myself up on a high rugged rocky narrow cliff, with Charles Laughton (whose acting I admire very much) directing me to get ready for the play. Below the cliff was a black leopard, who leaped and leaped up to reach me and tear me down. Only I was aware of the leopard, and, of course, was quite panicky, because I could not climb higher, could not get away from the leopard, because the tree I was holding on to was quite flimsy and weak. Charles Laughton simply said, 'Silly, very silly,' totally unaware of the black monster."

"I feel that you, Dr. Millet, were Charles Laughton . . . the black leopard that I feared so much in the dream is the priestcraft of the church which I still hate so deeply.

"Before I went to bed, before the dream, I wondered why it was that I hate and fear the priestcraft so much, why I cannot think of Ecclesiasticus without fear and doubt, why I feel so liberal and broad, particularly towards Judaism, why I do not feel that the church, with its traditional creeds, is the only way to salvation, and I found myself thinking of the experience that I had with my uncle when I was about 14, and had a discharge from the penis. This I had kept secret from him for many days, until I became alarmed at the flow. Then the horrible scolding, threats and anger scene occurred. 'Who was the woman? Do you know if you do not tell me the truth the medicine prescribed may do you untold harm, if you are lying? If this were known you would never be permitted to enter the sacred ministry?' Very innocently and very confused, I said, 'Who, what woman, I don't know any,' and he did not believe me. I lost all faith in him as a man and as a friend.

"I believe I am eliminating the horror and nightmare of my uncle and, almost by a categorical directive, not quite a compulsion, am finding the true Christ, the most desired apple on the tip-top branch of the tree of theological speculation. It is at least a change in my thinking. I am beginning to want to choose Christ, rather than choose my doubts, and fears, and hates."

He then related a dream that he had 3 weeks previously: "I had again a dream that was as sexual as it could be. I do not recall the particular details, but the main content was quite intelligible somehow. I was a great big man, strong and heavy, dressed in a grey suit, jolly, laughing and drinking with people, and the scene shifted, and I was with a girl who was nude. But she had on a steel brace with triangular reinforcements around her privates so that she could not be penetrated. I tried to make love to her, with the result that I had an emission and the dream ended abruptly."

"In the morning I noticed that much of the extreme tension had gone, and felt almost at ease; though the neck pains were still there the temple heat had lowered.

"I tell this because I am sure that the release of tension in the dream the night before is another matter that causes trouble and tension in me; and that sex is as much if not more a cause of conflict than the intellectual struggles I have mentioned.

"As I think of the dream, the black leopard is obviously sex. I have two Oklahoma clay pieces, one a black leopard lying down, the other a black leopard sitting up on its haunches, at ease, also. These I suppose give me the material for the dream."

In the eighteenth session the resistance to the therapist is openly stated and a renewed period of discouragement is related. He reasserts his unwillingness to accept any authority other than the spiritual authority of Christ.

"One thing that I have had on my mind is the dream in which Charles Laughton appeared who was directing me to play a role. When I identified you as playing the role of director, and myself as an actor, I was a bit proud that I was able to identify you as Charles Laughton because I do admire his acting, little realizing that I was actually telling you a part of my problem, which is that I do not trust anybody; that I was saying 'You too are making me act a part.' This came to me when you said 'I am not acting the part or role of a director telling you how to act a role.' At the interview consciously I was not aware of my offense, but your words did sink in because every now and then they arose in my mind. I think that I have identified you wrongly with my uncle, and my hostility in the dream is due to the fact that I really fear psychoanalysts, psychiatrists, professors, teachers, priests, lest they know what I am."

(Nineteenth session) "Last Saturday, after the interview, I hastened home to read the book that you had given me, "Healing, Human and Divine,"* and as I read "Body, Mind, Spirit" and read on to the paragraph on Sigmund Freud, I remembered that once in an article I had grouped Galileo, Darwin and Sigmund Freud with Jesus, (I just noticed I spelled Freud with an "n"— Freund, "Friend," and so I scratched out the "n") as men who had been inspired.

"As I read the chapter and came to the Devil-God paragraph, I found that I was enjoying "reading," and the whole picture of the destructive tendencies, the anxiety, the doubt, the fear, the hate, the heart beat, the temple pains, the neck pains, the spinal pains, which were so terrific that they compelled the suicide attempt, kept trying to get into focus.

"And so I've gotten to feel enjoyment again with thoughts. I have not been converted in the sense of a terrific emotional experience but I am beginning to feel more sincerely the needs of man in the Christ idea.

"If the idea of Christ has any value at all, it has by its origin, by its inner and deeper appeal, the value 'that the goals of the efforts of man to remove or achieve mastery over the obstacles of life' are worth the efforts, and that there is victory even in pain."

In the twenty-second session this seemingly increasing sense of confident conviction is further elaborated, with a slight tinge of triumphant defiance of past fears and guilt feelings.

The twenty-fourth session followed a month's absence from therapy. His report shows a period of continued philosophical reflection in a vein of hopefulness, followed by a resurgence of the old guilty fears and depressive ruminations. Eventually he brought up some infantile sexual memories and guilty fears attached to them. He went back once more to the dream of the black panther, and concluded that sexual guilt is at the bottom of all his troubles.

"I remember when I was about 7, playing in the street, a girl about my age was sitting on stairs, with her legs stretched apart and I could not help staring at what I saw.

"I feel somehow that the experience drove me unconsciously to get interested in origins because I felt I was staring at something that was forbidden. I must admit that I was experiencing pleasure at the sight and yet it seemed something I must not look at, but the curiosity was most driving. This happened before I came into contact with my uncle. I had no shame, no feeling of wanting to hurt her, but I wanted so much to look deeper and longer, with no sense of violence."

In session twenty-six he recalled what he considers his first sense of fear:

"I feel that my predisposition towards fear is a sort of an inherited psychological condition (father).

"Is it because the power and motivation in my unconscious is fear, that my heart does not seem capable of love and joy?

"I think I can recall my first sense of fear. Fighting with a gang; explosion of little cannon. I seem to have been way ahead of my gang—alone. When the

---

*"Healing, Human and Divine", Association Press, New York, 1957. (Chapter on "Body, Mind and Spirit", p. 23; John A. P. Millet, M.D.)

explosion went off the other gang attacked and my gang ran off. I was hit by a rock in my elbow and I could not explain to myself how I could tell my uncle what I was doing in a fight. I ran off and felt guilty, not because of running away but because I was hit."

On the day following this note he had a dream: "Last night a nightmare. Somehow in an upper room, and I took or was given a box of pellets which I spread around on the floor, and I lighted them and they went off. I escaped and apparently they were chasing me. And here I was with my coat swung open and hands in my trouser pockets as though enjoying the fact 'that I got away with that.' But soon others came, recognized me and in column formation took me as a prisoner. Somehow I got somewhere and three recognizance men barred my way but I got in, 'a jail,' and the prisoners ganged up on me and they began to fight with me. And in the fight some one tried to hit me with a blackjack on the back of my neck and I felt my neck had been broken, with terrific pain, but just before I woke one of the men said to the man who tried to blackjack me, 'You hit the wrong guy,' the man who tried to blackjack me had hit himself."

He then reported another dream on the night that followed: "Another nightmare. In a snow speed sled, going up a bridge. A line attached to something ahead that couldn't move. The line was rope—and a poisonous snake. It broke. I shouted to the colored man in the sled with me—'the snake's head is poison'—and tumbling down I awoke."

His associations to these dreams were given during the succeeding session (no. 27), after renewed self-analytical ruminations:

"The dream, nightmare of my conscience being blackjacked, has now been a source of great laughter. Every now and then I find myself laughing at the subtle tricks of the mind, the psyche, 'You hit the wrong guy' and yet that is what I have been doing so long to escape the self-accusing sensitive conscience or super-ego. The content of the dream is not only amazing but so enlightening.

"That dream of the blackjack. If anyone was knocked out more completely by a real blackjack I can't believe it. It was thorough.

"The dream of the sled, rope, snake, dark object—truck? The big dark object, the truck, I realize was something that obstructed the easy glide (even though up-hill) of the sled, namely, fear."

The twenty-ninth session is of special interest in that after giving an excellent account of the sufferings engendered by his neurosis, and expressing his conviction that he had used God as a scapegoat, he finds himself searching for a God whom he can trust and to whom he can dedicate his life and labor— the God whom he sees as the loving Father of the Christ:

"It is this that I now find myself interested in, not fanatically, not as an automaton driven by fear, but drawn by the love that I think I am capable of. In being at one, or whole with Him, rather than alone with fear; I know that I shall live, not as a saint, but at least helpfully, usefully, purposefully, and not make his creation vain and useless. I believe that was what Jesus Christ taught, but which I never grasped, because my personality was gripped by this horrible neurosis."

During the summer months that followed he continued to feel relatively free of tension and was able to enjoy his outdoor activities. In October he watched a TV program describing the physiology of the nervous system, which interested him. That night he related a most interesting dream which helped him to realize that his salvation lay in the 'God-given gift of reason.'

"That night I dreamt of being in a house, with a sort of central square column going to the roof, around which the other rooms were built, and I was working on the electric wires. Something was the matter, a short circuit somewhere, so that some lights did not function, though others did. Mother was present and my brother, vaguely, and she kept saying two women guests were expected for supper.

"But I kept working on the electric wires and I saw the two women arriving. I did not recognize them but I said, 'Mom, here they are'—and I kept working on the wires. I have a great respect for anyone who understands electricity and I felt the question of rewiring was a very easy thing because I have done simple wiring often. Somehow the women were lapping up a bowl of soup, but I kept working and I said, 'You do not know how serious this is; the light does not appear, there is something wrong. There might be a short circuit and a fire.' Somehow I got wires into this column. They were very inflexible, shredded, worn, but the wires themselves were thicker than ordinary electric wire, and were made not of copper but something like aluminum. Now as I forced these wires through I knew I went under some other wires in the column with my wire and I felt that, because the wire I was working with, shredded and bare, but strong, would short circuit the wires which too were bare in the column, and yet I took the chance, because I wanted light.

"Before I knew it there was a fire, a fire in the column, above the floor of the room and the room seemed to have become a salesroom, with salesladies who disappeared, except one who sat quietly during the fire.

"I did not ring the fire alarm for help because I felt I could put it out myself. There was a water hose in the back of the room which seemed to become an attic, and I fastened it to a water pipe and turned the water on. Someone nearby, who was not there before, said: 'No, not like that: the water goes only in one place, but diffuse the water like a mist, so it goes all over the fire.' I did that and then I directed the water in one stream to the one girl who sat in the salesroom alone, and she disappeared, and soon the column was full of smoke, and the fire was out; and as I became semi-awake the problem of getting the water out of the column became foremost and the idea of putting a hole in the column in the basement below came to me. Then the question of insurance bothered me; for though apparently I was ruined I still felt that I could not collect the insurance because the fire had been caused by my wiring, that is, it was my fault."

"The question of insurance of the damage may mean the question of my own salvation, or assurance, which is constantly blocked by the question of 'I am at fault: I wired wrongly: I am guilty.' There is, I think, a slight hope in this whole picture, that the short circuit did not put out all the lights, for there was one somewhere always lighted. I take this light as my faith in the God-given gift of reason, though it seemed a light outside of my electric circuit. The man who was not too distinguishable, who helped me to diffuse the water on the fire, I am sure was you."

After this interview he decided to see how he could get along through the winter without further help from me. He continued at his job, but gradually began to feel depressed again, until he finally became panicky, after 3 months had elapsed, was obsessed with suicidal thoughts, and called me to come to his assistance. I visited him in his apartment. I found him in bed, panicky, weeping, full of the old self-doubts, hopeless. I left a prescription and suggested he resume his work with me. He came to the office 3 days later bringing with him some notes and two dreams:

"The last two or three months I have been trying strenuously to ward off what I felt was coming on. I really wanted to stand on my own feet, without running to you. I kept before my mind the picture of strength, courage, and love. And so I took upon myself many things."

In session No. 38 he brought in some other notes, including a dream of the morning of the previous conference

"I was somewhere in a cathedral church. My part in the service was vague, except that I was to tell someone to read something from the prayer book, and I was standing next to someone who was to read. There were many people behind me and the officers of the church, like deans, bishop, etc., not too distinguishable in features, were in the sanctuary. I felt something was going to happen, I didn't know what, but I was trying to find the place in the prayer book, sort of nervously, even though I was sure what the page was because I thought I had it placed with a page marker. And then it happened, a sudden explosion, like a bomb, and everything was destroyed, except me, who was standing there, without trembling. The building collapsed but there were no shrieks of hurt people. I remember sort of coming awake, without fear, that is trembling, and was a bit afraid to open my eyes, wondering whether I was still alive, whether the bomb had killed me also. When I came conscious, that is awake, and realized that it had been a dream, then I got up, shaking, confused, quite weakened, yet alive."

"I feel as though the subconscious was saying 'I'm not trying to scare you, hurt you, I am trying to show you that working for the church is not your vocation. Let's get rid of it for you'."

He reported with considerable relief his ability to reconstruct his understanding of the nature of his illness directly following this previous conference.

His notes of a week later, 2 days before the session, show his identification of hell fire with the tortures which his compulsive allegiance to his church affiliations have subjected him, and again reveal a growing and desperate need to free himself from what he feels to be the intolerable yoke of church authority.

"The fire to me is the church, the super-ego, my uncle, the compulsion, the association with the fear that I have of my uncle, etc. I know I have this fear but the work I have constantly stirs up more fears, more hate, more despair. The answer is 'Get out, get out; you still can help and love people, sincerely, honestly, happily, in a different environment'."

"I have found myself now trying to build a belief in God which will be satisfactory to me, a God-head of love in which the theological father is represented by the creator of nature or beauty; the theological son by goodness; and the theological holy spirit by truth. This satisfies my mind, my heart, my soul, and I wonder why I never was able to do this till now. It is not a closed strait jacket—there is great room for expansion in love, in beauty, in truth, in goodness."

He then reported a dream: "Some strange badly lighted place, hotel I think, and I meet people, men and women, who at first seemed to like me: then a feeling of suspicion on their part gripped me, and they tried to tie me up, and tied a steel cable from a truck outside the hotel to the window, with heavy opaque glass, and the motor of the truck was started, as though to mix me up, strangle me, not to pull me out, but I was *not* strangled. The truck that was pulling me out was my sex instinct and the ropes tied around me (not the cable) were the bonds of theological and metaphysical slavery, which were mixed up with my urge to live and to be happy."

He did not consult me again. However, as the time neared for making his final decision to leave his job he became depressed and fearful and it seemed wiser to hospitalize him where he could be seen regularly and be helped to crystallize his emerging resolution. He was treated at the hospital for 3 months with psychotherapy and drugs and soon began to rally his forces again.

From this time on the patient lived in his country cottage, leading the life of a hermit, coming to the office once monthly to report progress and to discuss his activities and reflections. Three months after leaving the hospital he expressed discouragement over the continuance of head pain, although he felt increasingly sure that he was overcoming the guilty fears of which he had been a victim for so long. He no longer reported any dreams.

There was a gradual, although somewhat uneven progress toward a better state of mind, even though any suggestion that he make use of his talents for gain or community service were stoutly resisted. When I made one such suggestion he became acutely disturbed for a week or two. The echo of the uncle's authority seemed to ring down again through the years.

Toward the end of the fifth year of treatment, in the sixty-fifth session, he unexpectedly brought in two dreams:

"I was called by phone to hold a service in honor of a bishop. Without hesitation I said I would but I had no program, no order of service. There I was, in a parish house, made an announcement, said, 'This service is not in honor of anyone but God. It may be a testimonial to a bishop.' I grinned. 'What is your name?' I took the bishop's red and purple gown and said, 'I think this is yours'."

At last he restores the symbols of church authority to the proper officer and declares his worship to be for God alone.

"Then last night I had another strange one. When I used to walk down lower East side streets there were gangs, perverts, homosexuals, etc. Invariably I would go through there thinking I would be caught by them, would have to run. These people are the residents of my own mind whom I have created in my own mind. Last night on the way to see my masseur I lost my way, asked directions, soon got on the proper road.

Dream: I was driving the car, got lost. No lights on streets. Within a block or two saw two roughnecks. They stopped me. I didn't run away. Had fear but no fright. They said, 'Wait a minute—get out'. They took my car. I had a bunch of papers like law briefs in my hands. They tossed them into the car, said, 'If you don't do anything you won't get hurt.' 'What do you want of me?' 'Nothing, just get in with us.' I was afraid I would be late for a dinner engagement. 'Where is my car?' Two strong fellows picked it up, put it on other side of the road. They said, 'Come with us.' A great strong fellow came along. I shook his hands, 'My, you are a strong fellow!' 'You said it and if you don't do what I say I will kick the shit out of you!' 'Come with us!' Then he said, 'Here's your car. Run along.' "

Once more we have the theme of being overpowered by two strong men, only to discover that he is allowed to go his way unmolested when he shakes the analyst's hand.

In the sixty-seventh session he had abandoned his physiotherapeutic visits, explained the reason for his collapse under the implied command of the therapist to become more active, and affirmed his own conviction that he needed more social life. This affirmation seemed to be free of compulsiveness and to represent one step further toward the effective resolution of his unhappy isolation.

In conclusion, it has been my purpose in presenting this rather dramatic material to draw attention to what I believe to be an area of psychoanalytic research which has been largely neglected by psychoanalysts, the area of religious attitudes, convictions, doubts and conflicts. The dreams and written or verbal communications of the patient illustrate vividly the difference between the obsessional conflicts of a patient who has no conscious concern with religious beliefs and practices and those of a manifestly devout man whose lifetime of struggle with his conscience represented a wish to escape from the tyranny of an externally implanted need to believe certain dogmas in order to compose within the freedom of his own reflective thought a religious formula to which he could give personal allegiance. This conflict between the acceptance of dogma and striving toward some affirmation of spiritual values which transcend human capacity to achieve, but whose recognition as a reason for striving may be said to constitute the essence of the truly religious mind, is becoming increasingly widespread as the ancient dogmas fail to satisfy most educated men.

The patient whose material is presented here exhibits this need for recognition of a dimension of mental life which includes experiences such as reverence and awe, the appreciation of beauty and the exercise of the creative imagination in the search for a more satisfying explanation of the universe. Although unable to accept dogmas which his intellect found to be absurd he was unable to settle for the values of the humanists. Repeatedly, however, he was able to affirm a set of values which expressed his personal aspirations. Their representation in the life and sayings of Jesus provided his imagination with the model that he needed to give these values a meaningful reality. It is perhaps through such experience that conflicts not amenable to routine psychoanalytic therapy have often found their way to resolution.

Sandor Rado* in his classification of the different levels of motivation in treatment behavior, has selected the term *aspiring level* to denote the attitude of the patient most favorable to cooperation with the analyst. However, he restricts the term to signify the patient's eagerness to learn how to make full use of all his potential resources for adaptive growth. Such a definition, while not eliminating consideration of the role played in human life by the wish to direct conduct into patterns consonant with abstract ideals, including those embodied in the teachings of most viable religions, does not perhaps imply the need for including the study of such values as part of the psychoanalytic method. The reductive viewpoint of Freud, exemplified in "The Future of an Illusion,"† has encouraged psychoanalysts to consider that their obligation to their patients does not include the task of examining their religious attitudes. Where science ends and mysticism begins presents a real challenge to the dedicated student of human behavior. This fact should not deter us from attempting to evaluate the epidemiology of religious convictions and the different influences which they exert in promoting or delaying the resolution of conflict.

In view of the limitations of time and space, discussion of the familiar themes of incestuous guilt, castration fear, and sexual inhibition, so clearly illustrated in this dream sequence, has perforce been omitted. It is of interest that the resolution of his conflict—the struggle with the two strong and evil men—his uncle and his own conscience—is eventually conceived as having been achieved by the overcoming of sexual guilt through assertion of his right to acceptance through a re-definition of his religious convictions and of the meaning to himself of the Christian message. For him the aspiring level of treatment behavior was best maintained when he felt sure that both his defiance of doctrine and his allegiance to the inner spiritual message of his religion were given close attention and freely discussed.

---

*Psychoanalysis of Behavior, Grune & Stratton, N. Y., 1956, p. 252, Table I.
†Freud, S.: The Future of an Illusion. International Psychoanalytic Library No. 15, London, England, Hogarth Press, 1928.

A NEW TECHNIQUE FOR FACILITATING INSIGHT INTO DISSOCIATED MATERIAL*

By RICHARD G. ABELL, M.D.

THIS paper will show how verbatim tape recordings of psycho-analytic sessions can be used to facilitate the recognition of dissociated material and the development of insight. The importance of developing methods of recognizing and reintegrating dissociated tendencies is emphasized by Sullivan's[1] statement that the healthy development of the personality is inversely proportional to the number of the tendencies which exist in dissociation. He says that psychoanalysis proceeds by reintegrating the dissociated motivational systems and dissipating the parataxic influences of unresolved past situations through which the patient has lived.

These processes are facilitated by using the tape recorder in the manner in which I will now describe.

Tape recordings were made of the verbalizations of patients during psychoanalytic sessions and played back so that they could listen objectively to their own verbalizations. Their reactions were again recorded on tape and at the same time notes were made for further study.

It might be thought that patients would have difficulty in evaluating their own productions accurately, but the present studies demonstrate that exactly the reverse is the case. Under such objective conditions patients are able to evaluate accurately not only much more of the actual meaning of what they have said, but are also able to become aware of dissociated aspects of the personality and, through reintegrating these during continued therapy, to expand the boundaries of the self. In addition, they recognize more easily their parataxic distortions. I was surprised to find that this capacity was not limited to

*Work done with the aid of a grant from the National Institute of Mental Health to the William Alanson White Institute.

the 'adept,' but occurred consistently in patient after patient during the 9 year period in which I have been collecting these data.

The present studies consist of the reactions of 125 neurotic patients to tape playbacks. The patients varied in age from 15 to 56, and were of both sexes. These studies were made in the Young Adult Service of the William Alanson White Psychoanalytic Institute, and with my own patients.

Case 1: The first patient had been in therapy with me for 2 years before I started to analyze her reactions to tape playbacks. She was approximately 50 years old, was a graduate of one of our leading universities, is cultured and intelligent. In addition to being a wife and mother, she is successfully engaged in a profession.

I will describe her reactions to tape playbacks of 6 successive sessions 1 week apart.

After playing back to her a part of the first session she said, "There's a bland, upper society quality to my voice that I didn't know was there. It doesn't sound the way I feel. The machine substitutes an emotional impact that I don't feel when we talk . . . it sounds like a public speaker. When I sit here talking to you, I feel as if my voice were a monotone, but when I hear the recording, it sounds like a very good performance."

Her reactions to the second playback were as follows. "I hear a very familiar voice that I cannot place, but it doesn't sound like mine. What worries me is that I don't know who it sounds like. I like it very much, much better than I do what I think my own voice sounds like." I said to her, "What do you think your own voice does sound like?" She replied, "Dopey, much more monotonous, not nearly as clear or musical. I am amazed at the clarity of the tone. This is what keeps jarring me. I keep thinking that I don't always use my voice correctly, but this recording shows that I really do. What shocks me is that my voice is so effective here when I'm not trying to create an effect. I would expect to sound sullen, bitter and confused, but this voice sounds bright and cheery and charming." My patient continued, "I'm not yet conscious of all the things I hear in this recording that I like objectively." Then she said suddenly and brightly, "Oh, I'm beginning to hear myself talk like that recording."

In the third session she said, "I feel as if at the last session I was putting myself together for the first time. It was the result of hearing something in my voice in the recording—something that *could be me.*"

A portion of the tape made during the session was played back to her at its end. Her reactions were as follows: "My response to that playback is— how charming my voice is. Having realized that it is not sullen and bitter, I will now have to take the next step, that is, to think that *I am* attractive. You see from the way I'm dressed today that I do feel differently. But I wonder—the immediate thought is—is it true? Can it be I?" (I said, "This is a natural thought. It's hard to believe at first what is actually in the tape, but the recording is accurate and there is no appreciable distortion.") As she was ready to leave, she said, "My voice is lovelier than I think."

In the fourth session she said, "You know, my voice doesn't reflect the problems I think I have. After hearing the playback I begin to think that I am not elephantine and stupid and uninteresting."

In the fifth session she commented, "My voice still sounds higher class than I expect, but it doesn't surprise me as much as it did. When I first heard my voice it sounded too pleasant and cheerful. It didn't seem to express the miserable feelings I was having here. I'm surprised at my not recognizing my voice as me. It's too good for me."

In the sixth session she said, "I had a funny feeling about you last time when we were talking over my reactions to the tape. I felt that we were talking like two friends or colleagues. I wondered whether because I have made so much progress I wasn't beginning to feel towards you like an equal."

Case 2. Another patient of mine, John, a 38 year old man, who had been in therapy for 14 months, responded to hearing his voice played back as follows: "I didn't recognize my own voice. It was such a unique experience, hearing my voice for the first time. My voice is stronger than I thought. I thought I had a thin, raspy voice, but I don't, do I? I dissociate myself from my voice completely. When you played back the tape my initial reaction was, 'This is not my voice at all.' But I had to be convinced, because it said exactly what I said. When I did hear it, I was pleased and impressed by it."

Case 3. A 25 year old man I'm treating in psychoanalytically oriented group therapy is actually intelligent, attractive and well liked by the members of the group. However, he can't believe this. He listened attentively to the playback of his voice, with an incredulous smile on his face. He said, "It's funny, it sounded exactly like the Doctor's voice, but it doesn't sound like my voice. The funny thing is, I liked that guy who was talking, whoever he was. He sounded like a very nice fellow. I thought he sounded very pleasant." He laughed, and then said, "This is a schizophrenic experience. When I talk I think it's as if I will be talking through my father's skull, stiff and pompous. I think I can't be too likeable. When I hear that fellow out there I don't hear anything stiff or pompous. That fellow is not like my father at all. He's somebody separate. He ended by saying, "That was a terrific pleasure."

The recording of an interchange between 2 patients in psychoanalytic group therapy follows. My own comments are included.

Case 4. Doctor: Margaret, you've just heard your voice. Would you tell us what you think about it in comparison to what you think about your voice as you hear yourself?

Margaret: Well, I couldn't believe it was my voice. I thought this voice was lower pitched than mine, and sort of fuller and rounder. Really quite a nice voice to listen to—almost sophisticated. And I think of myself as having a squeaky voice that is constricted and high pitched, that irritates. That's the way I think of my voice. . . . Don't you think that this distorts the sound a little bit?

Doctor: No, not at all. No.

Margaret: Well, I thought it was like the two of you, but I didn't think of myself as having that kind of voice at all.

Doctor: Well, you see, you've got a control here when you hear my voice and Harry's voice.

Margaret: Yes, and it's the true voice then . . . Well, now, this may be my own devaluation of myself again. And yet I have a good singing voice. I know that.

Harry: I want to make a remark here.

Doctor: Yes, go ahead, what is your comment?

Harry: I feel that the Harry in the playback speaks much, much better than I do—grammatically much more correctly than I speak. And sounds more intelligent than I sound. This is my honest feeling from what I heard him say. I thought he was going to say things incorrectly, and in fact he didn't.

Doctor: He didn't, that's right.

Margaret: And actually, on the tapes, you sound very intelligent. But in the group I never gave you credit for being intelligent, because all I heard was the loudness and crankiness in your voice. Because that's the way my father was, loud and cranky. To me what you said in the group got across as ruhruhruh—keep out. It kept me from seeing what you're really like. You're really very intelligent, I can see it now, as I listen to the tape. [Here we see the recognition of a parataxic distortion.]

Harry: Everyone tells me I'm very intelligent, and I never believe anybody.

Margaret: And you know, you look intelligent, too.

Doctor: Now, Harry, you can see here for yourself, from the objective evidence, that you are intelligent.

Not all of the patients' reactions were positive. This depended in part upon the stage the patient had reached in his analysis.

Case 5. For example, a 30 year old man who had been in analysis for 1½ years, on hearing his verbalizations in the playback for the first time, said, "My reaction to my voice is negative. It sounded affected. What I said did not affect me as I thought it would. It sounded eager—trying too hard. There are a number of things that I would like to change. There is an emotional tone or quality that seems overdone. My voice is the stereotype of the non-productive intellectual who sits around and makes motions but does nothing."

Five days later he listened to a playback of a recording made at that time. Again his reaction was negative. He said, "I didn't like the voice—it seemed to be put on. It seemed false, in a way. For a good deal of my adult life I have acted out a part that wasn't mine. My Dad is rich. I am admired for my Dad's house and car, and I didn't do anything to deserve it. I wasn't made to work. At home they gave me the impression that home is a very safe place, that I was bright and when I got out into the world I could succeed very easily, but there was no hurry. They gave me the impression that when I decided to go out I could make a million dollars easily, and then come back home. It would take a couple of weeks."

This patient had been living at his parents' country estate outside of New Haven prior to therapy. He had a job in an engineering firm in New Haven but felt that he did not need to work hard. After a year he was dismissed. This dismissal made him take stock and it was at about this time that his reactions to his taped voice were first made. Prior to his dismissal he had really been unwilling to face his lack of productiveness on his job and in most outside activities. In fact, his passivity was out of his awareness; instead, he believed what his parents had told him, namely, that he was bright (which is true) and that he could succeed without effort (which was not true). He recognized his passivity in the manner in which he spoke in the tape recording and this helped to bring it into consciousness. At this time it became the subject of intensive study in his analytic sessions.

A year later, after he had made some constructive changes, which were reflected in his speech, another recording was made. After listening to it he said that he was surprised how well he sounded. Then he remarked, "An analyst sitting across from me pointing out that I am succeeding I can doubt because I think he is paid to do this, but I can't doubt the recorder for this reason."

It is interesting to note that this patient is now determined to mobilize his energies, has registered at a well known university for a Ph.D. in electrical engineering and is doing good work.

DISCUSSION

Dissociated material may be defined as topics or tendencies of which the individual became unaware in infancy and childhood because they were not noticed (that is, approved or disapproved) by significant adults. To quote Sullivan "For the expression of all things in the personality, other than those which were approved or disapproved by the parent, and other significant persons, the self refuses awareness, so to speak. It does not accord awareness; it does not notice; and these impulses, desires and needs come to exist disassociated from the self, or dissociated. When they are expressed, their expression is not noticed by the person."

In the case of the first patient what was basically dissociated was that she is attractive, intelligent and capable, in contrast to her concept of herself as "dopey, monotonous, sullen and bitter." When she actually heard her voice, she recognized that it was 'clear, musical, bright, cheery and charming." She expected to sound unintelligent and uncultured. When she heard her voice, she could tell that she was intelligent and that she had a cultured voice. She had felt that her voice was ineffective, but on hearing the tape she discovered it was effective, even when she was not trying to create an effect. It is interesting to see that the recognition of these dissociated aspects of the self was startling and shocking. It "jarred" her, she said, and it "shocked" her, which is in accord with Sullivan's statement that the integration of a dissociated tendency is a shocking experience. Essentially what happened during the course of these 6 sessions was that she discovered an identity of which she had not been aware—an identity that, I suggest, was a truer one than the one imposed upon her by her derogatory parents.

These findings are consistent with the view that a large part of what is in the unconscious consists of positive and constructive aspects, capacities and talents which have been dissociated. What remains in awareness is largely a negative sense of the self. This concept—that what is in awareness in the neurotic is largely negative and what is in the unconscious is largely positive—is in stark contrast to the Freudian view that the unconscious is, to a great degree, composed of dark, dangerous and destructive impulses. The implication of these findings for psychoanalysis is that one of the important goals of therapy should be to help the patient become aware of those good aspects of his personality which have been dissociated. They can then be incorporated into the self.

One can recognize dissociated aspects of one's self by listening objectively to tape playbacks and separate one's own identity from that of another person. This is illustrated by the patient who said, "When I talk, I think I will be talking through my father's skull, stiff and pompous." When he heard the actual playback of his voice he said, "That fellow is not like my father at all; he's somebody separate." So also Margaret, upon hearing the tape playback, realized that she had been reacting to Harry as if he were her father, and that this had prevented her from seeing Harry as he really was.

The last patient (Case 5), upon hearing the playbacks of his first two tapes, recognized from them his own lack of integrity. He had been groping toward this recognition in his analytic work prior to hearing these tapes. Listening to them finally convinced him. After a year of further analytic therapy, he was surprised at the degree of his improvement, but couldn't doubt it because he recognized it objectively from the tape playback. These patients are representative of the reactions of the other 119 patients included in this study.

These reactions demonstrated that the playback to patients of accurate tape recordings of their verbalizations does facilitate the recognition and reintegration of dissociated tendencies, the dissipation of parataxic distortions and the development of insight.

REFERENCE

1. SULLIVAN, H. S.: The Interpersonal Theory of Psychiatry. New York, Norton, 1953.

Discussion by Edith Weigert, M.D.

DR. ABELL has demonstrated that the tape recorder is a useful means of retrospective confrontation of the patient with his own verbal productions. Dr. Abell holds a mirror up to the patient, a mirror that he is not in the habit of using. I remember Dr. Sullivan once discussing the surprise effect of listening to his own voice. Freud aimed at such a confrontation in psychoanalysis when he asked the analyst to be like a mirror. But he also found in the course of his investigations that transference and countertransference prevent an unblurred ideal of mirror effect in the analytic situation. Sullivan called the exchange of analyst and analysand a participant observation which is influenced by the dissociations of the self system and the parataxic distortions in interpersonal relations not only on the part of the analysand but also on the part of the analyst.

The playback of recorded sessions to which Dr. Abell exposed his patients brought out important distortions of the self image that these patients harbored. In the majority of the demonstrated examples, there is the startle reaction of being pleased with assets that the patient had not before been aware of. This is a therapeutically favorable reaction. There are many patients so low in their self esteem, so imbued with authoritarian disapproval that the therapist is sometimes tempted in exasperation to ask "Is there not anything good about you?" Dr. Abell was able to convince some of these dispirited patients by the mirror effect of the tape replayed that there were hidden charms and strength, and a positive relation to the self which had not been recognized by him before. Even where Dr. Abell's patient recognizes a phony pretentiousness in his recorded voice, this discovery makes it possible for the patient to get rid of a borrowed identification, a troublesome defense reaction which did not protect the patient against anxieties and this discovery leads to a positive re-evaluation of what is his real ego strength. The patient who was identified with a hated father became able through the playing back of his voice to separate himself from the imposed identity. But such an experience can also lead to a discouraging self devaluation. I think here of the play of Samuel Beckett "Krapp's Last Tape" where a lonely alienated individual goes over his own taped recordings of past experience in mounting despair, or we may think of the image of Dorian Gray by Oscar Wilde where the portrait of the hero shows all the symptoms of dissolution and decay which he tries to overlook in himself in his daily living. In the original legend of Narcissus the self confrontation of the hero leads to a suicidal self infatuation. Dr. Abell has not mentioned such experiences of fatal self involvement or disillusion about the self in his patients. It seems very important that the confrontation with himself, the playing back of his own verbal production should take place in the frame of a positive therapeutic relation, it is important that the therapist conveys to the patient the insight that he is not identical with the distorting defenses, and that there is a more hopeful and constructive aspect repressed or dissociated which is recognizable and acceptable to the therapist.

The patient frequently considers his defenses as ego-strength, particularly when they are of the noisy, expansive type, and may underrate his warmth, his flexibility, his genuine need for solidarity and fellowship. The confrontation with his own voice, his verbal expression may stimulate the patient's alertness to his authenticity, his genuine, autonomous reactions in his own interpersonal experiences. But these discoveries cannot be made in complete solitude; therapeutic guidance is necessary. The mythological and literary examples that I mentioned before indicate the disheartening effect of self confrontation in the mirror experience. Dr. Abell's presentation is a worthwhile contribution to the techniques of psychotherapy and deserves to be tried out in further experimentations.

LSD AS AN AID TO PSYCHOANALYTIC TREATMENT

By CHARLES CLAY DAHLBERG

AS A PART of the psychoanalytic process we strive to recover memories, fantasies and emotions. LSD is the first drug, after mescaline, to be of help in this process because it does not cloud consciousness nor interfere with memory of the drug-induced events.

Lysergic acid diethylamide, better known as LSD 25, is related to the ergot alkaloids. In 1943, Hofmann, a Swiss chemist who accidentally ingested a small amount, referred to it as a "phantasticum" because of its effect in producing fantasies and hallucinations. There followed an enormous amount of work using this and other drugs in attempts to simulate and study psychoses. While LSD does not produce schizophrenia, it may be properly called psychotomimetic in that it can, under certain circumstances, cause symptoms (principally hallucinations) common to certain psychotic conditions. Depending upon other circumstances, there may be a variety of symptoms secondary to the fantasies and hallucinations.

In the 11 years since the first published report on the use of LSD as a stimulant to psychotherapy, there have been many studies. The principal ones are by Cohen and Eisner, Abramson, and Chandler and Hartman, and those reported at the Josiah Macy, Jr. Conference in 1959. Most workers use it to facilitate psychotherapy with hospitalized patients. Some outpatients have been treated while hospitalized for 12 to 24 hours. Clinical psychotherapeutic research on LSD has been more extensive in Europe than here. Results are similar to what we find, but little if any psychoanalytic research is reported. It appeared that a drug, which could cut through the intellectualizations and other dysjunctive processes which people use to avoid meaningful communication with each other and thereby to get to their fantasies and emotions, could be of use with many psychoanalytic patients.

255

My own work was started on a few patients who had long courses of psychoanalysis, generally with more than one analyst. They were all neurotics with serious character disturbances, but all had some anxiety, depression, and problems in sleeping or eating. They tended to have detached schizoid personalities with reasonably strong ego structures. It is generally agreed that psychotics, compensated psychotics, and borderline cases should not be treated with LSD. Because of the danger of suicide, seriously depressed patients also should not be given LSD except while hospitalized. The mystical nature of the experience can play into the hands of the paranoid personality and so the drug should be avoided in these patients in outpatient therapy.

Everyone who has studied the effects of LSD on man agrees that the drug causes the user to be profoundly susceptible to influence by his environment, which should be strictly controlled if it is to be therapeutic. Aside from the increase in time, a recording machine and extensive note-taking, my analytic sessions have been conducted like any to which the patient is accustomed. Other workers have used props, music and blindfolds to encourage fantasy. I have not done so because, while it is true that fantasy and acting-out can be stimulated in this way, verbal communication, which is at the heart of the analytic process, is diminished by such means.

The nature of LSD is such that it is necessary to have someone in attendance for at least 12 hours after taking the drug and a hospital should be available if an unexpected emergency should occur. These precautionary measures are not difficult to arrange and are readily acceptable to patients in these special circumstances.

Technique

I first broach the subject to the patient in terms of a trial with a new drug which is useful in helping some people to open up. Physiologically, it is absolutely safe, but the emotional effects can be dramatic. For that reason, and because it is an experimental drug, I have a trained person with each patient from the time they leave my office until the drug wears off. With some trepidation but with a good deal of interest, patients agree. I then allow a week or two to pass for any further thoughts about LSD to be discussed.

We then schedule a day on which both of us will have ample time, since it usually takes about 2 hours for the drug to take full effect. We then have a 2 to 4 hour session with a break at the end of each hour. The patient then goes home, accompanied by an attendant for the night. The following day the patient meets with me again to report significant events and sometimes to go over in detail my notes of the previous day's LSD session. I usually give the drug once every 3 weeks. The optimum frequency and total number of treatments is still to be worked out.

The dose I use is about 1 mcg./Kg. orally on an empty stomach. In the first session, I give a smaller dose of the drug; varying with the effect and size of the patient, the dose has been 60-90 mcg. This is usually subhallucinatory although there are illusions and visual distortions.

In the first session, I leave the patient alone for half an hour after he takes the drug; by then the sympathomimetic effects appear. These can be mild gastric distress, nausea, muscular irritability, light flashes, chills and flushing; they are not especially distressing if the patient expects them. Most of these symptoms pass in about 30 minutes. On the next visit, the patient waits an hour after the drug, and, if all goes well, by the next time he waits 2 hours. If the patient desires, he may have a sandwich 1 hour after ingestion of the drug, by which time absorption should be complete. The patient knows that I am always available if needed. By the end of the first hour, there are generally some mental symptoms and the heightened visual sensations about which so much has been reported.

The height of the reaction is during the period of 2 to 6 hours after taking the drug. We have a 2 to 4 hour session at which I take detailed notes or a recording. The drug wears off in about 8 hours after ingestion and the patient is ready to sleep. After each LSD analytic session, the patient goes home with an attendant who remains on call during the night. If the effects of the LSD are too upsetting, 25-50 mg. of Thorazine intramuscularly will usually quickly relieve the symptoms. I have never found this necessary nor have I had to hospitalize a patient using LSD.

Precautions

The person under the influence of LSD should not be left alone for any significant period of time. The world of LSD is a strange one. Ego boundaries are fuzzy and distorted even with the small sub-hallucinatory doses used; a word from me or a glance at a trusted person is reality orienting and anxiety reducing. This is especially true if analyst and patient are familiar with each other. For this reason, I insist upon at least 6 months experience with a patient and projective studies to confirm my clinical evaluation.

Case Studies

The following cases will illustrate the effects of the drug in producing rich, meaningful, emotionally charged fantasies and memories. The first case demonstrates the coming into awareness of the patient's basic fantasy which determined the character of her relationships to all important people.

Case 1: A detached, intellectualizing schizoid woman of 30 had had 7 years of analysis, about half of which was with me. Her only sibling was an older brother, the family favorite. She was unmarried and had sexual relationships with both sexes. The intensity of her emotional reaction during orgasm sometimes frightened her lovers. Her response to sexual frustration was bitter and hostile. While her sexual relationships were usually long lasting and not casually entered into, the other elements in her relationships were of much less importance.

Her images of herself were (1) a baby boy, (2) a noble youth such as an Indian brave, and (3) a man. Her sexual relations with men were felt to be homosexual, i.e., man to man; with a woman she was the man or a baby.

Under the influence of 65 mcg. LSD, she had well remembered, powerful emotional experiences which were more notable for their emotional than intellectual content and therefore offer difficulties in description.

In her fourth session, after saying that she never exposed herself except sexually, she moaned and said she wanted Lisa, her lover, to come and take care of her. "I feel like an infant—a totally sexualized infant—blood sucking."

"I'm having a tantrum inside. You are impatiently demanding what you want me to produce, never what I want. I never can know what I want."

"With Lisa I can lose control and be an infant. Now my Mommy is going away. I'm torn between you two. When my mind turns to her it calms down."

The patient wept for some time and then said, "I guess this is what I've been covering up so hard. This is exactly what it's like sexually. Pain, tearing, pulling conflict. Everything but the tears is what's in my orgasm. That's why it's so frightening to people. I don't know what it's about but this scene you've been witnessing is what I've been keeping from you for 4 years. It has the feeling of a storm. I'm calm now."

"I started singing—moaning—after my orgasms a couple of years ago. Like a baby singing. It's not out loud with her. It only comes out in sex and with LSD. It can't be put into words. I cut off a lot with Lisa but I get something important. I encapsulate the infant. Like muffling my ears and eyes so I could have something inside. The more I'm in contact with reality the less I have of this feeling."

She rocked and held her abdomen and spoke of the hole that was almost always in her belly.

In her fifth LSD session she alternated between feeling she was a man and a baby. She was startled to look in a mirror and see a woman. She realized that there were too many emotions connected with being a woman. These emotions paralyzed her. Her role, and therefore her feelings, as a man or as a baby were purer.

In her sixth session, after some mention of my life and family, she felt that she wanted a family but quickly realized that this was a desire to be a child in *my* family. She cried throughout this and seemed to be struggling. She mentioned a familiar childhood fantasy of living on a farm which had a large kitchen with a fireplace in it, and then said, "That's what Lisa means to me. The feeling I get about her is the same as that fantasy. The thing that's tearing me apart is that there are two ways of getting at the same thing.

"That was like a storm. I felt if I didn't say it, I would drown. It was one of the most impressive experiences I've ever had. You know, it's one of my favorite fantasies when I'm not on LSD. Maybe it's that I've lost connection with it. It was coming so fast. The image itself was benign. Those childhood fantasies are loaded."

Then she told how the image of her mother killed these fantasies. Her mother held out the promise of fulfillment but at a price which meant her life. Then she felt me near her and her mother appeared and got small, disappearing. "You did that. I feel protected. Did I ever tell you that when I make love I call 'Mommy'? That's the old Mommy."

She then told how she couldn't share anyone. "It's like I have to give up this wonderful feeling I have once in a while for feeling just *good* all the time." Then, panting and breathless she said, "Nothing is worth it. I won't! That's what I get in the orgasm. It's like being reunited. I wish I knew what this running out of breath was. It's not sex. Some flood of feeling takes my breath away. I feel that if I let go I'd be screaming with rage."

In her seventh session she felt what she described as "womby" and that I was very close to her. "That's the vegetative state I'm always looking for I guess. You've got me at an earlier stage. Wherever I am, it's the best. I don't want to move. I can't conceive of any change. There are no images. It's all physical."

As the mood changed, she said she had been preoccupied for the past few days with thoughts of her mother. She told of present examples of her mother's possessiveness and guilt-producing mechanisms. She mentioned that her brother was breast fed 6 months longer than she and blamed her mother's wanting to nurse him longer on the fact of his having a penis. She recalled her love for her brother and her feeling of being a girl at 3 but her desire for a penis starting about 5.

Then with a sudden rush she admitted to wanting to be a member of my family. "It's the little girl inside that wants it." She felt that any such wish was bound to be painfully frustrated. "It's there. It's a horror. That's why I couldn't let myself go and be a boy until I met Lisa—I'd be frustrated if I let myself want it. God how I wanted that! Those are the things I work so hard at not remembering. What I wanted so much.

"That's what those tearing LSD's were about. I knew they didn't have to do with the subject but with the *tearing*. I won't remember. I can't."

Crying through all this, she continued, "The flood was the *wanting*. It started by my remembering how much I wanted to be a boy—really remembering it.

"There's a way of looking at the feeling that I can do. We've talked *about* it many times but this is another way which really opened it up. No wonder I didn't want the LSD today."

After a while she related the above emotions to sex and said, "It's like playing brinkmanship with my own emotions. Tampering with the tidal wave. With every orgasm it's possible to go to the other side—or become flooded. It's exciting how close to the edge I can come without getting lost. And then the slight disappointment that I didn't get lost."

Then she told of how she had worshipped her brother and felt her parents had also worshipped him. She was afraid of him too. Her mother called him the king. The patient had to kill herself to make him laugh. She had an image of a golden-haired naked boy of 8 or 10. Her mother made people believe he was the most beautiful boy in the world. "But I couldn't make a dent in him. He wouldn't even let me worship him. God I was glad when he left home.

"I could never compete with him for my parents, so I think I aligned myself with him and then competed by becoming him. There never was a chance on my own. I don't think they ever saw me."

She sat up at this point and said she had become scared—she was getting so close to important things. Her need for Lisa was strong. "It must make me feel better about this."

On the following day, describing this session, she said she felt she had been experiencing the original impact of what she had wanted so desperately. "It came out of left field—a complete surprise. The two wants—to be a boy and to belong to my mother. They are much clearer now.

"Wanting to be a boy was really me. I expected to go to sleep and wake up a boy. Belonging was a fairy tale—like the fantasy of being in your family or being an Indian boy. I'd watch other families from the outside. Partly it's because I can never admit to not having a family."

She also told how she became a tomboy to be a better boy than her brother was. He was above the street games.

Her next session got to her having feelings of guilt about her brother. She had been unaware of a feeling of somehow having betrayed him. It was in this way that she explained the hostility he had for her and gave her some sense of being able to change it if she could only get forgiveness. "That must be why I spent the rest of my life making nice and I never know what for and I hate it."

The foregoing highly condensed account of five 2 hour LSD sessions omits my comments. They consisted of a small number of directing, reassuring, encouraging and interpreting remarks. Between sessions, we worked on the material and on events more related to present reality.

It is difficult to describe the role of the analyst in the aforementioned. Much communication was nonverbal, reassuring her and urging her to allow the fantasies to carry her where they would. There was also the force of the analyst felt in the expression of being torn between her Mommy and me. In this I represented the demands of reality and "Mommy" the mother of her infancy. In a later session where she felt a child in my family, she was experiencing the possibility of healthy growth and development. The image of her mother killed this but the sense of my presence made her mother shrink.

The dynamic situation in this patient's life had never been particularly unclear. She had felt rejected, had identified with her brother and competed with him for her mother and had consistently lost. Her father was a relatively minor figure who had during her preadolescence encouraged her in being a boy out of his own anxiety about the sexualization of their relationship. This then gave her an inadequate heterosexual orientation and eventually led to her homosexual acting out as a way of getting back to her infantile relationship with her mother.

The connection between this intense desire for her mother and her orgasm had not been clear before, nor had the transference desire to be a member of my family as a girl. These two elements were new; the latter to both of us. The latter is particularly interesting. She was not merely relating to me as a father but to a family with a father, mother and brother. It was this constellation which allowed her to be a baby girl again.

Aside from these new dynamics, the rest was never obscure but had been therapeutically useless to her. The LSD brought life into her understanding by the intensity of her emotional reaction. In this way the basic fantasy by which she lived was brought into sharp awareness; in essence that fantasy was being her mother's baby girl again. This had not been impossible to get without LSD, but under LSD the condensations were expanded and made vivid. All of the important actions in her life were related to this fantasy and until she was convinced of this she could not understand her life or develop beyond this relationship. Out of an unconscious hope of finding the tidal wave of mother-love again, she held off from developing any real relationships with real men.

Case 2: The next case is an example of a patient cutting through an obsessional substitution and coming quickly to the meaningful core of a specific problem.

This 29 year old woman had a schizoid personality with obsessional and hysterical features. Her complaints at the time we used LSD were of tension, feelings of inadequacy, fear of a heart attack, trouble sticking to things and quarreling with her parents and husband. Her principal interests were in money, her attractiveness, and getting attention.

She was married to a passive, mother-dominated man and was obsessed with her hatred of his doting mother. There were fairly long sterile periods with me in which she was occupied with tedious obsessional talking. I was usually unable to help her break through into more useful productions.

With 60 mcg. of LSD she had very emotional sessions. In the first one she spoke about her family and home and how oppressed she had been. She compared that to the feeling of freedom she had under the influence of the drug. She said she didn't want to think of her mother and then in a burst of emotion cried, "I can't go through this. My heart will stop. My mother said she wouldn't leave my father if I had something wrong with my heart. If only I knew I could live through this. I had to carry the responsibility for her life. The heart thing is so simple. My mother is trying to make me responsible for every one of her failures including that I wasn't a boy. She should take care of her own mother, but I do it. I had to be *her* artist. Now she is dying and she'll make me responsible for that. I don't want to be an invalid all my life. The only thing that has really upset me here is this woman. Everything else I can take. Poor damn thing. She treated me better than her mother treated her, but her mother stuck with her. Mine is modern. My husband's mother is old-fashioned too."

"So that's what's wrong," I said. "Yes," she responded, "she sticks with him. A bitch, but she sticks. I'm taking him away from her and she is jealous. I was too smart. I had to observe everything that went on" (at home), and she went on to describe her own mother's selfishness.

"I never dreamed there was so much about her in me. And all the lies. 'You have to love your mother' and I hated her. I finally told someone about that and they told on me." She described how nothing natural in her was wanted and how her mother pretended to be an old-fashioned loving mother but was really the fashionable love-goddess.

The patient said she was trying to be like her mother and also to be herself. She added, "I knew all this but not how I felt. What I didn't realize is how I was taking the responsibility for her. Isn't it funny. The problems I was so concerned with just aren't there. My mother-in-law doesn't matter. I was just driven wild that she was so possessive of her son and my mother doesn't care about me no matter what I do."

It can be seen in the aforementioned that the patient related to her mother under LSD with intense fear and feelings of responsibility for her mother's welfare. She expressed her strong need for mothering and jealous hatred of anyone who has a protective mother. Incidentally, a lot of analytic work had previously gone into her relationship with her mother and she had worked out a reasonably adequate relationship with her.

The LSD effect is much like that of sensory deprivation. In the latter, the internal sensations deprived of the ordering influence of external reality become exaggerated in importance, disordered, and somtimes appear as hallucinations. Since the effect of LSD is somehow to increase the importance of internal sensations, the result is a similar decrease in the relative importance of external reality. This effect can be increased by blindfolding which further diminishes the contact with external reality.

It is from these conditions that the therapeutic and antitherapeutic consequences of LSD flow. Panic, for instance, is avoided by maintaining friendly human contact.

Since defensive operations develop in interpersonal relations, defensiveness will diminish as contact with external reality loses importance. Since the patient is in a psychoanalytic situation, his attention will tend to be directed towards problems in living particularly from the point of view of history and development. Emotionally charged fantasies and memories will emerge. Expression of these will be less inhibited than ordinarily and the snow-balling or self-stimulating process which occurs reverses the mind's natural tendency toward condensation and results in the emotional and ideational elaboration of memories and fantasies.

The self-observing function of the mind remains more or less intact so the patient is able to see and remember the changes in interpersonal relatedness that occur with the increased contact with his inner self. One result of this is that since external reality is less intrusive than ordinarily, any intrusion by the analyst, being undiluted by other external elements, will have greater impact. This apparently paradoxical effect allows brief interpretations or assurances to be very effective. On the other hand, self-seeking or irrelevant remarks are clearly seen by the patient to be unrelated to him and therefore ignored.

Another result of the heightened contact with inner reality is that transference distortions can be quickly traced to their original interpersonal sources. The analyst being present and helpful while the transference distortion is being traced allows the transference to be split into source and reality. As one patient said,

"I feel an intense hatred for you. I see myself grinding you under my heel. Now it's my father I'm stepping on." Later he reported that at the same time these fantasies were occurring, he felt my actual presence in the room and had a sense of well-being about that.

The concept of a "basic fantasy" is particularly useful to describe what many of these people expose under the influence of LSD, as was clear in the first case. To the degree that a person has a basic fantasy rooted deeply in the past and to the degree that it is antithetical to adult modes of relating, that person will have problems in living.

The feelings brought out under LSD are very strong but the patient is not usually carried away by them. Contrary to some published reports, I have never had trouble keeping contact with my patient. The condition is very much like that in the later periods of successful analysis when the patient can be quite comfortable about feeling strongly his rational and irrational thoughts while at the same time detachedly observing himself and learning from the experience.

The time between LSD sessions is useful. I find the 3 week interval good because it minimizes psychological dependency on the drug and allows time to work through and extend the LSD insights. There is usually too much material from any one LSD session to be successfully integrated except over a long period of time.

LSD may possibly shorten many analyses, but, in my experience, the time element necessary for successful analysis is still long. Its important use is in opening up persons to analysis who are otherwise unlikely to be successfully analyzed at all. Those patients most likely to find it useful are the very defensive, resistant, intellectualizing psychoneurotics who fall into the obsessive, hysteric and phobic classifications, and the detached schizoid personality.

The kind of material I have described as coming from the patient can be reassuring and encouraging or it can be disturbing. It is valuable to open up hidden parts of the psyche but not if the patient cannot manage it. Naturally, the analyst must use his clinical judgment based on his knowledge of the patient and any other information he can get before starting analysis with LSD. There is neither a place for rashness nor overprotectiveness in psychoanalysis no matter what facilitating techniques are used.

REFERENCES

1. ABRAMSON, H. A., JARVIK, M. E., LEVINE, A., AND WAGNER, M.: LSD I. Physiological and perceptual responses. J. Psychol. 39:3, 1955.
2. ——: LSD 25 III. As an Adjunct to psychotherapy with elimination of fear of homosexuality. J. Psychol. 39:127, 1955.
3. ——: LSD 25 XXII. Effect on transference. J. Psychol. 42:51, 1956.
4. ——: LSD 25 XIX. As an adjunct to brief psychotherapy with special reference to ego enhancement. J. Psychol. 41:199, 1956.
5. ——, ROLO, A., AND STACKE, J.: LSD Antagonists: Chlorpromazine. J. Neuropsychiat. 1:309,1959-60.
6. BUSCH, A. K., AND JOHNSON, W. C.: LSD 25 as an aid in psychotherapy. Dis. Nerv. Syst. 11:——, 1950.
7. CATTELL, J. P.: Influence of mescaline on psychodynamic material. J. Nerv. & Men. Dis. 119:233, 1954.
8. ——: Use of drugs in psychodynamic investigations. In: Experimental Psychopathology. New York, Grune & Stratton, Inc., 1957, pp. 218-233.
9. ——, AND MALITZ, S.: Revised survey of selected psychopharmacological agents. Am. J. Psychiat. 117:449, 1960.
10. CHANDLER, A. L., AND HARTMAN, M. A.: LSD 25 as a facilitating agent in psychotherapy. Arch. Gen. Psychiat. 2:286, 1960.
11. CHOLDEN, L. (Ed.): Lysergic acid diethylamide and mescaline in experimental psychiatry. New York, Grune & Stratton, 1956.

12. COHEN, S. AND EISNER, B. G.: Use of LSD in a psychotherapeutic setting. Arch, Neurol. Psychiat. 81:615, 1959.
13. ——: LSD: Side effects and complications. J. Nerv. & Ment. Dis. 130:30, 1960.
14. COOPER, H. A.: Hallucinogenic drugs. Lancet 1:1078, 1955.
15. CUTNER, M.: Analytic work with LSD 25. Psychiat. Quart. 33: 715-757, 1959.
16. DAY, J.: The role and reaction of the psychiatrist in LSD therapy. J. Nerv. & Ment. Dis. 125:444, 1957.
17. DITMAN, K. S., WHITTLESEY, J. R. B., AND HAYMAN, M.: Subjective claims following the LSD experience. Unpublished.
18. EISNER, B. G., AND COHEN, S.: Psychotherapy with LSD. J. Nerv. & Ment. Dis. 127:528, 1958.
19. FELD, M., GOODMAN, J. R., AND GUIDO, J. A.: Clinical and laboratory observations on LSD 25. J. Nerv. & Ment. Dis. 126:176, 1958.
20. FRIEDERKING, W.: Intoxicant drugs (Mescaline and LSD) in psychotherapy. J. Nerv. & Ment. Dis. 121:262, 1955.
21. HAYES, J. S.: Clinical investigations with LSD 25. Research Dept. Bulletin, No. 1 of the Phila. Mental Health Clinic (undated) mimeo.
22. Harvard Medical School Symposium, Sensory Deprivation. Cambridge, Mass., Harvard University Press, 1961.
23. HOCH, P. H., CATTELL, J. P., AND PENNES, H. H.: Effects of mescaline and LSD 25. Am. J. Psychiat. 108:579, 1952.
24. ——, ——, AND ——: Effect of drugs: Theoretical considerations from a psychological viewpoint. Am. J. Psychiat. 108:585, 1952.
25. ——: Remarks on LSD and mescaline. J. Nerv. & Ment. Dis. 125:442, 1957.
26. ——: Pharmacologically induced psychoses. In: Sylvano Arieti (ed.): Am. Handbook of Psychiatry, New York, Basic Books, 1959.
27. ——: Methods and analysis of drug induced abnormal mental states in man. Comp. Psychiat. 1:265, 1960.
28. HOLLISTER, L. E., PRUSMACK, J. J., PAULSEN, J. A., AND ROSENQUIST, N.: Comparison of three psychotropic drugs (Psilocybin, JB 329 and IT 290) in volunteer subjects. J. Nerv. & Ment. Dis. 130:428, 1960.
29. HUXLEY, A.: The Doors of Perception. New York, Harper & Bros., 1954.
30. ——: Heaven and Hell. New York, Harper & Bros., 1955.
31. KATZENELENBOGEN, S., AND AI DING FANG: Narcosynthesis effects of sodium amytal, methedrine and LSD 25. Dis. Nerv. System 14:1, 1953.
32. KETY, S. S. (Ed.): The pharmacology of psychotomimetic and psychotherapeutic drugs. New York Acad. Sc. 66:417-840, 1957.
33. KLINE, N. (Ed.): Psychopharmacology. Am. A. Adv. Sc., No. 42, 1956.
34. Editorial: Hallucinogenic drugs. Lancet 1:445, 1961.
35. LANGNER, F. W.: Six years experience with LSD therapy. Unpublished paper delivered at the meeting of the National Assoc. of Private Psychiatric Hospitals, January 23, 1961.
36. LEWIS, D. J., AND SLOANE, R. B.: Therapy with LSD. J. Clin. & Exper. Psychopath. 19:19, 1958.
37. LINDEMANN, E., AND CLARKE, L. D.: Modifications of ego structure and personality reactions under the influence of the effects of drugs. Am. J. Psychiat. 108:561, 1952.

38. MALAMUD, W., AND LINDEMANN, E.: Analysis of psychopathological effects of intoxicating drugs. Am. J. Psychiat. 90:853, 1934.

39. MARTIN, A. J.: LSD treatment of chronic psychoneurotic patients under day hospital conditions. Internat. J. Soc. Psychiat. 3:188, 1957.

40. MORSELLI, G. E.: Contribution a la psychopathologie de l'Intoxication par la mescaline. Le probleme d'une schizophrenie experimentale. J. Psychol. Norm. Path. 33:368, 1936.

41. MURPHY, R. C., JR.: As quoted in: The Use of LSD in Psychotherapy. Abramson, H. A. (ed.) New York, Josiah Macy, Jr. Foundation, 1960, p. 224.

42. NEWLAND, C. A.: My Self and I. New York, Coward-McCann, Inc., 1962.

43. POLLARD, J. C., BAKKER, C., UHR, L., AND FEUERFILE, D. F.: Controlled sensory input: A note on the technic of drug evaluation with a preliminary report on a comparative study of sernyl, psilocybin, and LSD 25. Comp. Psychiat. 1:377, 1960.

44. SANDISON, R. A.: Psychological aspects of the LSD treatment of the neuroses. J. Ment. Sc., 100:508, 1954.

45. ——, AND WHITELAW, J. D. A.: Further studies in the therapeutic value of LSD in mental illness. J. Ment., Sc. 103:332, 1957.

46. SAVAGE, C.: Variations in ego-feelings induced by LSD. Psychoanalyt. Rev. 42: 1955.

47. ——: The resolution and subsequent remobilization of resistance by LSD in psychotherapy. J. Nerv. Ment. Dis. 125:434, 1957.

48. SMITH, C. M.: A new adjunct to the treatment of alcoholism: The hallucinogenetic drugs. Quart. J. Stud. Alcohol 19:406, 1958.

49. STEVENSON, I., AND RICHARDS, T. W.: Prolonged reactions to mescaline: A report of two cases. Psychopharmacologia 1:241, 1960.

50. THOMPSON, C.: The role of the analyst's personality in therapy. Am. J. Psychotherap. 10:347, 1936.

51. WHITELAW, J. D. A.: A case of fetishism treated with LSD. J. Nerv. & Ment. Dis. 129:573, 1959.

52. WIKLER, A.: Mechanisms of drugs that modify personality function. Am. J. Psychiat. 108:590, 1952.

53. ——: The Relation of Psychiatry to Pharmacology. Baltimore, Williams and Wilkins, 1957.

54. Ataractic and Hallucinogenic Drugs in Psychiatry. World Health Organization: Technical Report Series No. 152. Geneva, 1958.

Discussion by Max Fink, M.D.

IN THIS optimistic study, Dr. Dahlberg reports on the use of a hallucinogenic drug to stimulate psychoanalytic interactions, and suggests that LSD is useful to "recover memories, fantasies and emotions" and "to get through the intellectualizations." The technique is simple, requiring two principal modifications: that of extending a single session to many hours, and the need for a companion in the post-treatment period. Dr. Dahlberg reports no complications in 50 LSD sessions in 4 subjects and suggests no limitations other than those implicit in patient selection. In the 2 case summaries, he notes increases in the expression of emotion and feelings, the richness of fantasies, in the recollection and clarity of memories, and in receptivity and tractability in the interaction. The observations are asserted to be related to the drug effect, and while not stated explicitly, it is assumed that increases in verbalization, recollection and receptivity are helpful in psychoanalytic therapy.

The report confirms therapeutic studies using similar techniques by Chandler, Sandison, Abramson and Cohen. While it may be helpful to discuss the technique, especially to ask Dr. Dahlberg for his criteria for selecting patients for this therapy, I would like to focus on two assertions in the report—that LSD alters patient's verbalizations, and that the LSD experience is therapeutic.

The assertion that LSD administration alters verbalization is one that is testable, and such investigation appears necessary as a foundation for the therapeutic and theoretic superstructure delineated by Dr. Dahlberg. In an earlier draft of the report, Dr. Dahlberg lists 10 observations of his sessions descriptive of the interaction. Linguistic analysis provides measures which may be related to these observations, and which may provide the operational bases for assessing the reported interactive changes. Dr. Dahlberg notes that after LSD "the expression of emotion is quite open"; "expression of feeling toward the therapist is open and there tends to be an increase in dependency feelings"; and "fantasies and associations are rich and free." In psycholinguistic analyses, these descriptions may be reflected in such measures as an increase in the use of adjectives, the variety of words, and in references to the therapist.

Another aspect noted is ". . . a curious exaggeration of the fundamental way of relating . . ."; "embarrassment is at a minimum and matters which have previously been held back are spoken of more freely" and ". . . defensive measures may be discarded." In linguistic terms, these views may be reflected in the use of personal pronouns, the present tense, alterations in rate of speech, *etc.* Similar operational suggestions can be made about the observation that subjects exhibited increased receptivity and increased recall.

In our laboratory we have undertaken such psycholinguistic analyses with drugs. We confirmed the observations of Weinstein and Kahn that after intravenous amobarbital, speech was marked by increased use of denial, displacement, minimization, third person, and future and past tense.[1,2] With other drugs, notably anticholinergic hallucinogens, we noted significant decreases in these measures. In another study the diversity of speech was measured using the type-token ratio (TTR) as the index.[3] With amobarbital, there was a decrease in the mean TTR, reflecting a greater repetitiveness in speech, while with the anticholinergic compounds there was an increase in mean TTR—reflecting a greater variety of speech.[4] Among the compounds in the latter class was LSD, after which there was an increased diversity of speech on these measures. It is possible then that Dr. Dahlberg's descriptions of the changes in the interaction after LSD may be clarified by similar psycholinguistic studies.

Dr. Dahlberg asserts that the effect of these changes in verbalizations are salutary. This is a most tenuous conclusion, since neither the criteria of efficacy, nor the methods of evaluation, nor the relation to control data are presented. There are at least two major changes in this treatment—the interpolation of a drug, and the extension of sessions of interaction to many hours. Perhaps this latter element alone may be as potent in altering behavior as the administration of the drug. Was this not the conclusion reached by some observers with regard to the use of amobarbital or methamphetamine as therapeutic adjuvants?

I would like to congratulate Dr. Dahlberg on his enthusiasm in exploring this therapy, and commend the techniques of experimental psychiatry to his attention. Techniques sufficient to verify his observations of altered communication and the therapeutic efficacy of LSD are available and such studies may substantiate the inferences with which he concludes his report.

REFERENCES

1. FINK, M., KAHN, R. L., AND WEINSTEIN, E. A.: The amytal test in patients with mental illness. J. Hillside Hosp. 4:3-13, 1955.
2. ——, AND ——: Changes in language during electroshock therapy. *In:* Hoch, P. and Zubin, J. (Ed.) : Psychopathology of Communication, New York, Grune & Stratton, 1958.
3. JAFFE, J.: Language of the dyad. Psychiatry, 21:249-258, 1958.
4. FINK, M., JAFFE, J., AND KAHN, R. L.: Drug induced changes in interview patterns: Linguistic and neurophysiologic indices. *In:* G. J. Sarwer-Foner (Ed.) : Dynamics of Psychiatric Drug Therapy, Springfield, Ill., Charles C Thomas, 1960, pp. 29-44.

THE COMBINATION OF PSYCHOTHERAPY WITH DRUG THERAPY

By PAUL H. HOCH, M.D.

I PROPOSE to focus attention on the *clinical point of view,* which should not be complicated by inadequate "basic science" considerations. In diseases or disorders in which essentially the etiology is still unknown, the therapy employed is of necessity symptomatic rather than causal.

In practice, the main questions are: (1) when should drugs be used alone without psychotherapy; (2) when should psychotherapy be used alone without drugs; and (3) when should the two methods be used in combination. In the latter case we must ask when and how should combined treatment be employed? There are numerous statistics available regarding drug effects, but most of these have been obtained on overtly psychotic individuals treated as inpatients in mental hospitals. Much less is known about the efficacy of tranquilizers, antidepressants, antianxiety compounds, etc., in the treatment of ambulatory mental patients which comprise the milder forms of schizophrenia, depression, and in particular, the large number of psychoneurotic patients.

The main problem of combined treatment pertains to the neuroses. We could assume the best treatment for all patients would be a combination of drug treatment and psychotherapy; if we go into this matter more thoroughly, however, this assumption is not tenable for several reasons.

Large psychiatric hospitals are not organized and equipped to give individual psychotherapy to every psychotic patient. They are able to give individual therapy to a selected number of patients and group psychotherapy to others, but the vast majority is not able to receive direct psychotherapy. This pertains to patients under drugs or other somatic treatments. Today those which can be considered indirect forms of psychotherapy are given in many hospitals and are based upon the organization of the hospital, within the therapeutic occupational, recreational, or other milieu. These treatment approaches have, of course, a therapeutic effect but they are not what we would call direct organized psychotherapy. In this connection the question can be raised whether or not it is necessary that all psychotic patients should receive drug treatment in addition to psychotherapy. This is a controversial issue. There are those who feel that psychotherapy for a psychotic patient is not valuable; there are those who feel that only psychotherapy is able to help. Many psychiatrists take a middle-of-the-road stand.

The important question is how much psychotherapy is needed for those psychiatric patients being treated with drugs? To what extent can drugs replace psychotherapy and *vice versa?* The original attempts of organized psychotherapy in the functional psychoses rested on the assumption that these disorders were of a psychogenic origin, therefore being similar to the neuroses, and should be treated with psychotherapy. Those who visualize the origin of these "functional" psychoses as "organic" in nature do not feel that much can be accomplished with psychotherapy. But, it is obvious that many of these patients, even at a time when they are free from psychotic manifestations, show many abnormalities in their overt behavior in daily life. The experience gained in mental institutions is that many schizophrenic patients show a marked improvement and even an elimination of symptoms with drug treatment alone. On the other hand, the relapse rate of these patients is quite high, sometimes reaching approximately 30 per cent. *However, if they receive psychotherapy in addition to the treatment this relapse rate can be cut in half.* When the drugs reduce or eliminate the gross psychotic state, patients with a more favorable psychodynamic make-up, inner strength, and resources are able to adjust to different environmental situations. This is true even though certain adaptational impairments characteristic of the disorder may still remain.

When should drug treatment be introduced in the psychotherapy of schizophrenia? First, in patients who are autistic and negativistic, rendering contact with the therapist is tenuous. It is here that tranquilizing drugs are able often to ameliorate these emotional patterns, thus permitting a better accessibility. Second, in depressed schizophrenics; some individuals do well with antidepressant drugs, and if too much anxiety or tension is present, a mixture of antidepressant and a tranquilizer can be used. Third, many paranoid patients who are under strong tension benefit from tranquilizing medication if they can be induced to take it. Hebephrenic and simple schizophrenics are the least accessible to drug therapy and psychotherapy either alone or in combination, but there are many exceptions to the rule. We find patients in all categories of schizophrenia who are refractory to drug treatment or psychotherapy, but we should not apply too many diagnostic prejudices. We should try to apply treatment to all, including regressed hebephrenics.

In patients suffering from depression, drugs are also used to ameliorate or eliminate the syndrome, but have not been able to replace fully electroshock treatment. We have not been able to confirm reports which indicate that over 80 per cent of the depressions respond to drugs. We find that only about one-half of the depressions respond to available drug treatments; in the other half, electroshock treatment remains necessary.

Depressed patients do not pay sufficient attention to therapy with the possible exception of reassurance. The ambivalence present toward most decisions and in relationship to the therapy is a formidable barrier to treatment. Of course, the suicidal danger is always present. Such patients make great demands upon the time of the therapist. The use of antidepressants, therefore, is of great importance and permits the therapist to do more for such a patient than merely give him reassurance and emotional support. It is still an open question as to what extent psychotherapy alone or in combination with drugs is able to prevent the recurrence of a depressive attack. Based on available statistics and our own observations which are numerous, we are not impressed that psychotherapy, drugs, or electroshock therapy are able to prevent the reoccurrence of a new depressive attack. Essentially all treatments available permit us to cut the depressive episode short. The above statement applies to practically all depressions with the exception of some reactive depressions; these may respond to psychotherapy and recurrence after such treatments is not seen as regularly as in other forms of depression.

One of the most controversial points is the use of drugs in the treatment of the psychoneuroses. We have much less reliable information regarding their efficacy in this treatment than about the influence of the drugs in psychotic patients. The different compounds—tranquilizers, energizers, antianxiety drugs—are prescribed in large quantities and practically every physician today prescribes one or the other of these to patients where an emotional symptomatology is present.

We believe the great resistance in some psychiatric circles to the use of these drugs is essentially based on the psychiatrist's experience with neurotic patients. Of course, every case must be individually evaluated. It is more or less obvious that many psychoneurotic patients should be treated without any drug adjuvant provided their treatment would not be facilitated were the drugs to be administered. The decision to use or not to use a drug is often determined upon the matter of degree of symptoms present. We have psychoneurotic patients who are not markedly crippled by the intensity of their symptoms. There are other patients, for instance—some anxiety states or phobic states—where the anxiety is so intense that the patient is not able to function even relatively well. When the use of the drug eliminates the anxiety, these persons are more comfortable and are able to partake of psychotherapy. Some psychiatrists have expressed the fear that if the anxiety in these patients is eliminated, and the patients are comfortable, they would lack the motivation for psychotherapy. This may happen in some cases, and as in many schizophrenics, some of them will have the inner strength and resources to solve their conflicts providing their tension and anxiety is reduced; nevertheless, in many instances they are very well aware of the fact that even if they are more comfortable they have many problems which must be resolved. In many instances where the neurotic patient accepts only the drug therapy and does not want psychotherapy, the motives are not so much the patient's lack of interest in psychotherapy as his inability to obtain or afford it. In such situations the patient tries to be content with the use of the drugs alone.

The use of the drugs in psychoneurotic patients encounters various objections. It has been claimed that drug administration interferes with the so-called transference relationship. If the patient experiences a degree of hopeful emotional dependence upon the therapist, the introduction of a drug, even if it leads to some complications, does not interfere seriously with the patient's cooperative treatment behavior. The patient usually feels that the therapist is using every weapon at his disposal to help him, that he is aware of the considerable suffering of the patient, and is trying to make his symptoms more bearable. This usually increases rather than decreases the patient's hopeful emotional dependence, hence his cooperation with the therapist. The idea that the patient must be uncomfortable for effective psychotherapy is open to question, and it should be re-examined in the light of present-day knowledge.

Regulating the use of drugs in relationship to the patient's mode of cooperation is now a part of the therapeutic procedure. If the therapist considers the drug in one compartment and psychotherapy completely in another, it is obvious that a constructive fusion cannot be accomplished. We feel this is probably one of the most important problems in endeavoring to appraise properly what one treatment may or may not do.

This brings up the question as to who should do combined treatment. It is obvious that it should be done only by those who are equipped to do so who have a working knowledge of psychotherapy and drug therapy. Acquiring knowledge in both fields is not so difficult or so complicated that it cannot be done. It is not good policy to have drug treatment entrusted to one physician and psychotherapy to another. The handling of the patient by two different therapists who do not fully coordinate these therapies may confuse the patient. It is rather common that the patient tries to "trap" the therapists into complicating statements, misinterpretations, and recommendations. This, of course, interferes seriously with therapy and is objected to by many—and rightly so. The treatment of the patient should not be carried on by a "committee;" it is preferable to have the drug therapy and psychotherapy in the hands of one person in order that the aforementioned difficulties may be avoided. The therapist prescribing the drug must be constantly aware of the feelings described by the patient in order to enable him to integrate his knowledge of the drug action and the patient's feeling about it into his psychotherapeutic maneuvers and aims.

Some psychiatrists and patients have expressed fear that drugs would also slow associations and would reduce the uncovering of unconscious material. It has been stated that the dream material produced under the influence of the drugs is less voluminous. All the mentioned observations are valid in some patients but they do not apply generally. In many patients the ability to associate is far better when drugs were used than when they were not. This is due to the fact that the patient who was blocked by anxiety or other emotional overcharge is relaxed by the drug. A large dose of tranquilizing drugs can slow down the mental processes; however, this is not the case if the dosage is not excessive. Some feel that drug effect can be replaced by psychotherapy, namely, that if a patient has frequent psychotherapeutic contacts, he does not need the drug because the treatment sessions are sufficient to reduce his anxiety and tension. This may be correct for milder neurotic disturbances, but it does not hold for those which are more severe. It is correct to state that less drugs are needed if the patient is seen frequently. In such cases, the dependency upon the therapist replaces drug action. However, a complete interchange between psychotherapy and drug action does not exist.

The production of dynamic material is not affected negatively provided the drug dosage is not excessive and the patient's attention span is not reduced. Interpretations are followed just as well as in a drug-free state. If such a patient is not completely dominated by his symptoms, interpretations can be given and absorbed by him more readily without the constant weighing of how ego-damaging the interpretations may be. As for the patient gaining insight into his conflicts, it has become more and more recognized that this can be present intellectually or emotionally, but this still does not necessarily mean an improvement of the patient in respect to handling a conflict. Indeed, the patient may function quite well without having detailed insight into his conflictual structure.

Some therapists have mentioned that persuasion and suggestibility have been changed under the influence of drugs. The reactions to drugs in this respect is highly individual; it is possible we may see both. In this respect also the regulative role of the therapist is of great importance.

The great difficulty which confronts many patients is the inability to translate the gains they have made during therapy into action. Many psychotherapeutic failures are on this level. It is here that the use of drugs in conjunction with psychotherapy is important. Many patients are able to translate therapeutic gains into action with drug therapy. Very often these gains are blocked by excessive fear or other neurotic resistances. The judicious use of drugs gives the patient a better and greater executive radius. This is as important in treatment as the use of drugs to reduce anxiety for the sake of improving contact and also to prepare the patient for psychotherapy. The drug may have a special role in acting-out patients.

Apart from the treatment of psychopaths, we are concerned with acting-out tendencies in the neurotic realm. This may be by using alcohol in excess or engaging in self-damaging or environmental-damaging activities, which even though they cannot be labeled antisocial, are, nevertheless, most troublesome. A great deal of blind submission and blind defiance is involved. In many such patients today, for obvious reasons, only supportive treatment is given. More active therapy can be applied with the provision that some of the patient's hostility can be curbed by the drugs. In such instances we sometimes use one or the other of the tranquilizing drugs, preferably one of the phenothiazine compounds. In contrast to aggression one of the great handicaps to psychotherapy is the apathy present in some patients. Often the motivation for psychotherapy is present but the energy for its effectuation is not. In such cases, energizers or other stimulating drugs administered in relatively small dosages are successful. This is also true regarding the use of amphetamine. Many of these patients are often dropped from therapy as uncooperative or they terminate their treatment under some pretext. Therefore, in many instances, the carrying through of psychotherapy to its conclusion is dependent upon the use of a tranquilizer or an energizing drug. Instead of accepting the patient's rejection of psychotherapy, we should try to use it in combination with drugs to overcome this resistance. We have seen the successful conclusion of therapy which would have been impossible without the use of drugs.

The use of drugs in combination with psychotherapy may lead to certain physical or mental complications. Familiarity with adverse drug effects is an absolute necessity for every therapist using them. Some patients complain about lethargy and weakness, or about being driven or overstimulated if stimulants are used; other patients may complain about feelings of depersonalization or of feeling strange, peculiar, and out of contact. In some patients this occurs only if the dosages are relatively high. Occasionally, however, this may be encountered even with the administration of small dosages. We have observed patients, who, after a while, accustomed themselves to the drug and lost their strange feelings. In others, however, these feelings persisted and when the drug was withdrawn and the symptoms disappeared, a reintroduction of the drug promptly produced the same complaints. Both somatic and psychic complications are important in a psychotherapeutic setting. This is not because these complications are considered by some as dangerous, but because these symptoms produce a disagreeable psychological effect. Drug adjuvants to psychotherapy are used in patients who are anxious and apprehensive and they may respond to a drug-produced complication with an increased amount of anxiety and disappointment. In our experience patients who receive systemic psychotherapy can be induced to take another drug even though they had a negative experience with one or else they willingly cooperate in an adjustment of dosage, and their faith in the therapist is usually not shaken. This happens only if the therapist is able to explain to the patient some of the more common side-effects. In such a case the patient can be immunized against the emotional impact of such a complication and the psychotherapy may remain unimpeded. The role of drugs does not necessarily have to remain the same during the treatment of an individual patient. In one case one may begin with psychotherapy, then add the drug, discontinue the drug, and continue with psychotherapy. Variations in such treatment schemes must be adapted to the patient's needs.

We have a considerable amount of knowledge as to how drugs influence the psyche, and especially the emotional operations, but treatment with drugs remains empirical. We know that the tranquilizers relieve excitation and anxiety. They have a sedative action but they do not interfere with consciousness to such a degree as barbiturates, scopolamine, or others do. Productive symptoms such as hallucinations, delusions, etc., are influenced because the emotional overcharge is reduced. These drugs alleviate the symptoms but do not eliminate the basic structure of the psychoses or neuroses.

The same is true about the energizers and antianxiety compounds used either in the psychoses or neuroses. The effect of the tranquilizing drugs seemingly occurs in the midbrain and the reticular substance, but how this is accomplished in chemical terms is still hypothetical.

The action of psychotherapy is probably somewhat better understood than that of the action of the drugs because in terms of communication and interpersonal action patterns. However, if we cut through the considerable amount of verbiage and theoretical reasoning concerning how psychotherapy acts we must say that many psychotherapeutic results are still meagerly understood. For instance, why different psychotherapeutic approaches have very similar treatment results remains unexplained. We do not share the idea that psychotherapy is a superior treatment because it eliminates basic problems, whereas the drugs are only a symptomatic palliative. Both treatment methods have specific functions. The drug treatments are essentially quantitative in that they are able to reduce anxiety, tension, and emotional overcharge. Conversely, the stimulating drugs increase emotional charge. Even though the drugs used today do not effect every function of the psyche, grossly speaking, the aforementioned pharmacological effects are constant.

We are all aware of the fact that with neurotic individuals the con-flicts are less important than the ability or inability of the patient to cope with them. We are sure that future research will enable us to strengthen the patient's ability in coping with the conflicts. In this respect the future will indicate a better integration between the organic, psychodynamic, and social approaches. These all deal with neurotic individuals today but they are also in isolation from each other. Integration between all these aspects into one operational whole is the future aim of psychiatry. We believe that integrated psycho-dynamics and psychopharmacodynamics will elucidate many obscure problems and will aid in evolving a more effective therapy.

NAME INDEX
(Principal References in *Italics*)

278

SUBJECT INDEX

(Principal References in *Italics*)

---

*The Editor is indebted to Miss Sevilla Laird for her aid in the preparation of the Name and Subject Indices.

Céremony of Silence — "Cool it"

Appr Central Ritual —

Bali

(1) Be Aware
when you Have
(2) Subvocally wakes Th —
(3) Referent Focus & Plenary
(4) si f
(5) wms & ofter Pabs Synch
(6) Relate to Pleasanty —

Also —
More
Future
Truths

"The Circle of News"

P. 101 / 102 xx !

Body Ritual = Olympics
Ballet